# Megalies

# Megalies

A Memoir

LODOVICO BALDUCCI

RESOURCE *Publications* · Eugene, Oregon

MEGALIES
A Memoir

Copyright © 2014 Lodovico Balducci. All rights reserved. Except for brief quotations in critical publications or reviews, no part of this book may be reproduced in any manner without prior written permission from the publisher. Write: Permissions. Wipf and Stock Publishers, 199 W. 8th Ave., Suite 3, Eugene, OR 97401.

Resource Publications
An Imprint of Wipf and Stock Publishers
199 W. 8th Ave., Suite 3
Eugene, OR 97401

www.wipfandstock.com

ISBN 13: 978-1-62564-408-4

Manufactured in the U.S.A.

to Claudia

All the stories concerning myself, Claudia, Grace, Father Serra and Don Oreste are factual. The others are true but they have been modified to protect the privacy of the individuals involved

# Introduction

"You are now and you will always be my beloved son!" With these words the mother of Ted Bundy bade farewell to her child a few hours before he was electrocuted for serial murder. Ted Bundy had brutalized and murdered at least 30 young women in rampages that involved seven different states and terrified entire communities. He was on the "most wanted" list. The news of his arrest and conviction was received with universal relief, and his execution was celebrated with champagne popping outside the chamber. If we believe the newspaper interviews, most of the victims' families expressed "a sense of closure" with his death. Nobody came to mourn him.

His mother expressed no wish to prevent his execution. She elected instead to make a statement that defied both the hatred that demanded his execution and the electric chair that killed him. Her love survived all instruments of death, and nobody could take it away from her nor from her son.

The words of Bundy's mother condense the message of this book that concerns unconditional love, transfiguration and redemption.

Unconditional love. The mother acknowledged that the heinous crimes of her son could not be justified. Perhaps she even hoped that the execution might melt some of the hatred that had isolated him, since his arrest, into a cage of burning ice. She bled for the victims' untimely and brutal deaths and understood and sympathized with the feelings of the victims' families. But despite the pain her son had inflicted on entire communities and on herself, she still held him as her beloved son. For the believers, like myself, she was telling God: "If you want me, you have to take my son with me. You cannot ask me to choose between the love I have for You and that I have for him: As You should know, love is not negotiable. I allowed my son to be executed. I won't allow him to be damned."

Bundy's mother had understood that love can only be unconditional, because the persons who need love most are the ones who are lovable least!

She learned the most difficult of all lessons, how to love the unlovable. She had seen her son naked and hapless when he came out of her womb to face a hostile world, which for him would be difficult to tread given his illegitimate birth. She heard him begging for attention and affection that only she could provide. In discovering their unique relationship she discovered her own sacredness; that is, her own unique mission. That discovery led her to commit her own life to her son, without knowing whether he had a future and what that future would bring. The fact that he became a serial murderer and the target of universal hatred reinforced rather than silenced her love, because that is when that love was most needed. The vision she had of her child at his birth was not dissipated by the fog of hatred and destructiveness that embedded him on the convict's bench or in the national media. She knew that a unique diamond does not cease being a diamond because it has been buried under a thick layer of dirt and because other people have cast it as a pebble.

To be able to see beyond the moment, to gain a vision of the whole person as endowed with a unique role that no other person can fulfill in his or her stead, is what I call the experience of a transfiguration. The Gospels provide reference of a transfiguration. Peter, James and John are terrified and awed as they witness their teacher, a carpenter who might not even have been able to write, enlightened by a supernatural light and entertaining the two pillars of the Jewish faith: Moses and Elijah. That vision, more than his miracles and his teachings, supported their loyalty to him through their own martyrdom.

I contend that the experience of transfiguration is necessary in everyday life to persist faithfully to one's commitment; that is, to practice unconditional love. I don't see how a marriage can survive without the spouses having transfigured in front of each other. When Claudia, my wife of more than 40 years, led me down a dangerous ski slope in the Italian mountains that I would have never considered negotiating on my own, I saw in her much more than the joyful companion of a Sunday escape. I saw in her the person whose enthusiasm, whose trust, whose affection might have revitalized the sense of my own sacredness. That vision sustained my commitment to her throughout the darkest moments of our marriage. More than a persisting memory, that vision is the awareness of an alternative time, of a perpetual present that underlies all the moves of my life, the unchangeable that underlies all changes, the unity that underlies multiplicity. Likewise, when I face the task of communicating to one of my patients that the end is near and no form of Western medical treatment can help him or her, I try to see behind the waning flesh, the skeletal face and bent shoulder, what that person represents for himself or herself and for his or her family. Only the experience of this transfiguration allows me to convey a living word of compassion, make the patient feel that I do indeed take part of his or her pain.

Bundy's mother's unconditional love brought redemption in several forms and ways. First, it redeemed the victims' families of the hatred her son had engendered and that might have accompanied them for the rest of their lives like solitary worm, a tapeworm that prevents any form of growth, because it destroys an organism from inside and prevents access to all forms of nourishment. Her love told the victims' families: "I am one of you; like you I have lost a beloved child through no fault of my own. I deserve your allegiance." Implicit in this allegiance was the forgiveness of her son, as you cannot at the same time be in solidarity with a person and hate that person. In other words, she made possible forgiveness for her son by the victims' families. She redeemed herself. Had she distanced herself from her son, as I see parents do when their children do not fulfill expectations, she might have avoided the acute pain of seeing him dying, but she would have lived with the worm of guilt for having abandoned her son when he needed her most. And she redeemed her son in two ways. First, she sheltered him from the public hatred that had targeted him. If there is such a thing as Catholicism's erstwhile purgatory, it must be a kind of a storeroom where the souls are deposited until the resentment and the hatred they have generated throughout their lives have waned. She freed him from that purgatory.

More important, she demonstrated that no matter how atrocious the crimes of her son, love could transform those actions in a source of universal and perennial good. Through her love his actions became an occasion for universal forgiveness. I'll try to explain. We are all familiar with the Hatfield-McCoy family feuds. In some regions of the Italian countryside (Sicily, Calabria, Sardinia, Corsica; this last region belongs to France but its inhabitants speak mainly Italian) such feuds are still active. Generation after generation of individuals (until now men, though women in recent years might have demanded to be part of the endeavor in the name of equality) learn how to hate and to kill each other in the name of a forgotten ancient offense. This hatred becomes more widespread and pervasive with each generation, as the family becomes a tribe of related individuals and risks involving an entire region until somebody takes the initiative to ask for forgiveness and says "the buck stops here." Only God knows how much more hatred the hatred for Ted Bundy might have spread, had his mother not taken the initiative to say: "The buck stops here."

The actions of Ted Bundy represent an extreme expression of everyday occurrences. I don't know a single person who is not overwhelmed by the emotional debts left unpaid by previous generations and carries with himself or herself a form of resentment that metastasizes to all relations like a cancer that metastasizes to different organs. In my case, until I made peace with my parents and grandparents, I could not help but to transfer my resentment to all the people I came to know including my friends, my girlfriends, my wife's family. What I am trying to say is that we all need the redemption that Bundy's mother effected.

Redemption is a typical Jewish concept, centered on the figure of the redeemer. This was the man who paid the debts of a family member and prevented the sale of that family member and his family as slaves. Slavery was the punishment for unpaid debts, according to Mosaic Law. In Christian beliefs, which developed in a Jewish culture, Christ was the redeemer of humanity as his death paid for the debts contracted by our progenitors and freed humanity from the slavery of sin and death. But the aspiration to redemption is present in all cultures, even those that precede the Judeo-Christian tradition. The great Greek mythology expressed both the aspiration to redemption and the human tragedy of not being able to achieve it. In his book *The Labyrinth of Solitude*, the Mexican philosopher Octavio Paz, who won the 1990 Nobel Prize, states: "History has the cruel reality of a nightmare, and the grandeur of man consists in his making beautiful and lasting works out of the real substance of that nightmare." I see this statement as a call for redemption as the ultimate goal of human life by a person who did not profess any form of religion. In his book *Sor Juana Inés de la Cruz, o, las trampas de la fe* Paz could have not been more critical of the Christian faith. Likewise another Nobel Prizewinner, Ernest Hemingway, an avowed agnostic, in his book *For Whom the Bell Tolls*, reminds us that we are all connected, that the debts of a person are the debts of the whole humanity.

The premise of this book is redemption as a universal aspiration and effecting redemption as the only activity able to fulfill the most demanding human expectations. Redemption makes life worth living. In my view life is a journey of discovery, rather than the travel toward a safe apron. The pursuance of a safe apron distracts humankind from the joy and the satisfaction of discovering redemption. The frustration of being unable to reach this safe apron is the source of all addictions. Not being able to obtain their goals, oblivious of the joys of discovery (from the scent of flowers to the masterpieces of art and nature, to human affection) people look for solace in chemicals, sex, overwork. The mother of all lies, which may take innumerable forms, is the existence of a fleeting safe harbor that can be reached by pure human effort. Only confronting and acknowledging this lie one can redirect himself or herself to the tasks of redemption, directed by unconditional love, inspired by transfiguration.

As I am a physician and have spent the last fifty years of my life in the medical field, I will focus on medical lies to illuminate the paradigm. The role of medicine, of course, is to enable people to begin and to continue their ongoing journey of redemption. Instead, in its practice in the West, divorced from spirituality, medicine has become perverted into promising medical solutions to human problems. Health has become one of the many illusory safe harbors detouring humans from the road to redemption. Humans are coerced to divert resources corresponding to trillions of dollars toward the goal of an impossible physical perfection that would never satisfy the human aspiration of redemption, even if it were reachable.

The safe harbor of physical perfection is really not different from the safe harbor of the perfect home, the perfect vacation, the perfect family, the perfect job or the safe harbor to fame to be achieved as a scientist, a sports hero, an artist, a literary genius or a successful political leader. I was still living in Italy during the World Cup of 1970. Italy beat Germany overtime in one of the most exciting games in the history of soccer. After the game the roads in all Italian towns were spontaneously invaded by a rowdy crowd celebrating this memorable victory. My intellectual friends were ashamed. "Why do we not see similar manifestations when one of our scientists gains the Nobel Prize?" "What is the difference?" I would ask today.

Perhaps the common enemy underlying these detours from the road to redemption toward the road to addiction and self destruction is a faceless and chameleonic power that aims to maintain humanity in a condition of self-centered slavery, like a dog pursuing its tail. Blindfolded by the promise of an impossible safe haven, humans are unable to partake of the joy of freedom, to look beyond oneself in the search of one's role and mission. This nameless power thrives on hatred, because its very survival depends on human life being disposable. The vision of transfiguration that allows one to see in each and every human a unique player in a greater design is the only antidote to the destructiveness of this power. Transfiguration generates unconditional love and, with that, the joy of redemption. The insidiousness of this power was best described by Pier Paolo Pasolini, an Italian homosexual author and essayist who came out of the closet when doing so put both his life and his livelihood at risk. Proud of being different, Pasolini stated in one of his essays: "The majority of people is always wrong!" That was the best indictment I ever heard of the myth of representative democracy that has been long enshrined as the ideal form of human freedom. At that time democracy was reigning in most countries of the Western world and, despite that, homosexuals were demonized because of their perceived "difference." As Pasolini clearly saw, representative democracy is representative of the power of the mob! Democracy was just one more of those illusory safe harbors that distract human beings from themselves and silence their aspiration to redemption. Representativeness is one more of those lies on which power thrives.

Perhaps the best example of how this power has been enshrined as the supreme human achievement comes from the proposals to clone human beings. Without stepping into the ethical debate related to cloning, I ask its proponents: "Who among you would like to clone Jesus Christ, or Francis of Assisi, or Luther? Or Calvin, or any major Christian leaders?" No! The interest is to clone beauty, intelligence and physical fitness; that is, those characteristics that favor the achievement of power, not those that spread love and redemption! Though most people profess devotion to love, their actions and choices testify devotion to power!

Perhaps the most controversial proposition of this book will be the statement of my Christian faith as the only source of unconditional love and the only effective antidote to the lies of power. My Christianity rests on three legs. They are the Christian message, the act of faith and the awareness of spirit.

The Christian message acknowledges the subjection of humankind to evil and offers a way to redemption. The sacrifice of Christ on the cross tells all of humanity: "The buck stops here; I have taken upon myself the hatred that has imprisoned your humanity in centuries past. Now you can elect not to hate anymore, because your hatred is dead with me. In fact, in my death you are offered the way to effect redemption by your own suffering. I made you partners of redemption, which allows you to freely exercise your aspiration to unconditional love." I am unaware of any other religious beliefs offering the opportunity for ongoing redemption, for the ongoing exercise of unconditional love. Equally important, the Christian message is historical, not philosophical; it took the flesh of a man and the body of an assembly, the church that survived more than 2,000 years.

The act of faith means to believe in something that is not evident by itself, based on the authoritative testimony of a person. My act of faith relies on the testimony of two Catholic priests who, at different time of my life, prevented my self destruction, because they knew better than I did what was good for me. Their faith showed them what was good for me. My act of faith also rests on the joy that the Christian faith brought into the lives of some of the people I have met, a joy that I found contagious.

Finally, there have been moments in my life where I could not help but feel the direct intervention of God, like the time when I thought I had lost my beloved wife on a dangerous mountain wall, as I will narrate to readers who join me on my spiritual journey. A fictional TV character, Father Ryan, once asked: "Who is the crazy one? The one who hears the thunderstorm and believes it is the voice of God or the one who hears the voice of God and believes it is a thunderstorm?" The reader will decide. I certainly am inclined to see the intervention of the spirit in all events of my life.

## CHAPTER 1

# The Mother of All Lies

"Just lie! Make it up, dammit!" I said. "How can you expect to become a physician if you don't learn how to lie?"

The third year medical student wore a crisp short white coat, starched, fresh from the laundry, a designer tie and long styled hair. He proudly sported a stethoscope around his neck and an ophthalmoscope in his front pocket. He appeared genuinely stupefied. His expression was a mixture of disbelief, dismay and politeness. Wary about arguing with his teacher during the first day of his clinical rotation, he owed it to himself, to the sense of his own dignity, to rebut statements that sounded to him nothing less than egregious. Frantically he was trying to read my expression. He hoped I was joking. That would have offered him a way out of a dangerous confrontation even if he did not appreciate a sense of humor behind my comments that he judged very inappropriate.

I had asked him what the blood sugar level of his patient was. "I am sorry, Dr. Balducci, I forgot to look it up," he answered, hoping that I would have lauded his honesty and his candor. My inciting him to lie caught him by surprise and astonished him. All of a sudden he had heard from the voice of the teacher that a medical team was not a Boy Scout troop. My duty as a teacher was to be after him, and his duty was not to be caught with his pants down even if had to resort to a lie. For the young man entrusted to my tutoring, this was going to be a long two months!

Days later the vice chancellor called me into his office. He told me to tone down my rhetoric and to respect a student's personal values. The son of a well respected practitioner in town, that third year student could have caused us a lot of problems with the community had I persisted in my cynical truth-telling. To survive dire economic times, the university needed to do a lot of fund raising. The suspicion of a farming-oriented Southern legislature inclined to see in a teaching hospital a Frankenstein laboratory contrary to basic Christian teaching in virtually every scientific experiment did not help either. The promotion of the lie as the most successful way of practicing medicine by me—a foreign-born faculty member who claimed to be an agnostic—would have jeopardized the support of the Medical School by a small Southern town closing ranks around a number of Baptist churches professing the power of the revealed truth.

Thirty years later the same medical student, now a prominent brain surgeon, wrote me this letter:

Dear Dr. Balducci,

Your lesson about lies has been the most durable and meaningful of my entire medical career! I wish to thank you for having opened my eyes and for having allowed me to pursue a very successful profession. I also hope you will forgive me for the embarrassment and the pain I caused you when I reported you to the dean. That was the immature reaction of a young man who had grown up in privilege and had kept his eyes wide shut about the realities of life up to that point. You opened my eyes! Your incitation to lie was the most truthful lesson I ever received, maybe the only candid statement I was handed during my medical school and residency. It made me aware of having grown embedded in a web of lies that was going to suffocate the real self I was desperately looking for. Thanks for providing the scissors to cut the web and make myself free.

Very truly yours . . .

Of course I was moved in learning that after so much time he had understood what I had been trying to tell him. The expectations that the faculty was putting on medical students and medical residents, like the expectations that patients eventually would bestow on these future doctors, were and are totally unrealistic. The only way to meet those expectations was and is to take shortcuts. More important: It really did not matter what the patient's blood sugar was; what mattered was to know whether he was or was not diabetic. I did not expect an exact answer from the third year medical student. All I wanted was a correct answer.

Here is an example of how young medical doctors learn to masquerade as all-knowing wizards: "If you have been up all night to take care of patients and did not have time to read about your patients, it means that you have slept too much," Eugene Stead, M.D., chairman of medicine at Duke University, used to tell his house-staff. Whether Professor Stead should be considered an icon of medicine or a sadistic abuser of young people is not the issue here. The issue is that to meet his expectations, the house staff had no choice but to lie—because, being human, at some point they needed to sleep!

When did I learn this lesson myself? Perhaps when a prominent professor from New York came to visit the residency program where my wife, Claudia, and I were interns. During the morning report he sat at the head of the table without a smile, without even an expression of sympathy for young men and women in scrub suits, trying to vanquish, with gallons of coffee sipped between yawns, the fatigue of an additional sleepless night. None of us had time to shave or to comb our hair. His gelid eyes pierced our faces digging for faults that he would, with relish, underline and punish. His stated goal, endorsed by the American Board of Internal Medicine that he had the privilege and honor to chair, was only to improve the program and make us more responsible physicians. I imagine he saw as role models the Egyptian taskmasters compelling the Hebrews slaves to build the pyramids, whipping them to death. The survivors would have learned from their experience to become stronger men.

He interrupted my presentation about a woman admitted during the night (she suffered from an abdominal mass and anemia) to ask me what the peripheral blood smear looked like. Looking directly into his dead eyes with my firm eyes, compelling my mouth to withhold an explosive yawn, I answered with the firmest voice I could muster, "She had microcytic anemia with target cells." Of course I had not looked at the peripheral blood smear in the middle of the night. But my lie made him happy! Happy that I had lost a few precious minutes of sleep for an activity that was completely and utterly irrelevant to her treatment and that could have waited until the following morning.

"Let's hope I am dreaming!" I was telling myself. "He must be 60 years old, an age when most people enjoy a stroll in the park with the family dog or take care of their grandchildren. Instead this man flew three hours on an airplane, for what? Just to make sure that I unnecessarily lost more sleep!" The situation felt like being trapped in a Kafka tale.

During the Middle Ages the abbots of monastic orders used to break the pride of new monks by forcing them into strenuous exercises that appeared futile to any reasonable person, such as carrying water in a basket from a river to the monastery three miles away. The visiting professor clearly felt that practicing medicine was a religious exercise needing unconditional submission. Thanks to this blind submission to the gods of medicine of their times, the disciples of Dr. Benjamin Rush in Chicago killed more people with phlebotomies (bloodletting) than the yellow fever they pretended to cure.

In the steps of Benjamin Rush, the visiting professor got his own victim, thanks to my dear wife, who never could learn how to make things up. She presented the case of a young black prisoner with renal failure who had been denied dialysis because he had proved to be an "unreliable patient." This means he could not be expected to follow medical advice. In the days before Medicare had approved dialysis for every patient, a committee was charged with deciding who would receive dialysis and who was doomed to experience complete renal failure. It could have been called a death panel indeed (perhaps impaneled by the same people who are concerned that universal medical coverage may lead to pulling the plug from grandma's ventilator).

That committee—composed of physicians, nurses, psychologists, and social workers—correctly decreed that dialysis would have posed an unnecessary risk to the welfare of this individual. Feigning distress, with deep sighs for the fate of this black prisoner, the professor accusatorily barraged my poor wife and the specialists on the committee: "How can we accept nowadays that anybody die of renal failure? You must go back to the renal specialists and ask them to reconsider their troublesome decision."

During this Broadway-worthy performance I could not help thinking: "Son of a bitch! I bet that if you were to find one of your house staff comatose on the floor you would fire him instead of taking care of him. And now you pretend to be beset with compassion for a prisoner you never met!"

The renal people heeded the professor's sham plea, as they really were given no choice. As a result the poor black prisoner traded a painless death from kidney failure with the most painful of deaths from peritonitis caused by peritoneal dialysis, courtesy of truthfulness in medicine.

Here's what happened to the poor black prisoner: During the night, trying to go to the bathroom, the young man pulled out the dialysis catheter dwelling in his abdomen. For him it was nothing more than an annoying intrusion of his intimacy by people he did not trust and did not like and mainly did not understand. As a result of this operation all the bacteria that had covered the walls and the floor of the penitentiary and that had lodged in the grooves of his hands, so deep that none of our disinfectants could reach them, gained access to his peritoneum. An autopsy revealed the bacteria did feast on it for a few days by literally gnawing it piecemeal. The infection had skinned him alive from inside out.

He died this painful death owing to the pretense of compassion by a man, a Master of the American College of Physicians, in whom the practice of medicine and medical politics had long ago dried up any human sentiments. Or maybe a man whose feelings had been strangled by the chain of lies he had nurtured throughout his life.

The foundation of the young black prisoner's death was the worst type of lie, the lie feeding on the truth. It was true, as the sanctimonious professor implied, that medicine discriminated against the minorities and the poor. The discrimination occurred when a group of privileged people at the National Institutes of Health or at the head of some private foundations decided to invest a substantial amount of money in the development of kidney dialysis instead of promoting welfare and education for everybody. *That's* when the discrimination occurred—not when the dialysis was denied to the prisoner on the assumption, validated by the events, that it would have turned against him as an instrument of torture and death.

The lie I had urged the third-year medical student to tell was a little white lie in pursuit of a patient's ultimate healing. But, in fact, Western medicine is built on lies that undermine the patient's ability to heal. There are lies that divorce physical healing from spiritual healing. There are lies that prop up technology and pharmaceuticals as the only true answers. There are lies that say doctors can successfully intervene in patients' lives while displaying not one whit of compassion. There are lies that say that the doctor always knows best.

Allow me a brief literary example from my native Italy. Giovanni Verga, a Sicilian engineer turned writer at the beginning of the last century, has crystallized the alienation of the poor by the medical system in his masterpiece *I Malavoglia*, first printed in 1881. The Malavoglias were a fisherman family who tried to improve their status by exempting themselves from the rules of the local bosses. After losing their only asset, their fishing boat, during a tempest, the family had a downfall from which they could not recover, as they had lost all social support when they had challenged the village leadership. Even the closest friends skirted the Malavoglias for fear of the bosses' revenge. The patriarch of the family refused to declare bankruptcy, as he felt duty-bound to honor his commitments and pay his debts. As a result the family was evicted and scattered. The life of each child was disrupted. The second daughter was disowned and forgotten after she found no solution to her problems but to sell her body in a brothel catering to sailors.

Eventually the patriarch developed cancer and was interned in the hospital of Catania (the major city of the area), where he felt like a stranger in an environment that had not been generated by him or for him. This stern individual had preferred to make himself and his family homeless rather than dishonor it with insolvency; he could not muster sympathy for a daughter who had chosen prostitution over starvation. He had faced death every night on a capricious sea ruled by unpredictable weather. He had endured innumerable wounds of his flesh and fractures of his bones when trying to subdue his boat to the strait's currents, without as much as a cry, without even a complaint. In the regimented environment of the hospital he had become a pawn in the hands of a player he had never met. He had lost the only thing that had mattered to him: his control over his own life, which for him was tantamount to his dignity and his honor. He had been disempowered and dishonored. That was too much for him to bear. He fell into a deeply depressive mood and died of starvation in a forgotten corner of the establishment, much earlier than his cancer could have killed him.

The situation is emphasized in few majestic scenes of the movie version of the book. *La Terra Trema* (*The Earth Trembles*) is a prize-winning cinematographic masterpiece directed by Lucchino Visconti in 1948. For this production the director refused to hire professional actors and engaged fishermen who spoke only Sicilian dialect on the set. When programmed in Italian theaters, the movie was shown with Italian subtitles. This organization sent a powerful message: the Malavoglia patriarch spoke a different language from the nurses and the physicians who were supposed to take care of him. The director asked: How could they possibly help him or how could he ask their help if they could not even communicate?

Our visiting professor from New York would have answered this dramatic question with the mother of all lies, the one on which he had based a lifetime of lies: "They did not need to communicate because the doctors knew what was good for him. Health is an objective good that benefits all people irrespective of their origin, beliefs, religious affiliations and sexual orientations." In other words there is an objective truth and an objective good identified by reason and independent from whom and what people are.

When I urged the third year medical student to lie, I must confess that my statement was more than a rhetorical device to attract the young student's attention and to break the young man into the reality of medical practice. It was also an expression of my deep anger toward a lie that had haunted most of my life up to that point and that had led me to the threshold of self annihilation. One could say that I practiced lying as a way of life throughout the initial 30 years of my life, and I had grown progressively more conscious of the burden of lying, including mostly the inability to generate the love I craved (and even worse to express the love I wished for and I did not know how to share). A hidden message for that medical student and all medical students I tutored up to that time was "welcome to the unhappy world of lies," the same way an attractive woman left a message on the bed of her unknown partner after a one-night stand: "Welcome to the world of AIDS!" Like that woman I was eager to destroy other lives with the same lie that had threatened to ruin mine. In my view, my ability to lie had been a major asset in becoming a successful physician.

This book chronicles the history of my recovery, of how I found in my Christian faith the only effective bulwark against the destructiveness of lies. It wishes to be a message of hope for those human beings who feel like I did—that their life is overwhelmed by a pervasive and possessive lie.

I hope also to unmask some of the more obvious lies of Western health care and thereby show the patient how to arm himself or herself against them in negotiating our brave new world of pharmaceuticalized medicine. I hope that, in doing so, future generations of medical students will have a greater hope of being infused with compassion and grace during their medical training rather than robbed of the last vestiges of their humanity. And, of course, that patients will have a greater shot at being healed.

CHAPTER 2

# Pregnancy, Prostitutes and Death

## *Real Life Stories*

"Lawyers and prostitutes have clients; doctors have patients." This used to be one of the favorite mantras of one of my more beloved mentors and role models, Dr. Sandy Spiers. A Briton (maybe I should respect his wishes and call him a Scotsman) born in Australia and who emigrated to the States in the early '70s, Dr. Spiers was a bright hematologist who developed the cure for a rare disease (hairy cell leukemia) and who advanced the treatment of both acute myelogenous leukemia and large cell lymphoma. Though compassionate in his practice and caring toward his trainees, Sandy was also known for blunt statements that reflected a deep sense of humor that never abandoned him even in the darkest moments of his career. Later, I will outline how he was penalized by the medical bureaucracy for having cured five patients without having kept up all necessary paperwork. One may look at his action in this way (and I do): He had thrown a life ring to five drowning people without wasting time finding out whether the ring had undergone all the proper safety checks. (Sometimes medical bureaucracy promotes a safety that kills.)

His statement meant to convey his deep conviction that human life cannot be considered merchandise, and consequently a patient is never a "client." He balked at the current tendency of the profession to use this nomenclature; that is, to equate the search for cure and healing with the purchase of a new television set, a car, or a bag of groceries. Put another way, he felt, as I do, that medicine should be at the service of a person, which means that medicine, like any other human activity, should help the person to live and preserve his or her values.

Personal values are the central theme of the way I look at the practice of medicine as well as the filter through which I view my spiritual journey. The lie of our society, including medicine, the one that I called the mother of all lies, is the pretense that human values are independent from the person. The problem with setting up human values as independent from the person is the resulting concerted effort to disdain and destroy what is personal. Perhaps this dichotomy of individual and culture (or, if you will, of society, of environment)—an idealist philosopher like Johann Gottlieb Fichte or Georg Wilhelm Friedrich Hegel would have called it the conflict of "self "and "no self"—is as old as humanity; it is just the experience of living. But in our society—due to globalization, instantaneous communication, dissolution of the nuclear family, disappearance of a common language fostered by common beliefs—the destruction of the personal values that define a person has taken an accelerated pace never before seen. Is this dissolution irreversible? I will try to illustrate how medicine can help (or threaten) personal values.

"Why did my daughter not get an abortion yet?" thundered the powerful state senator in the halls of the hospital without any consideration of other patients' families or of his daughter's privacy. With his pointed beard and long hair, Sen. Bailey looked like Colonel Sanders in a double-breasted suit. Unlike that of the friendly colonel, his attitude was anything but benign. He seemed eager to shoot the first cannonball against "them Yankees."

For the first and perhaps only time, this Southern politician who had run innumerable battles on the state Capitol to outlaw abortion, sodomy and family leave was in full agreement with our activist, feminist and lesbian head nurse. The young girl did not know what she was doing and should be coerced into an abortion by people who knew what was good for her. Under the leadership of the nurse manager, the nurses on the floor threatened to withhold life-saving chemotherapy unless the young woman elected to terminate her pregnancy.

Susan Bailey was 19, unmarried, unemployed, eight weeks pregnant and just diagnosed with acute myelogenous leukemia. A high school dropout who had experimented with all types of drugs and all types of bed partners, men and women of all ethnic origins, she had been disowned by her conservative family. In the previous three years she had been living on charity or doing odd jobs or indulging in prostitution and drug peddling.

She already had two abortions. Now, with the imminent threat of death, she was staunchly fighting to preserve her pregnancy. "I knew I was going to die soon," she admitted to a social worker who interviewed her during a remission of her disease. "And if I had killed the baby in my womb, I would have felt as if I had died twice, as if I would be forever dead. I perceived that pregnancy as a guarantee of my survival. An abortion at this time would have felt as if I had aborted my own life! So far I had been a nuisance to my family and a reservoir of sexually transmitted diseases for the people I partnered with. I did not want to be remembered like that! I wanted to leave something alive, growing, a living witness that my life had not been a complete mistake, an abortion itself."

She was a prophet, which in ancient Greek means a spokesperson for God. Nineteen years later, her child is a six-foot-three sports star in an ivy league college and the pride and joy of his grandfather, who sports him around town to his political rallies as proof of his unyielding opposition to abortion and as a living witness to the fact that a life in the womb is a God-given gift nobody has the right to refuse!

"Doctor, I want you to meet Jeff," he told me at an official dinner as I happened to sit close to him and his grandson. "He knows that you and I protected his life and his mother's wishes, when everybody else wanted to destroy him in the womb!" I had a hard time holding back tears, but I also could not help asking whether he really meant it. Of course the young man subscribes in full to his grandfather's political stand. He is a leader of Christian conservatives in college. He has enshrined his mother as a heroine of the pro-life movement (fully deserving, I wish to add). I believe he also signed a commitment to preserve his virginity until the time of his marriage.

To be fair, Senator Bailey put his money where his mouth is. After Susan's death, five years following the diagnosis of leukemia, he raised millions of dollars for the support of unwanted pregnancies and has toned down the campaign rhetoric. His focus now is on nurturing pregnant women in need rather than penalizing abortion seekers and abortion providers.

This happy outcome was reached only as part of a monumental struggle. After Susan's diagnosis, I sat down for an hour with the senator, his wife and his older son to explain that it was all but impossible to perform an invasive procedure on an adult patient without her consent. "She is not an adult," snapped the Brooks Brothers-suited brother, who, at 29, was already a CEO of a major financial institution. "She is a goddamned addict whose brain has been turned to ashes by drugs and syphilis. I bet she does not even know who the father is of that bastard who is going to rob my legitimate children of part of their inheritance. I can't believe the law can't protect the assets of mine and my brothers' children. I can't believe the law can compel me to support a bastard with my hard work. You should have had the bitch sterilized as soon as she started having her periods." With this last sentence he looked straight at his mother, who was gulping silent tears in the corner. He paced the room up and down as I was wondering whether he might try to beat me up in lieu of his dejected sister.

The senator also had a hard time containing himself. More polite than his son, he could not help but grumble against those liberal laws that protected the lowlifes instead of the tax-paying hard-working people. Eventually, after the intervention of hospital lawyers, they realized there was no way to get Susan to kill her unborn child for any reason. Only the mother thanked me for the time I devoted to them. The whole family's attitude changed, however, when Susan went into remission. Sober and reinvigorated both by her pregnancy and her disease, she became most welcoming to the same family she had slammed the door against, and the family, including the brother, were moved by her change. I know that they celebrated when baby Jeff was taken home, and then again when Susan went to nursing school to pay back the care she had received in the hospital and to help other leukemia patients. Unfortunately her disease recurred just after she passed her licensure exam, but at that time she was at peace with the world and died six months later holding the hands of her four-year-old and her father.

We also had a meeting with the rebellious nursing staff and a psychologist who tried to defend the nurses' viewpoint. To them it was explained that to disregard the doctors' order simply because they objected to a patient's carrying on her pregnancy was a form of mutiny associated with criminal penalties. It was also pointed out that it was not a good idea to protect a baby's integrity by killing the baby, as they had claimed that their main concerns were the malformations that chemotherapy could induce. Finally, they were shamed into doing their homework. There is no proof in the medical literature that chemotherapy is teratogenic (that it produces fetal malformation) with very few exceptions that did not apply to Susan's case.

The case of Susan Bailey was definitely extreme, and it could not be repeated today in the United States. An appointed ethics committee would unanimously conclude that the patient's autonomy cannot be overturned and that an abortion against the will of the pregnant woman is all but a form of violence comparable to rape with battery. I chose to describe this case because it highlights, by being extreme, the issue of personal values in medicine. For whatever reason Susan felt validated by her baby, and the preservation of her pregnancy was worth more to her than the cure of her disease, which the nurses and her father felt, incorrectly, the pregnancy might have jeopardized. What she expected from medicine, and what medicine fortunately helped her to do, was to carry her pregnancy to term. The alternative response of official medicine, from the mouths of her nurses, was that her baby should be discarded the same way one empties a urinal, as a nuisance that stands in the way of cure. And of course everybody should know that cure is the absolute goal of medicine even when the patient is not interested in it. Technological medicine had taken a life on its own with its own set of values that are independent of a person's feelings and wishes.

Two more aspects or themes of Susan's case deserve mention. The first is redemption. In ancient Israel the redeemer was the man who agreed to pay the outstanding debts of a family member. Thanks to the generosity of the redeemer the insolvent debtor and his family could escape the fate of being sold as slaves. The Baileys needed redemption. The father's political and economic ambitions had estranged him from the very values that formed his electoral platform: the protection of the unborn life. Paradoxically he was ready to destroy an unborn child that interfered with his ability to promote policies that protect the unborn. One may add that his ambitions had also estranged him from his children. The promiscuous oft-stoned Susan and her coldhearted brother were two sprouts from the same roots, two fruits from the same tree. Neither of them had learned how to love because neither had ever felt loved. The unwanted Jeff and the disowned junkie Susan brought love back into a family that never learned to love, that was craving love but did not know how to love. Just as the death of Christ brought life to a death-enslaved humanity, the death of Susan redeemed her family from the slavery of suspicion, disaffection and hostility. She made a sacrifice of her life and of her pregnancy that brought together with the adhesive of love a family of which each member was lost in his or her own desert and did not know how to find their ways home.

Sacrifice derives from the Latin *sacrum facere,* which means to render sacred, reserved for a special use. Susan's physical suffering—endured through her long disease and her death, her emotional suffering during her solitude, her spiritual suffering from the disdain, the disregard and the open despisement bestowed on her and her child—had been the currency that redeemed the debts left unpaid by generations. Stockpiled on family life, those debts had transformed her family into a living tomb. When I think of Susan Bailey I conjure in my mind two images quite different in their demeanors that led to the same glorious outcome. The first is that of the Virgin Mary who accepted becoming a single mother in a culture where just the suspicion of promiscuity might have led to death by stoning. Like Mary, Susan carried on a pregnancy because she had faith in life though she might have never learned who was the source of that life, and her faith was reinforced rather than weakened by all the external pressures to have an abortion that were founded on seemingly reasonable arguments. In her heart of hearts she felt that her faith in life was stronger than the worldly reasoning that made abortion seem like a reasonable choice. The second image is that of the prostitute who washed Jesus' feet with her tears and dried them with her hair. Of her Jesus said: "Her sins, that are many, are forgiven because she has much loved."

I said Susan had been a prophet. When she told the social worker that she wanted to leave a print of herself, to continue living in her child, she did not realize the scope of her declaration. She was just thinking of a child who would link her life to her surviving siblings and friends, kind of a living memory. Yet, her inspired words implied that her death and her living child would bring healing to a family on the edge of collapse, would redeem centuries of unpaid debts that had overwhelmed that family's emotional and spiritual reserves. The redemption of her family from the slavery of lovelessness filled the thirst for love of all people she had touched. While talking of the birth of his own child to King Ahaz, the prophet Isaiah unknowingly predicted Christ's birth. Likewise, talking of her own child, Susan prophesied the redemption of her family and friends.

In the same vein I could not help thinking of the special role prostitutes had in the history of human salvation. According to the letter to the Hebrews, Rahab, a prostitute from Jericho, had been the first person saved by faith. American King James Version: "By faith the harlot Rahab perished not with them that believed not, when she had received the spies with peace." Inspired by a God she had never known, she had concealed Joshua's explorers and allowed the Hebrew conquest of Canaan. Without her intervention dictated by her faith in the work of an unknown (to her) God, the elected people would have never settled in the Promised Land and the birth of the world redeemer would have never happened. The chosen people would have been deselected forever. They would have been lost in the Sinai Desert as were millions of other shepherds destroyed by tribal feuds.

According to Genesis, Jesus was the descendant of a prostitute, a whoreson. (Genesis 38: 12–23) Tamar had remained a widow and childless. By Hebrew law she should have married the younger brother of her deceased husband, but her father-in-law, the patriarch Judah, had withheld assent. The resourceful young woman, defying the patriarchal society in which she lived, dressed herself as a street whore and in that fashion copulated with Judah, who had not recognized her. As a payment for her sexual services, she asked of Judah a comb and a ring. A few months later, when Tamar's pregnancy was discovered, Judah wanted her burned to death for adultery as prescribed by law. (Genesis 38: 24–30) Then she showed Judah the items with which he had compensated her. Repented, Judah acknowledged his own sin and allowed her to marry his younger son. She gave birth to twins;

one of them, Perez, is said to be the ancestor of King David. Again, without Tamar's resourceful disguise and sexual commerce, Jesus might have never been born.

And according to the Gospel the resurrected Jesus first appeared to Mary Magdalene, a prostitute, rather than to his righteous and unbelieving apostles. Without the intervention of a prostitute, the resurrected Jesus might have never been recognized, the Christian church would have never begun, the world's redemption would have never been effected, the death of Jesus would not have amounted to more than one of a thousand deaths from violence, disease or starvation that occurred every day in remote corners of the world.

Why Mary? one may ask. Because, thanks to the forgiveness of her many sins, she had gained the most from Jesus' redemptive death. Unlike the apostles who had their families and their jobs to go back to, she only had Jesus. Without Jesus her life had neither goal nor sense nor support.

It is difficult at this point not to see a parallel between Susan and the Magdalene. I don't know whether Susan had any formal religious beliefs. But because of her poverty she recognized her unborn child as her only asset. Worried about the preservation of their own privileges and prejudices, her parents, her siblings and her caregivers had seen only an encumbrance in a child who ended up becoming the redemption of many. A street peddler is in a better position to appreciate a dawn or a sunset than a man protected from nature by the walls of his mansion. As the Nobel Prizewinner Marguerite Yourcenar said in her 1929 novel *Alexis,* "When it is dark we are more clairvoyant because our eyes do not deceive us."

The Greek novelist Nikos Kazantzakis crystallized the role of the prostitutes in the history of salvation in his 1948 novel *The Greek Passion.* During the Turkish occupation of a small Greek village it is the village prostitute rather than the high clergy of the Orthodox Church who offers her own life for the liberation of her people.

The second theme is medical arrogance. This was not the first time and certainly won't be the last I have heard a proposal to perform an abortion on a woman who is about to receive cytotoxic chemotherapy.

"Lodovico, butt out! This is the real world, and you don't know or understand anything about it." A young woman on the phone screamed these words at me. I had mentored her during her oncology training, and she had just opened a private practice. She considered me then, and continued to consider me even after this episode, the most trustworthy of her mentors and counselors. More than once my wife and I had socialized with her and her husband, and we even gave her a baby shower for the birth of her first baby. And yet she could not tolerate what she perceived as an inappropriate intrusion in her domain. The case involved a 32-year-old woman with early stage breast cancer. After surgery that had removed tumors and lymph nodes, she needed six courses of chemotherapy to reduce by 5 percent the risk that her cancer would recur. She was also twelve weeks pregnant. I had called my former trainee, who had asked for my advice, to let her know that the abortion of this woman was not medically indicated.

Let's look at this case as dispassionately as we can. The pregnancy was not in any way threatening the mother's life, in which case I would have been ready to perform an abortion myself (even if I were to be excommunicated by my church). The benefits of chemotherapy were minimal, and so were the risks of fetal malformation. So where was the indication to abort a desired pregnancy outside of the prejudices of the treating physician imposing her view on a vulnerable patient?

And yet another case: "I can't believe that you are keeping this baby!" Every three weeks Jen and Judith hammered a 40-year-old woman with this refrain. The woman was receiving chemotherapy for breast cancer, and they were part of the medical team. Like many professional women, the patient had married late, at 37. After two years of unfruitful attempts, she succeeded in getting pregnant and like Susan wanted to preserve her pregnancy at any price. Breast cancer was discovered when she was five weeks pregnant, and chemotherapy began at the sixteenth week of her pregnancy, when the risk to the fetus was negligible. Jen was a victim of spousal abuse, we learned later. Her husband beat her regularly, and he got particularly incensed if she did not regularly shave her pubic hair. He liked hairless crotches because it made him feel as if he were copulating with a young girl. He also had subjected her to sodomy several times without her consent. Judith was a middle-aged woman, a proud volunteer of an organization promoting abortion. After her stormy divorce, 20 year earlier, she had developed hatred for men and all that concerned men. When her only daughter became pregnant at age 22, she tried to coerce her into an abortion. I believe the reader can judge for himself or herself how dependable were their professional recommendations to a woman concerned about protecting her pregnancy more than protecting her own life from cancer.

In treating a pregnant woman with cancer, there may be two medical reasons to consider abortion. The first is the concern that the pregnancy may accelerate cancer growth. This possibility has never been demonstrated. If anything, there is some evidence that a pregnancy may be beneficial in the cases of leukemia and lymphoma, but I am the first to admit that the evidence is feeble at best. The second reason is the concern that cancer chemotherapy may hurt the fetus. On this topic there are plenty of studies based on the outcome of pregnancies during chemotherapy as well as on fetuses that were spontaneously or medically aborted. While it is clear that chemotherapy may increase the rate of stillbirths, it is open to question whether it may cause birth defects. Perhaps the strongest support for this hypothesis comes from a study published in the Annals of Internal Medicine in 1980. In pregnant women with Hodgkin's disease who carried their pregnancies to term, the incidence of chemotherapy-induced birth defects was 10 percent, and in most cases these birth defects would not be seen to prevent a productive and happy life. The only exception is an unusual drug, aminopterine, that has been abandoned for more than thirty years (I never had the opportunity to use it), which has been associated with a high risk of birth defects.

Besides being based on false pretenses, the argument for abortion in pregnancy completely ignores the fact that the abortion is not necessarily a safe procedure and that we ignore, at least in this country, what the short and long term complications of abortion could be. To my knowledge nobody has studied the emotional impact of abortion on a woman already distressed by the diagnosis of a deadly disease. Like corporate polluters who refuse to even study the issue of global warming, and who put their profit ahead of the very preservation of the world, abortion proponents refuse to even consider that abortion may have disastrous medical consequences.

I am clearly an abortion foe, and I won't even pretend to be unbiased about the issue of abortion. I use the abortion example because it is one of those I know best and where I can best describe the lethal influence of medical arrogance. This issue is a mirror of how the power that medicine confers on the professional may be used to hurt vulnerable individuals. I have already mentioned how Dr. Rush killed more patients than he purported to cure of yellow fever with bloodletting.

As a veteran oncologist, I still remember how melanoma patients underwent ferocious amputations in the hope of curing their disease. Forty years ago a melanoma clinic looked like a hospital in a war zone given the number of amputees who attended it. I even remember a young man who had undergone, willingly, the amputation of his penis. The reason for this legal maiming? An observation in 1912 indicating that melanoma, a cancer of the skin, had a tendency to recur within three centimeters of the place where it was surgically removed. From this questionable observation the dogma was derived that only a 5 cm margin-free resection could guarantee a cure. Two Italian studies revealed that a 1 cm margin was sufficient, at least in the case of the so called "thin " melanoma, in the early 80s. Only in 1993 the first American study was published supporting the Italian findings. When Dr.Charles Balch challenged the dogma and proposed a study of a shorter (1 or 2 cm) margin, he was treated like a Dr. Mengele by the Human

Investigation Committees. Medical ethicists felt that the study was immoral because the smaller margin might have been associated with an increased risk of melanoma-related deaths, and they spoke eloquently against the study. Thanks to medical ethicists, we may still disable the majority of melanoma patients with the promise of a cure. In my experience an assembly of bioethicists can be much more dangerous to human health than a combination of cancer chemotherapy drugs has been to the unborn child. Perhaps the most humorous (were it not tragic) example of medical arrogance concerns a 1700 German gynecologist who recommended that physicians wash their hands after having examined a woman and prior to examining the next one. At that time, wealthy women delivered their offspring at home and the poor ones were admitted to the hospital, three in each bed. The death from puerperal sepsis (infection) in the hospital was higher than 40 percent! By washing his hands after each visit and prior to the next one, the visionary physician reduced the rate of puerperal death to a lower level than that seen in home delivery. Yet, he was derided by his colleagues and scolded by the medical society for carrying out such a mundane study.

As a footnote, I'll add that I witnessed the practice of putting three pregnant women in each bed in Dakar, the capital of Senegal, in a ward called "high risk pregnancy." One may wonder whether the pregnancies were at high risk before or after admission to the hospital.

The next case is somehow the mirror image of Susan Bailey's. I felt I had to include it as an acknowledgement of my own bias against abortion and to establish some type of balance in a narrative that is highly charged with my own emotions.

I had met Daisy Green when she was twelve and I was a medical intern. At that time she was a shy girl with braces on her teeth who had not started menstruating yet. She had been taken to the hospital because she had developed juvenile diabetes and her mother wanted her to benefit from consultation with the institution's renowned diabetologist. Besides her shy smile and her braces, I remember that she was always asleep when we entered her room during morning rounds. In the hospital she was taking advantage of the absence of adult supervision to watch television late at night.

Fourteen years later I met Daisy again. Now she was a proud young executive of our hospital, engaged to a medical student who planned to become a family practitioner. The wedding was scheduled after her fiancé's graduation, and they planned to move to Oregon shortly thereafter for his residency. She had already found a job in the hospital where her husband was scheduled to intern. After meeting them at a number of hospital functions, Claudia and I became kind of adult confidants for the jolly young couple looking toward a promising future.

Four months before the wedding date, Daisy discovered she was pregnant. Even before she informed her fiancé, she ran to our house in tears. It had been the first time that they had complete sexual relations (how many times had one heard this "first time" story in the case of an unwanted pregnancy!), she declared between sobs. What was she to do? She dreaded to idea of walking down the aisle on her father's arm in a white dress and with a four-month tummy. Her grandparents, her cousins, her aunts and uncles — all would be flying in from all over the country (and even from Europe) for the wedding. More than two hundred people would be congregating to witness her shame.

Claudia and I sat at her side with an affectionate expression for this confused "quasi daughter." We knew only too well that it would be virtually impossible to influence her decision. It was clear that she wanted our approval for an abortion. While we could not endorse such action, which was contrary to our principles and our beliefs, we could certainly express our emotional support and reassure her of our unconditional love. And that is what we tried to do with our silence, our expressions and our availability. To listen to Daisy, we interrupted a busy evening during which I had planned to prepare a scientific presentation and Claudia to perform a laborious quality-assurance review of her staff. Both our tasks were due the following morning.

For an hour at least she shared with us anecdotes of her family life. Between ages six and 18, when she left home for college, she had never missed a single Sunday school class or Sunday service. When her 19-year-old brother came home stoned on pot his father did not talk to him for a month and threatened to report him to the police. Likewise she was very sternly scolded when she came home smelling of booze from her school prom. Her parents' living room was replete with wedding pictures of her mother and her aunt in white dresses that revealed the family commitment to virginity. Her fiancé's father was a conservative preacher who had worked with Jerry Falwell to establish Liberty University. The young couple was contemplating joining a medical mission in an African country through Falwell's church. After these and many other stories illustrating how the concomitance of pregnancy and wedding were all but unacceptable to her and her fiancé's family, Daisy concluded: "I cannot do this to them. Tomorrow I will talk to Dr. Finch (her gynecologist) and ask for an abortion. I put myself into this trouble, and I have to solve it myself."

Claudia hazarded a comment. "I believe you should at least talk it over with John. After all he is the father and should have something to say about it."

"No, he is studying late at night for his final. If I involve him in this I may compromise his very graduation. No, I have to take care of it and I will." She started singulting in Claudia's arms. We realized nothing we could say would change her mind. After saying that she could spend the night with us, we kissed her goodbye. She drove home.

Three days later she called us from home. She had had the abortion the day before. John thought that she was bedridden for a couple of days due to flu and heavy periods. She planned to be back to work next week. How did she sound? Distant? Sad? I don't know of any adjective that could convey the tone of her voice. The best comparison I can use is of a person who has just received a major disappointment. Maybe a student who has just flanked an exam for which he or she had studied hard. Or an employee who after a disastrous job interview realized he would never get the position or the promotion. Or a lover who has just discovered that her partner is cheating on her and that their marriage plans are crumbling. We did not hear from her anymore. Surprisingly we were not even invited to her white-dress wedding that took place on the established date at the established time. I am sure it was not an oversight. She did not want to face through us the decision that changed her life. She wanted to pretend that her abortion had never happened, had been just a nightmare. The last we heard from some mutual friends a year later, she had experienced marital difficulty. But this really does not mean anything. Whose marriage is not in trouble during the first year of a medical residency? You don't have to invoke the abortion to explain it.

The case of Daisy is germane to this chapter in two opposite and yet converging ways. First and foremost, it is a statement of patients' values and autonomy. No matter how much one abhors abortion, as long as abortion is a legal form of birth control it was the ethical duty of an abortion provider to terminate Daisy's pregnancy. I am sure that all but the most ardent abortion supporters will find Daisy's motivations silly, to say the least. In general, when we hear a defense of abortion, we hear about women who cannot afford to raise their babies or who have been victims of sexual violence. But to abort a baby so that you can wear a white dress at your wedding without shame? To abort a baby to pretend virginity? That idea is especially ironic given the common wisdom that one cannot enter a commitment to live with a person without establishing sexually compatibility. Gimme a break!

I asked a colleague, as a joke, during the wedding of her brother, if she thought that her new sister-in-law was a virgin. "I hope not," this good Catholic girl retorted. "We are in the twentieth century!"

Perhaps the closest case to Daisy's I had seen occurred in Italy. A medical student's girlfriend inquired in our department of obstetrics about the possibility of an abortion. Birth control had failed; her diaphragm had punctured as she was copulating. "I don't want to have a baby I have not planned for," she stated. As absurd as this pretense of control may sound, I still find it more dignifying than a white dress at one's wedding. Yet, as providers, we should not judge another person's values. Daisy deserved an abortion as she valued a pretense of virginity on her wedding day more than her maternity.

The second point is how medicine may influence personal and social values. It is legitimate to ask whether the availability of legal and safe abortion makes it a duty for medical professionals to abort a baby for people in Daisy's condition. Many times I have heard some of my male friends condemn a single mother because she decided to carry her child to term. They perceived it a form of punishment or even of exploitation of the man who unwittingly released his semen between her thighs, oblivious of the fact that few a drops of transient pleasure might be transformed into a lasting life. Perhaps this issue was crystallized best in a New York Times opinion piece (hardly a pro-life publication) around 10 years ago, by a certain King (I have forgotten his first name). He and his wife were practicing Roman Catholics and at the same time belonged to the New York intellectual elite. During his wife's pregnancy, the development of the baby still in the womb became retarded. A number of well- meaning friends started asking what they were waiting for in putting off an abortion. There was no proof of that the child was dead or deformed, only that the fetus was developing slower than normal. Eventually, the pressure of condescending or benevolent expressions and comments became so heavy that the couple decided to have an abortion—even in the absence of what are called medical indications. They regretted the decision since and, as a form of penance, annually celebrated the birthday of the unborn child on the anniversary of the abortion. A case of retarded fetal development had threatened to compromise their status within the New York intelligentsia, had they not chosen an abortion.

But the pressure is not limited to abortion, of course. A simple anecdote related to a patient of mine may illustrate this. This German lady living in the United States had received chemotherapy for breast cancer, and she had become bald, as happens with most patients receiving cytotoxic chemotherapy. A cruel joke in Utrecht, Netherlands, asked: "How do you recognize the tombs of Pinedo's patients if you fly over the graveyard?" Punchline: "They are those where the grass and flowers fail to grow." Pinedo was chief of oncology at the Catholic University of Utrecht and one of the best known oncologists in the world. While my lady was sitting in the clinic waiting room minding her own business, another woman asked her: "Do you want everybody to feel sorry for you because you have cancer? Why don't you wear a wig or a hat?" What was originally presented as a choice or an opportunity, to wear a wig to conceal one's baldness, all of a sudden had become a social duty, to the delight, of course, of the medical-industrial system that thrived on the addition of new duties and new values. If he had lived today, Francis of Assisi would probably have been excluded from the majority of churches because his poor attire was considered inappropriate.

Finally, one may ask why a staunch opponent of abortion as I am appeared to be supportive or at least uncritical of Daisy's decision. The answer to this question is very simple. If I had a daughter and my daughter decided to have an abortion, I would feel it my duty to take her to the abortion clinic. We don't quit loving our children or our friends because we disagree with their decisions. I admire the mother of Ted Bundy, the serial woman killer from Florida. The night before he was executed she called him and told him: "You are forever my beloved son."

CHAPTER 3

# The Case of Peggy Sue

Susan's and Daisy's case illustrate what I mean about personal values and how these values should lead the medical practice rather than the other way around, as is happening more and more often. The case of Peggy Sue crystallizes this issue most clearly. The case involves a clear-cut decision between pregnancy and cure, without the emotional overtones of the abortion choice.

"Doctor, I expect a definite answer to this question. If I get pregnant, will I be able to carry my pregnancy to term without harm to my baby? This is all I wish to know. With all due respect, the other issues are my personal business!"

Perhaps Peggy Sue was a little irritated with me, but mostly she sounded frustrated. For forty-five minutes I had avoided her question, trying to convince her to receive a life-saving allogeneic bone marrow transplant (one in which the donated material comes from a different, though often related, individual). This procedure would most certainly have cured her newly diagnosed chronic myelogenous leukemia. But bone marrow transplant carried a risk of death of around 15 percent. Also there was a 50 percent chance that the chemotherapy in high doses preceding the transplant would make her sterile forever. So, the attempt to cure her disease implied a 70 percent chance that she never would enjoy the experience of a pregnancy. Begrudgingly she had chosen to delay that experience until her husband had completed his medical residency. As an accomplished high school teacher, she had a master's degree in English literature; she had supported the family budget during the so called "slim years" of the residency. When the time to carry her dream to fruition had come, leukemia had struck. It was diagnosed from a routine blood count the very day she went for the first obstetric check-up, to get ready for a pregnancy she had dreamed of since she was a girl. The fourth of five children, four sisters and one brother, Peggy Sue had always seen in maternity the accomplishment of her womanhood.

As children, her sisters and she had played a game of betting who would be the most prolific mother. They came up with the most elaborate names for their future children. As a Christmas gift once she received a Cabbage Patch doll. In receiving this gift, popular in the '80s, the recipient was asked to sign a commitment to take care of the puppet as if she were a real baby, including nursing her thrice a day, bathing and strolling her once a day. She honored this commitment until the day of her wedding, probably a Guinness world record. She decided to enshrine the doll among her dearest memories then, so as not to trouble her marriage with the presence of a previous child.

I felt ashamed after her terse statement. It dawned on me that I had not listened to my patient; instead I gave her my standard talk on chronic myelogenous leukemia. Even a used car salesman listens to his customers and will not offer a Cadillac to somebody asking for a Honda. But clearly, at some unconscious level, I felt that a doctor does not have to listen to his patients, as a doctor knows what is good for a patient irrespective of what a patient wants or is. I always was proud to say that a physician is not a used car salesman. In this instance I proved it.

In the case of Peggy Sue, I unmasked to myself and to the world the nature of the difference: medical arrogance and condescension. The almighty doctor knew what the patient should have done, for her own good, of course. Even worse, I had betrayed the trust of one of my trainees. Reginald (Peggy Sue's husband) had entrusted the care of his wife to me after two other oncologists had fumbled her expectations. Very popular among my residents, I was considered the "doctor's doctor," the highest honor that a resident class may bestow on one of their teachers. Most residents, staff and colleagues came to me first when one of their family members or friends was diagnosed with cancer. He sent Peggy Sue to me because I was renowned for my compassion and my ability to listen. Now Peggy Sue' s few words made my self esteem crumble: I had rested on the laurels of my fame and forgotten that one has to start again every morning to build this trust!

"Look, Peggy Sue," I said, looking to the floor instead of trying to establish eye contact as I generally do with my patients. Though she was half my age I perceived her as a mother reproaching a child whose lack of attention had badly hurt someone's feelings. "Maybe to say I am sorry is not enough, but I beg you to accept my apology, if you can. You came to see me to unload your concerns, and I completely overlooked them to give you a forty-five minute lecture that you probably had already heard three times and had perfected with your own research. I am ashamed to have wasted your time and to have ignored your concerns. If you give me another chance I would like to try to care for you one more time."

As I raised my eyes to her face I was struck by a benign, accepting smile on her face, a smile that conveyed trust and acceptance. This message was confirmed by her few meaningful words.

"Yes, Lodovico, let's try again. I have full trust in you."

This was the first time she had called me by my first name. I encouraged the residents and their spouses to be on a first-name basis with me. My large, imposing presence (and maybe my sarcasm and sometimes unpredictable behavior) discouraged most of them from accepting this invitation. By calling me Lodovico she signified that a new day had started in our relationship, that the air had been cleared from hurt and misunderstanding. My heartfelt apology had worked.

"Though the behavior of any disease may change, I don't see any reason why you should not get pregnant and should not be able to carry your pregnancy to term. Your white count is fairly low, the percentage of blasts in your blood is less than 1 percent; you don't have any complex genetic changes, and I can't palpate your spleen. Even without treatment you may live at least another three years, and with treatment more than five. Your chances of having a normal pregnancy are not different from those of a woman of the same age as yours. I have only two recommendations: Try to get pregnant as soon as possible, and delay the treatment with interferon for the first three months of the pregnancy, just in case, as the safety of interferon during embryogenesis is not established."

This time her smile became an enlightening and warming sun, and she hugged me as a daughter hugs a father who has just satisfied her most intense desire. Ten months later she gave birth to a healthy girl. Concerned that interferon might have increased the chance of a stillbirth, she delayed the treatment with interferon. That decision might have cost her her life, and she was told so.

The christening ceremony was particularly touching. Maybe more than fifty people were present, including her parents and her four siblings, each one with his or her rowdy brood. The small children acted impatient for their turn to hold and pamper the newborn cousin, and from time to time the parents had to break up a little fight because somebody tried to cut in line. I did not think my turn would ever come, and I was ready to leave when Peggy Sue and Reginald overwhelmed and disappointed the small crowd and walked toward me with the baby in her arms. "Lodovico, please, hold Anna Sue before you leave. She belongs even to you. We don't know whether she would have ever been born without your help." Claudia and I became, informally, Anna Sue's honorary grandparents.

Reluctantly, Peggy Sue agreed to give up the nursing part of her maternity experience. I did not want to delay her treatment any further, as her blood counts had increased, her blast percentage had doubled, and I believed I could palpate her spleen tip. But she was firm in delaying her bone marrow transplant for at least another year. "I want to enjoy my baby for a full year," she claimed in a tone that did not admit objection. She sounded like a general giving orders to his staff instead of looking for advice, but she was too graceful to be compared to any military officer I had ever met. Perhaps we were lulled into an unwarranted sense of security, because two of her sisters were what we called "full matches," meaning that their bone marrow was completely identical to Peggy Sue's, and risk of a rejection after transplant was negligible.

At the end of the year the disease became more aggressive, entering what we call an "accelerated phase." The percentage of blasts had increased to 6 percent and the platelets count had increased. Worst of all, she had developed multiple cytogenetic changes that represent an ominous sign. Despite my recommendation that we proceed immediately with the transplant, she wanted to have one more Christmas with her baby. Two months later she was in what we called blastic phase. Treatment with chemotherapy was instituted, but she failed to achieve a complete remission; that is, to clear her bone marrow completely of leukemia, a condition that is almost indispensable to a successful transplant.

We decided as a desperate attempt to try a transplant during aplasia (that is when bone marrow has been completely destroyed and the new bone marrow had not formed yet). The initial signs were encouraging.

Every day Reginald or her parents took the little girl for a visit to her mother through a glass wall, as she was in complete isolation. Mother and daughter had a silent talk made of smiles that could last an hour or longer. On the fourteenth transplant day her blood pressure dropped, and her consciousness became obfuscated. She was transferred to the ICU and went on a ventilator: an overwhelming infection with a fungus called aspergillus had obliterated her lungs and seeded her skin with little ulcerated nodules. Her skin started looking like a piece of tapestry eaten up slowly by woodworms. After fourteen days of ventilation her blood pressure could not be maintained anymore; the oxygen in her blood was barely adequate. Clearly the situation had become irreversible, and Reginald had to make the painful decision to discontinue the ventilator and let her peacefully die, which happened hours later. I will always remember that while we were moving her to the ICU, half conscious, she had the strength to tell me with a mouth that had turned into a painful wound: "Thank you, Lodovico."

The same joyful crowd that had congregated for the christening of Anna Sue had turned into a mourning crowd at the funeral. Yet Anna Sue, surrounded and pampered by her little cousins, appeared as happy as a two-year-old can be. She seemed to enjoy the gift of life that she had received from her mother, who had sacrificed her own life. That is what Peggy Sue had craved most to see! The transformation of joy into mourning was certainly a somber and sad experience but was not disheartening. By witnessing both the joy and sadness of the same people, I experienced the unity of that family, able to treasure any type of life experience. While they mourned Peggy Sue, they had treasured her death. In their heart of hearts they were aware that the death of Peggy Sue had established an even deeper bond among them that was the main source of comfort and hope. That funeral was like a tree that loses its leaves during the winter so that it can renew them greener in spring.

The case of Peggy Sue speaks for itself, yet some comments are in order. Clearly Peggy Sue had known all her life what her values were and, despite this, the medical system, impersonated by me in this case, tried to twist her values in the name of a cure that she did not want. Unlike the cases of Susan Bailey and Daisy Green, Peggy Sue knew very well what she wanted and so did her husband. And still it took her kind but firm reproach for me to listen. What is wrong with us? Why have we grown so much apart from the patients we are supposed to serve?

The answer to these questions would require a book on its own. It is clear, for example, that specialization has removed the responsibility of the physician for the care of the whole person and has restricted the scope of our practices. If a patient has a heart attack while in my clinics, the only thing I must do is to call an ambulance and send him or her to an ER where an emergency room physician will direct the patient to the proper specialist. I am absolved of the care of that patient until (and if) the heart attack is over.

But what is germane to this book is the loss of a common language, so that a patient becomes "a client." A Buddhist Chinese store owner may sell produce to individuals of all ethnic origins, sexual preferences and religious affiliations, even if he does not speak the language of any of them. All he has to do is to sum up the cost of each item and present a checkout bill. If the client cannot find the wanted item, he or she has no other recourse but to try another store. In lieu of being a person who listens and advises, the physician had become the clerk at the end of the checkout counter. Undoubtedly, patients and society have been as responsible as physicians are for this change. The rejection of any behavior that may be construed as paternalistic, or worse patriarchal, limited the scope and the sphere of a patient-physician interaction. Of course paternalism was offensive and by no mean I do endorse a return to the bad old days when "father knew best." The rejection of paternalism has constructed as paternalistic any suggestion or recommendation of a concerned physician who has not the least intention to intrude in a person's personal decisions. And there is a widespread public conviction that medicine is just like merchandise, trial tested and reliable as a car that leaves the shop. Yet, especially when dealing with serious or terminal diseases, the patient looks for a compassion and understanding that most physicians are untrained to provide, as the case of Peggy Sue clearly shows.

In the old days, as recent as the time when I grew up, medicine was practiced in small communities where people spoke the same language. By that I don't mean the same idiom. I mean that the words had the same meaning. In the small city where I was born, in the middle of the Italian countryside, green meant the color of the grass, and yellow that of the sun. In the civic club where my father used to spend his free hours, green meant the smoke-saturated color of a poker table; yellow the color of the Strega liqueur. So the need for a doctor as a sounding board was limited. Even then, however, the doctor had to take initiatives on behalf of a patient that might compromise his or her license, livelihood and freedom. Let's not forget the heroic doctor of the 1959 novel *Return to Peyton Place* who decided to testify on behalf of a girl who had been a victim of rape and incest.

Nowadays this common language has all but disappeared, especially in major metropolitan cities. But even the population of small villages has changed. When I was a child, there were less than a thousand black people in the whole of Italy. Now you can find numerous colonies from sub-Saharan Africa in every small town, including the one where I was born. Religion is a source of common meaning, but the majority of the European population and more and more people in the United States do not acknowledge affiliation to any organized church. The challenge for patients and physicians to find a common language in the middle of ethnic, religious, linguistic and cultural plurality, with the background noise of television, internet, and Twitter, is very real and very discouraging. It cannot and should not be dismissed with generic platitudes such as "physicians have to learn to listen and to be compassionate," as if it were within the power of the individual practitioner to absorb these qualities without role models in the profession, in the society and even in their own families.

The case of Peggy Sue and Reginald provided a turning point in my professional life as it proposed a solution to this vexing problem, which Peggy Sue's statement compelled me to acknowledge and address. While the ultimate solution may consist in sharing the same set of beliefs, I recognized that a solution is possible even in the multicultural multiethnic world in which we find ourselves. The solution consists in what is called a "value history." That means before anything else to try to know the patient, to inquire about what the patient expects from the visit, and to discern the patient's life goals. In the case of Peggy Sue, the goals were spelled out by the patient from the beginning. Peggy Sue was a modern woman, married to a physician, and she had been mapping the trajectory of her life since childhood. Her self confidence married to her knowledge allowed her to be assertive.

Peggy Sue was a rare exception. The majority of patients are ambivalent about what they want to hear and what they want to have done and are still intimidated by the figure of the doctor, no matter how friendly the doctor may act. "Do you realize how intimidating you are?" a patient asked me during a town-hall meeting at the institution where I worked. I must admit I was astonished. An illustration of this: It is very common for a patient to ask the nurse who discharges them a number of questions they should have asked the doctor, simply because they feel more confident with the nurse. Now I try to remember to close every interview by asking, "Are there any more questions?" But even so the questions to the nurses persist. "I did not want to take too much of your time" . . . "I did not want you to think that I was questioning your competence" . . . " I did not think you should have been concerned with my personal problems" . . . These are common justifications for not asking critical and vexing questions.

And let's be honest, physicians are people, too, and they don't want to open cans of worms that they are not comfortable in addressing. Patients' vulnerability gives them an edge in prescribing a treatment that may be correct for the theoretical entity called disease, but they may be at a loss to address the personal situation of a patient. A manual instructing providers how to conduct a medical interview recommended that one avoid seeing the patient again at the time of discharge from the clinics in order to avoid questions that may require of the physician further investment of time and emotions.

The advantages of a value history cannot be overstressed. First, it allows the physician to deliver that form of personalized care that supports patient satisfaction. This is particularly important in the case of a deadly disease such as cancer, whose ultimate outcome is commonly death. When one has little time to pursue his or her options, it is more important than ever to prioritize these goals, as the case of Peggy Sue taught me. Second, the doctor-patient relationship is a venue of compassion. It is a truism that you cannot feel compassion, a form of allegiance, for a person you don't know, and values, or life goals, are the defining features of each person. Third, a value history allows you to advise the patient at critical turning point in the trajectory of his or her disease.

For example, if a patient whose cancer has metastasized to the liver tells me that his major goal is to die without pain, I will advise that patient to forgo any further treatment, as death by liver failure is commonly painless. If the same patient tells me that he desires to live nine more months to reach some prefixed goals (a wedding, an anniversary, a graduation) then we will explore together alternatives to prolong life even if systemic chemotherapy has failed. Same disease, two different goals, two different treatment approaches: that is what we call personalized medicine.

Fourth, a value history makes a patient a partner in his or her treatment. When the treatment plan is discussed and accepted by the patient, this relieves the physician of the responsibility for an adverse outcome. Fifth, a value history facilitates the difficult end of life decisions more completely than an important but legal document such as a living will. Last, but certainly not least, the value history restores the basic tenet of medical ethics, the doctor's commitment to serve the patient and not him/herself. This derives from the Kantian second imperative: "Remember to consider humanity always as an end and never as a means." Irrespective of each practitioner's different philosophy, this imperative is the basis of any medical practice funded on mutual trust.

Another aspect of the case of Peggy Sue deserves mention. It shows the difference between curing and healing. Though often associated, cure and healing are two different outcomes that should be separately assessed and pursued, especially when cure is not realistic. Peggy Sue was healed in the absence of the cure because she was able to maintain and pursue her life goals, her values, in spite of the disease. She did not allow a deadly disease to interfere with her life. I learned from her that healing is always possible as long as a person is aware of his or her life goals. Of course, if you don't know where you are going, all roads will take you there, but you will never be happy with the destination you have reached.

The next case underlines once more the difference between cure and healing.

Chief Alexander was the chief of a disbanded tribe of Native Americans. He came to see me when his prostate cancer, metastatic to the bones, had become castrate resistant; that is, it progressed despite the withdrawal of his male hormone testosterone. The only treatment option for him at that time was chemotherapy with docetaxel. He confided to me that his life goal was to finish writing the history of his tribe, which would have been lost forever after his death. This time I leveled with him:

"How much time you need, Chief?" I asked.

"More or less six months."

"Without chemotherapy you will have approximately nine months to live. You may have pain, but we can take care of it with radiation; with chemo we have a 50–50 chance of adding six more months to your life, but you may not feel up to writing anything."

"Then forget the chemo," was the verdict.

He worked day and night to complete his book. He avoided the night cup of whisky that had cheered his earlier life, not to be distracted from his work. He even did forgo the Sunday lunches with his large family, which had been a tradition since his older daughter had married. She hosted her parents and sibling in a large house in the country. Twice we gave him radiation to assuage his pain, and once he received another treatment (radioisotope sumerium) to quell the pain in many different areas of his body. He used narcotics very sparingly and only when the pain kept him from sleeping. He died a week after he had sent the manuscript to the publisher. Before dying he scribbled a barely legible thank you note addressed to me for allowing him to live his life in its entirety.

One may ask why I was able to heed Chief Alexander's question immediately, while I did not listen to Peggy Sue until she scolded me. The answer is that physicians, as any other human beings, cannot help but be biased. Chief Alexander was a man in his 70s who had lived a full life and had a disease that was incurable by any stretch of imagination. I had no problem in sympathizing with his desire to forgo a few months of life in order to reach his life goals. Peggy Sue was a beautiful young woman, married to a young man I loved, and she had a disease I considered curable. Though she had spelled out her life goals from the beginning of our encounter, in my heart of hearts, almost against my will, I was hoping that she would change her mind. I don't believe this type of bias can be avoided, and I consider silly the statement, "I am unbiased!" I feel like asking, "You mean that you are not human?" That is why it is so important for doctors to give room to the patient to object to our approach and to emphasize that we are interested in knowing his or her values.

The last case brings back the issue of money as a reflection of values, often an important barrier in a doctor's conversation with the patient.

Georgios was a laborer from Greece who had immigrated to this country as a young man and, working as a brick layer and later as a supervisor, had made a small fortune he planned to bequeath to his three children. Two of them were medical doctors (a surgeon and a cardiologist) and the third one, a daughter, was a psychologist. Like many old people he thought that his contributions to Medicare would take care of all his medical expenses after age 65, and so he considered it an unnecessary expense to buy supplemental health insurance. Two years after surgery for colon cancer he developed metastases to liver and lung. Unbeknownst to his children, he came to see me. (I had given him chemotherapy after the original surgery to prevent the recurrence. Unfortunately, it had not worked.)

"Doctor, how much time do I have to live?" he asked.

"If all the treatments work, between one and two years."

"And without treatment?"

"Probably six months."

"Will I have a lot of pain?"

"I don't think so. Death from liver failure is generally painless, and hospice will take care of your pain if it develops."

"How much will the chemotherapy cost?"

"I am sorry, Georgios, I don't have an answer to this question. I will send you to the business office."

He came back the following day. "Doctor, I am not going to do it. It looks like I will have to pay around $30,000. My wife can live two years on that amount of money. And, by the way, Doctor, don't talk to my children even if they call you. Tell them that I forbade you from giving information. I will talk to them."

"Dear old man," I thought with tears in my eyes as I saw his small figure disappearing down the driveway, "how wise you are!" He was short, probably five feet four, and sturdy. His hands and shoulders were disproportionately large when compared with the rest of the body, revealing a lifetime of hard manual labor. The hands in particular were punctuated by corns, scars and keratosis (the red skin that precedes the development of skin cancer). He wore one of those cloth hats that are typical of golfers but, in his case, revealed anything but a life of leisure. It was to protect him from the scorching sun during long working hours.

Though we may be uncomfortable in talking about it, Georgios taught me that values are reflected in the monetary cost one is ready to pay. I learned later that with the money he saved by rejecting a treatment that might have proven all but useless, he paid for a trip back to the old country with his wife to visit the family he still had there. After making arrangements for his wife's support, he asked hospice to come by his house to offer their services, and he died four months later. One of the children called me to thank me on behalf of the family for the care I had delivered. Though he and his siblings disagreed with their father's decisions and would have liked for him to live longer, they did not insist that he receive chemotherapy. They had known that throughout his life the main life goal of their father's had been to take care of his family's welfare. To interfere with this last decision would have been to prevent him from being himself, from living his values up to the end of his life!

CHAPTER 4

# Uncle Titti
*Human values and retirement houses*

WHEN MY WIFE'S UNCLE Titti developed cancer of the colon he came from San Francisco to be operated on in Tampa to be close to the only family he had in the States. Eventually he settled in Florida, hopping from one old folks' home to the next. These residences were decaying hotels in downtown St Petersburg that reminded one of the Residence Vauquer in Balzac's 1835 novel *Pere Goriot*. This was an old house that the widow Vauquer used as residence for destitute elders, where everything from the smears of water that had destroyed the paint on the walls, from the torn upholstery of the chairs, to the smell of rotten food, indicated the worst aspect of aging: the aging person who ceases to care for him or herself.

Uncle Titti was a fiercely independent man. At 16 he left his Italian family and enrolled in the Italian Marines, where he was awarded a silver medal for extraordinary courage in saving one of his comrades who had fallen into the open sea during a fire. While serving in the Italian embassy in Peking he was imprisoned for several years by the Japanese, whose language he learned. He eventually established some lasting business relationships with his very captors. After the war he got involved in the hotel businesses first in Australia and then in the United States, and from 1951 through 1988 when he moved to Florida he had lived in San Francisco. Though he had been married for almost forty years he had multiple mistresses, and he had sired at least one child out of wedlock with a Thai woman. Many, including myself, may find his lifestyle objectionable. My goal is not to criticize Uncle Titti, however, but to emphasize that he was a man who enjoyed and cherished his freedom of movement more than he did family life, wealth and prestige. I might not have shared his values, but I recognized he had something to live for.

Eventually, as he aged, he was robbed twice in his residences, he was tricked by an Italian friend into lending him half of his poor savings without guarantees, and he was mugged twice in the street. From the hospital where he was admitted after one of these assaults, a well meaning social worker called us to arrange for an adult living facility, as it was not safe for him to live alone anymore. We practically shanghaied him from the rat-hole in which he was living in Saint Petersburg and took him to what was defined as a dignified residence. Though this imposed a sense of dignity from outside, for Uncle Titti it was the beginning of a yearlong agony.

On the second day in the new residence the associate director, a young woman who could have been his granddaughter, scolded him in front of the other residents because he had used the tablecloth instead of a napkin to wipe his chin. His poor eyesight had not allowed him to locate the napkin before some sauce fell on the table from his lips. One week later my wife and I were called for a conference with the director, a well-dressed divorcee with a styled hairdo who had made it her life's mission to run a well-oiled enterprise by breaking the backs of recalcitrant elderly. With him sitting at the end of the table we were told that unless his attitude changed he would be released into the street. He was considered very disruptive to the life of that peaceful community. His fault? He complained loudly that nobody helped him to have his eyeglasses fixed. He reminded a staff member that he used to go out of his way to accommodate the needs of his guests when he was a hotel manager. The service provided by the facility was subpar, in his opinion. This claim was promptly relayed to the front office and had been taken as a final act of insubordination by an irreducible rebel who, instead of enjoying the collective activities designed for the old people, wasted his time on futile grievances.

This meeting reminded me of a meeting we had the year before with the principal of our son's Catholic school, a nun who was unhappy with our boy's unruly behavior and threatened him in front of us to stop him from graduating unless he became kinder and more compliant with school rules. This time, however, an 83-year-old man instead of a 13-year-old rambunctious teen-ager was sitting on the convict's bench, all for having voiced his displeasure with the service provided by his golden prison, for which he was peeling off $2,000 — a sum more than his monthly income.

And those collective activities he was supposed to spend his time enjoying? They consisted of once-a-week events: a comedian entertaining people mostly in wheelchairs, a bingo game where the guests were allowed to lose or gain no more than five dollars, and an outing to the shopping mall. How could a man who had traveled five continents and spoken seven languages be content with these community activities? Uncle Titti had met the most powerful people on earth including three U.S. presidents, the Shah of Iran and two popes. He had rubbed shoulders with celebrity sports coaches and opera singers, not to mention his amorous pursuits. Uncle Titti, an Italian marine, was an independent and irreducible vagabond, and the jailer in her Armani designed uniform was not going to succeed in adding his feather to her cap. From that day Uncle Titti became taciturn and withdrawn. He lost weight, appetite and interest in life. He died a few months later in a hospital where he did not need to be and with a new $50,000 pacemaker for which there was no reason. (I am a medical doctor; I can say this.) It had been inserted on the pretext that he had felt dizzy and thus he might have had an arrhythmia—never documented.

The lie underlying these examples of human estrangement is that health is an absolute good deserving to be preserved at whatever price and whatever sacrifice, irrespective (and that is the heart of the lie), irrespective of the person. The lie is one taught every day in U.S. medical colleges. The truth is never acknowledged by the Western medical profession. In truth, there are no good effects independent from the individuals to whom they are directed, and medicine divorced from the patients it is purported to serve may turn into a form of punishment and abuse.

Claudia, my beloved spouse, had the silver medal Uncle Titti earned with his bravery framed. The frame now hangs over her desk, visible to her many visitors. It shines as a family badge of honor. She and I did not particularly care for Uncle Titti while he was alive. Though sometimes he might have been fun, he had become more and more an intrusion in our personal life, especially in the late years, as his memory was fading and he had grown more dependent on our support, including our finances. To tell the truth I resented having to share my hard-earned money with a man who had not been prudent enough to save enough resources for his future and had wasted all of his assets on whores, gambling and all types of entertainment. He never sent a penny to his natural daughter even when she had become a widow and had to fall back on public welfare for herself and her two small children. In the meantime he had no qualms about flying around the world to watch the final games of the World Cup or to shower his many mistresses with expensive gifts. The last time I saw him alive was in the ER of Tampa General Hospital where he was admitted for a severe infection, probably due to intestinal perforation. I practically abandoned him there, deaf to his pleas that I stay by him. I resented having to interrupt my busy schedule, to heed the manipulation of an old crook. To my lasting regret, I let him die without the comfort of Catholic last rites, because when I called the priest it was way too late.

I am saying these things to explain that our need to enshrine Uncle Titti's medal was certainly not inspired by a special devotion to his memory. That shrine honored unselfishness in time of danger, camaraderie, taste for freedom and enjoyment of all forms of personal expression, from art to sport successes. In spite of his shortcomings Uncle Titti had lived those values. Those values had survived the abuse he endured in the old people's residences and the assaults in the street. In the retirement center where we conspired to imprison him those values had been run over and all but disdained. After his death we were inspired to restore and cherish those values. We had learned that when one fails to recognize any asset in another person considered undesirable or a loser, when one judges a person an unqualified failure, one destroys a part of oneself; one mutilates his own humanity..

CHAPTER 5

# Uninformed Consent
## Dr. Mengele and the Ethics Committee

"But Doc, it feels as if something is missing...."

"Not to worry, boy, everything is all right."

This conversation took place at the University of Chicago medical center in 1941 between Dr. Charles B. Huggins and an elderly black man whose testicles Dr. Huggins had just removed. I heard that the operation had been performed without the patient's knowledge. It certainly had been performed without his signed informed consent, as no Human Investigation Committee nor Institutional Review Board to supervise experiments on people had been deemed necessary at that time. (These boards and committees are standard practice now.) Doctors were expected to do whatever they judged appropriate for the patients, and their actions were not subjected to any form of quality assurance, peer review, practice guidelines or clinical pathways. I would not be surprised if the patient had not been informed. Still, when I was in medical school in the 1960s, it was common practice to experiment on patients or to subject them to unconventional treatment without seeking informed consent.

Twenty-four hours after this likely abusive intervention,, the man walked out of the hospital free of pain and enjoyed two more pain-free years with his family. For more than six months, the man had been confined to his bed, suffering excruciating bone pain from metastatic prostate cancer, tossing and turning night after night trying to achieve an impossible solace from his torment. He had lost forty pounds, and his relationship with his family had been limited to grunts that meant that he did not want to eat, nor to talk, nor to take part any family activities. For six months he had only hoped to die as quickly as imaginable to end the pain of his crucifixion.

After treating a few more similar cases, Dr. Huggins published a seminal paper demonstrating that testosterone, the main male sexual hormone, stimulates the growth of prostate cancer. Removing the main source of testosterone — the testicles — led to relief of disabling symptoms and prolonged life in the majority of prostate cancer patients. For his experiments involving prostate and breast cancer, Dr. Huggins won the Nobel Prize for medicine in 1966. Most research on these two cancers still stems from his observations.

If we were to judge the experiments of Dr. Huggins according to the current ethical standards of human investigations we would probably recommend that he be jailed for egregious violations of patients' autonomy. And yet, thanks to his pioneering work, not only the patients he treated but also millions of men around the world over the next seventy years were granted a number of productive and enjoyable pain-free years despite the metastases of prostate cancer. The ends may not justify the means in principle, yet when we are dealing with suffering humans it is virtually impossible not to exert some form of deception. In the case of Dr. Huggins this deception provided critical benefits both to his patients and to all of humanity.

One way to look at Dr. Higgins's experiments is that by failing to inform the patient (if it is true that things went that way) he violated the patient's autonomy and betrayed his trust. He should be punished for it, his medical license should be revoked, and his findings ignored, even if they had been of benefit to millions of other human beings. This is certainly the way a modern Institutional Review Board would look at it. In promoting the censure of Dr. Huggins and in blocking the application of his findings in clinical practice, the Institutional Review Board would be inspired by a lie enshrined in the Beaumont report that regulates experimentation in human subject. The lie consists of the delusion that dozens of pages of so-called informed consent are an essential instrument to safeguard patient's autonomy.

But there is another way to look at it, and this other way makes the Institutional Review Board's standing a lie inspired by the mother of all lies. This is the conviction that truth is objective, independent from the person, and as such it may be summarized — or more properly diluted — in a sea of printed words. The other way to look at it is that Dr. Huggins was dealing with a human being who was suffering unimaginable pain preventing any meaningful human interaction. Based on his clinical observations and animal experiments, he had reason to believe that he could help this human being and many more like him by removing his testicles, which in the present circumstances were of no use to the patient. He had been trusted with the task of taking the course of action most promising to restore the patient's health and welfare, and he did, saving in the meantime one and millions of lives. He did what he had been asked to do. He fulfilled his professional duties to the end

The Institutional Review Board bureaucracy cannot distinguish between the interventions of Dr. Huggins that improved the life and the quality of life of millions of cancer patients and those of Dr. Mengele, that Nazi executioner who conducted sadistic experiments of no medical interest on scores of unwilling Jewish prisoners who were not even accorded the protections currently bestowed on experimental rodents. The Institutional Review Board bureaucracy is unable and unwilling to accept that a patient may trust his or her doctor to do the right thing in an emergency. Had an Institutional Review Board existed in 1941, most likely it would not have approved Dr. Huggins's research protocol, based on the ethical principle that under no circumstances should human beings be mutilated for investigative purposes. On the same principle the Institutional Review Board would have condemned millions of women to the pain of metastatic breast cancer, which at that time could only have been relieved by removal of the ovaries.

Even if the Institutional Review Board had approved the research, approval would have taken at least nine months of bureaucratic torture during which responsible Institutional Review Board members would have spent sleepless night tormenting themselves over the position of a comma or of a colon or semicolon in the informed consent document. And they would have expected the gratitude of the millions of real patients undergoing real unmitigated suffering that divorced them from the human consortium due to metastatic cancer, They had protected the sacrality of the process and had sacrificed to the process millions of human lives. I set on a board for 15 years and I believe that the people sitting on it are decent individuals volunteering their time to an activity aimed to protect the integrity of human investigations. The problem is that they receive instructions preventing them to distinguish legitimate human research that needs to be approved urgently from research that may exploit or harm patients. They are instructed to regard with suspicion any research protocol coming across their desk, and since most of them have no medical training or knowledge they are unable to make a life-saving distinction..

Do you think I am exaggerating, that I am making it up? Think again! For a few years the hospitals associated with the University of South Florida have not been able to perform life-saving research on trauma victims because the Institutional Review Board lawyer could not find a way to secure an appropriate informed consent from a patient who was comatous and had no designated health-care surrogate. While the closest relative might have signed a consent form "in lieu" of the patient for medical treatment, the lawyer opined that this prerogative did not extend to authorizing clinical investigation, on the assumption of course that every clinical investigator was a potential Dr. Mengele. Patients kept dying unnecessarily from trauma in order to preserve their autonomy.

Let me give you another example, this one closer to my heart. A friend of mine, Dr. Angel Markov, a genial Bulgarian refugee with a degree in medical engineering, had studied a drug, fructose 1–3 diphosphate, that held promise in making blood transfusions — and their associated complications — obsolete. The drug also held the promise of preventing death from any form of shock, whether it is because of trauma, a failing heart, infection, bleeding or loss of blood volume. The drug never could be developed in the United States because the Italian company that had developed the drug did not have the resources to carry it through the expensive process required for drug approval. The ethics committee represents without doubt a substantial part of this expensive process. When a good friend of his, a faculty member at the University of Mississippi, underwent a cardiac transplant and suffered a prolonged cardiac arrest, Dr. Markov tried in vain to have some life-saving fructose administered to him. Without the approval of the Institutional Review Board the patient was not allowed to use a life-saver that could have kept him from drowning, even though he was a faculty member, and the chairman of the department of medicine interceded for him. To its credit, the Institutional Review Board made no exception: Everybody had to be subjected to its rule of death! Perhaps the worst consequence of Dr. Mengele's crimes has been the worldwide call for control of human investigations through ethical committees. Not even in his wildest dreams could he have fathomed that he would end up taking millions of lives, still counting, with the complicity of medical ethicists!

Of course I support medical ethics. Ethical behavior is the only acceptable form of human interaction. The patient-physician interaction by its nature is uneven. As such it calls for protection because of the patient's vulnerability. What I do not support is the lie that patients are protected by signing a lengthy document whose completion may prevent the timely delivery of life-saving treatment. What I do not support is the lie that the patient has no right to trust a competent physician to recommend the most promising treatment in his or her circumstances even when this approach requires thinking outside the box and taking some risk. What I do not support is the lie that a cumbersome process that increases the cost of medical care to the point of becoming unaffordable is essential to protect patients' autonomy. What I do not support is the mother of all lies, on which the ethics committee misgiving is founded, that there is an objective truth, independent from the human experience; that is, independent from the person.

## CHAPTER 6

# A Tale of Two Frauds

BUILDING ON DR. HUGGINS's discovery, in 1968 the Veterans Administration Cooperative Urological Research Group (VACURG) began exploring the possibility that giving prostate cancer patients estrogen may be as effective but less traumatic than orchiectomy (removal of testicles) in suppressing the growth of prostate cancer. In 1973 they conclusively determined that DES, or diethylstilbestrol (at a dose of 1 mg per day), was as or more effective than orchiectomy. DES had some problems, as any medication does. Some men experienced breast enlargement, which could be prevented by irradiation. A few experienced blood clots or fluid retention. By and large, however, estrogen proved effective and better tolerated than orchiectomy. The hormones did not cause loss of libido (sexual desire) nor hot flashes nor anemia nor osteoporosis, which complicate orchiectomy in virtually 100 percent of cases.

For some unexplained reason, not supported by any research data, the most common regimens to treat prostate cancer between 1972 and 1984 involved a higher dose (3 mg) of DES, which was associated, not unexpectedly, with an increased risk of side effects.

In 1984 a new bomb dropped: A group of researchers reported in the New England Journal of Medicine that daily injections of leuprolide were as effective as the 3-mg dose of DES in controlling metastatic prostate cancer. Leuprolide is an LHRH analog, a substance that, chemically, effects castration. (In high doses, it is sometimes used on pedophiles for this purpose.) While leuprolide (marketed as Lupron) induced intolerable hot flushes in about 15 percent of men, it was associated with a negligible amount of blood clots, and for this reason it was proclaimed the winner of the contest. Prominent urology professors roamed the country using the doom-and-gloom M (for malpractice) word. With their pockets lined by hefty Big Pharma's honoraria, they claimed that from then on it would be malpractice to use estrogen in men with metastatic prostate cancer. The words of these self-appointed experts could have been used as evidence in any judicial trials against any doctor so misinformed as to prescribe estrogen.

In declaring Lupron a superior form of treatment when compared to orchiectomy and estrogen, they concealed inconvenient facts. An orchiectomy, which was good for a lifetime, then cost less than $1,000. The cost of estrogen was a little more than $20 a year, while Lupron cost more than $5,000 a year (just the wholesale cost). When one added the cost of administering the injection, the yearly total rose to $15,000. The current cost of administering Lupron or one of its analogs (Zoladex, Eligard and Tristar) is more than $50,000 per year per patient. Also, they failed to inform the public that preservation of the testicles was wishful thinking. After a few months of treatment, the testicles wane—almost as if the patient had undergone an orchiectomy!

Four years later, a follow-up study was published in the Critical Review of Oncology and Hematology, a European journal of which few physicians are aware, unlike the New England Journal of Medicine. The follow up showed that estrogen had delayed the progression of the prostate cancer in 15 percent more patients than Lupron. By then, estrogen had been removed from the market. The estrogens had three characteristics that contradicted the free market principles on which Big Pharma thrives: They were effective, cheap and safe. As such they did not attract the backing of the Western medical establishment.

The study and marketing of Lupron epitomizes how easily a fraud may be made legitimate in medicine. At least four steps in the process lend themselves to promoting such frauds: the design of the study, the promotion of the drug, the disregard of price, and the handling of scientific data.

As mentioned before, it had never been conclusively established that DES at the higher dose (3 mg) was more effective than the lower dose (1 mg), despite adoption of the three-times higher standard throughout the United States. On the patients' bodies, however, the triple dose was definitely three times as toxic. The study that should have been done long ago, which was never done due to lack of financial incentive, was the comparison of the two doses of DES. Perhaps the lower dose would have effected tumor control just fine and with fewer side effects. At least one study performed in the UK showed this to be the case. The federal government could have well supported the study, which if performed might have cost a million dollars but saved several billion over the next few years. But, traditionally, the bureaucracy is penny wise and pound foolish, especially so when it is responding to calls for lower taxes and less government, the mantra of right-wing politicians, Tea Partiers and Republican administrations.

To trust a drug company with a financial interest at stake to run a clinical study is like having the fox guard the chicken coop. But this simple truism does not find understanding in a population enamored with the lie that free market and financial incentives are the source of all scientific and human advances. So Lupron makers found a good excuse to compare their product with what was considered the "standard" dose of DES. Predictably, the prescribing of DES was associated with increased risk of blood clots, so it became easy for Lupron to become what was called "the new standard of care."

This expression, "standard of care," is another major lie, founded on the lie that disease is a well defined and reproducible entity and that the human component is at most secondary. This deceitful expression lines the pockets of two interest groups: trial lawyers and Big Pharma. Trial lawyers find in the concept of "standard of care" a unique opportunity to crucify conscientious physicians who are trying to tailor a medical treatment to the personal characteristics and need of each patient.

How did this affect me, as a doctor practicing cancer medicine? After this series of events, had I prescribed estrogen to a patient too poor to afford Lupron, or to a patient unwilling to suffer the complications of Lupron, I might have become a defendant in a lawsuit if the patient had developed a blood clot. Had I let the patient die in massive disabling pain, nobody would have sued me because I had not betrayed the current "standard of care." So you can see how well the phrase "standard of care" protects the public—sometimes not at all!

Almost forty years ago a friend of mine, a resident at the University of Mississippi Medical Center, sole support of his wife and two children, was moonlighting in the emergency room of a small city. In came a drunkard who had fallen on broken glass and was bleeding like a fountain from his radial artery (the blood vessel that supplies the hand). The surgeon on call refused to show up to examine the patient on the pretense that the patient needed a vascular surgeon (but really because the patient was destitute, and the surgeon would have had to interrupt his sleep for nothing). My friend had to make a quick choice. If he had sent the patient to Jackson, 150 miles away, to the attention of a vascular surgeon, the patient would have definitely lost his hand. The hand would not have been able to endure three hours of travel without blood. But, ironically, my friend would have been clear of any charges that he had not followed the standard of care. If he had tried to repair the artery himself, he might have saved the man's hand, but he might have exposed himself to a lawsuit in case of failure, as he had no training in vascular surgery. As it turned out, he followed his professional conscience and successfully repaired the radial artery. But the situation could just as easily have resolved with the conscientious young doctor ending up in court. So it goes that the protection of human subjects through the law sometimes means more damage for the same human subjects. My friend, whom we'll call Dick, died about ten years ago of cancer after working all his life trying to help his fellow man. Not many people would have acted as he did that evening, because I know very few doctors capable of putting the patient's interest ahead of their own and their families.' And I can hardly blame them as long as the law, manipulated by trial lawyers, puts their livelihood at risk. I guess that Dick, who died too young, might be one of those called "too good for living!"

In aiding and abetting the proclamation of a standard of care for almost every disease, Big Pharma finds a convenient excuse to charge patients or their insurance companies ridiculous prices for products that sometimes are more expensive the more useless they are. An example is pralatrexate, which has become standard of care for people suffering from peripheral T-cell lymphoma, because the drug extends by nine months the survival of one quarter of the patients, at a cost that may be as high as $400,000. This is but the tip of the iceberg of deceptions and lies.

That message that Lupron was the new standard of care for hormone-sensitive metastatic prostate cancer was reinforced by professors of urology traveling from conference to conference. They issued a number of "expert opinions," a new category of learning based on the bias of self-proclaimed experts all holding up the M (for malpractice ) word. This marketing—disguised as scientific information or continuing medical education (CME)—was completely legal at that time and was fully tax deductable for the corporation. So the prostate cancer patients, and the public, paid for their own deception. Nowadays this type of deception is much more expensive for the drug companies. They must provide so-called "unrestricted grants" to companies that provide CME instruction and credits—companies that will eventually hire one of these experts for a higher price. The presentation of the expert will be carefully reviewed, including the slides and the literature he or she will quote. The expert will be made to declare his potential conflicts of interest prior to the presentation, and medical reps are not entitled to sit in during the conference, all to avoid any appearance of undue influence. While all this apparatus seems to protect the integrity of science, such precautions could have not done anything to prevent the fraud related to Lupron. The data published in the New England Journal of Medicine clearly showed that Lupron was associated with decreased risk of blood clots, and nothing in the CME apparatus would have obliged the expert to report the follow-up data of the Critical Review of Oncology and Hematology or to compare the price of Lupron to that of estrogen and orchiectomy. He or she could have still bestowed the curse of malpractice from the height of his or her chair on any physician who prescribed estrogen out of consideration for the patient's finances and quality of life.

Patients were informed that, from now on, orchiectomy, defined a barbarous procedure, would be declared obsolete. Thanks to Big Pharma's great new medication, men would be allowed to maintain their bodily integrity until death (which was also a lie, as the testicles fade like snowballs under the sun when men take Lupron and similar medications). What was never mentioned was that this privilege of preserving these disinflated balls would cost Medicare and private insurance (that is, ultimately taxpayers and the patients themselves) additional billions of dollars every year. It is ironic that the company claimed that from now on, men would enjoy the freedom to choose among different treatments for prostate cancer without mentioning the cost of this privilege. How many people in their right minds would choose to pay $50,000 a year to preserve dysfunctional and waning testicles or to avoid the small risk of blood clots in their legs? And yet, in the name of individual freedom, all women in the country and most men, who have better things to do than being concerned about preserving their testicles to the end of their lives, are compelled to pay for the idiosyncrasy of few individuals misguided by the ubiquitous advertisements of Big Pharma. This is certainly not my construct of freedom!

Cost in medicine is always a thorny issue. Most people would agree that almost any price is worthwhile to save the life of a person with a curable disease. But when it comes to choosing a form of treatment in lieu of a second that brings few advantages in terms of cure or survival, it is legitimate to ask how much an individual would wish to pay, how much society wishes to pay.

One of my most memorable patients was a 78-year-old lawyer with metastatic prostate cancer, whom we'll call Mr. Henry. Still working full time, he used to come to my clinic in a dark suit carrying a leather briefcase filled with legal documents, which he scanned carefully behind his thick glasses, waiting patiently for my visit. When the time came to undergo castration, he had no doubt and chose orchiectomy despite the insistence of his urologist that he submit himself to serial Lupron injections. Each injection would have paid the urologist twice as much as the orchiectomy! His insurance and Medicare would have shouldered the whole financial burden of the pharmaceutical treatment. But he would have felt like a thief, he confided to me, in imposing on the fellow subscribers of his insurance and on taxpayers the ridiculous price of a caprice that to him had no meaning! Consistent with his clairvoyance and his firmness of purpose, when his disease progressed three years later and his kidneys became obstructed, he selected a quick and painless death from renal failure. With a kidney stent he could have gained six months to one year of life complicated by pain, infections, hospitalization and disability, and he decided it was not worth his while.

I caught hell from a member of my staff. "Why did you not tell him that with a stent he could have lived long enough to see the birth of his new grandchild?" protested Jeanine tearfully. This was the first and only time I saw Jeanine, my nurse practitioner, cry. A fiercely independent woman gifted with intelligence and beauty, a full-time professional and mom, confident that it is always morning in America, according to the dictates of Ronald Reagan, Jeanine seldom expressed her emotions or her distress at work. But she loved, as I did, Mr. Henry and did not want to part from him.

"I did not insist that he get the stent because I admire him and I envy him!" was my answer. "It takes not just lucidity, but also self-confidence and faith to face death the way he did, when no reasonable alternatives are available. Maybe this was a greater gift of love for his grandchild! What if his son could not assist his wife during the delivery because he had to take care of an ailing father or attend his funeral! He also spared more than $100,000 in medical expenses that his grandchild's generation won't have to pay!"

A very private person, Mr. Henry never indicated whether he was practicing any type of formal or informal religion, but I could not help seeing in his decision not to delay his death a sacrifice comparable to that of Christ's, an act of love supported by faith, a vision of humanity as a purpose and not a means, the embrace of a destiny higher than and beyond oneself.

I would choose exactly as Mr. Henry did, or at least this is my intention. And yet Mr. Henry and I and all the Mr. Henrys in the country are compelled to waste our money to support interventions that we don't approve of and we would not choose for ourselves. In his case these included a dream of testicle preservation and end-of-life intervention aimed at making death more expensive, prolonged and painful.

I support my church, Children International, and the work of a missionary nun in El Salvador. The money I would pay to conserve balls without physiologic function or esthetic impact of some fellow men would help support the growth of five hundred children in developing countries every year or save the lives of scores of children affected by cholera and other epidemics. But in the name of my freedom I am not allowed to make that choice because of the Big Pharma-manipulated standard of care.

Big Pharma thrives on legal economic deception. Until recently, when "financial toxicity" became recognized as a major complication of cancer treatment—people who survive cancer for five years are four times as likely to declare bankruptcy than those without cancer—it was considered bad taste to mention cost and price at a scientific meeting. It sounded as if we were saying, "Our role is to treat the disease, not to save the person. It is not our problem if the person is dying destitute. As long as he or she does not die of the disease we meant to cure, we can declare victory." One more time we go back to the mother of all lies, to the faith in an objective good independent from the person. And on this lie all forms of advertisement, including the medical ones, have built their castles of lies.

One may say that the voice of the patient having financial troubles has been choked by these triumphal songs of victory. The pain of those who died after investing their lifetime savings in the empty promises of medicine, the struggles of those who survived and remain indebted for years were dismissed a negligible "collateral damage" in the fight for life. When he reported that he had been arguing with the insurance companies until his mother's death, that his and his mother's very livelihod had depended on welfare thanks to expensive, and in her case useless, medical interventions, President Obama tried to give a voice and a face to these anonymous victims of the medical war. Whether this courageous speech helped or trampled his political success is still to be seen.

Some pharmaceuticals have been approved in the past twenty years on the evidence that they improved the quality of life of patients. This provision has many merits, as it indicates the medical system's supposed concern for the whole person. Yet the cost may be paramount in these circumstances. Let me give you an example. Erythropoietin, a drug I helped develop and market, was shown to improve the quality of life of cancer patients, without affecting their survival, at the cost of $10,000 a month. To demonstrate that the drug was worthwhile, should we not have run a randomized, controlled study comparing the quality of life of a group of patients receiving erythropoietin and another group of patients given $10,000 a month tax free? Or alternatively should we not have charged all patients during the study the equivalent of what they would have had to pay once that the drug was approved (from $2,000 to $5,000 a month, according to their carrier)? During the study the patients received the drug free, so the results were biased in favor of quality of life as the patients had no financial drain.

In other words, when the only effect of a drug is to improve quality of life, it is important to establish how detrimental the drug's cost will be on the quality of life. We cannot ignore the fact that resources are limited and that availability of money means availability of choices, especially for patients with limited resources and limited life expectancy. The cost of a treatment that is alleged to improve quality of life may prevent the dying patient from taking that dream trip with his or her spouse or making a reconciliatory visit with an old friend or an estranged spouse or an estranged child before facing death!

The same comments may be made about breast-conserving surgery. Partial mastectomy followed by radiation therapy is considered equivalent to total mastectomy (removal of the whole breast) in the treatment of breast cancer. Partial mastectomy is preferred by most women as it preserves the breast. (After treatment the breast has only esthetical function, as surgery and radiation eliminate any sensation from that organ. No matter what, the breast ceases being a sexual or a sensual organ.) Breast preservation is accomplished at a cost that is thrice as high as total mastectomy, in a conservative estimate. Until recently breast preservation also implied a more prolonged treatment, with daily visits to the radiation-therapy suite for up to five weeks. It is interesting that former First Lady Nancy Reagan selected total mastectomy for the management of her own breast cancer. It is reasonable to surmise that the First Lady of the United States had more important things to deal with than the loss of her breasts.

Finally, the case of Lupron shows how scientific data may be handled to the advantage of the drug company that sponsors the study and that owns the scientific data. The original Lupron study was published in the New England Journal of Medicine, arguably the most respected medical journal in the world, and was highlighted in major metropolitan newspapers that saluted the end of the barbarous orchiectomy. The follow-up study that denounced the superiority of estrogen over Lupron, four years later, was published in a journal of which very few oncologists, let alone physicians of other specialties, were aware. Suppression of the study by the company proved unnecessary, because estrogen had already all but disappeared from the market. The use of the M word had scared oncologists and urologists throughout the country from prescribing the cheaper alternatives to Lupron. Not to mention that some loopholes in the reimbursement system allowed clinics to charge several-fold the price of the product for its administration. So who needed estrogen anymore? Certainly not the physicians, certainly not the pharmacy that had little or no profit margin on estrogen. Just those poor souls who had no health insurance or were not able to pay the hefty Medicare copayments and who have no voice in nor control of a privatized health-care system. Once again Marie Antoinette, reincarnated in the medical industrial system, disdains the starving crowd pleading for bread and offers them instead overpriced cake. But while the poor were deprived of the only life-saving medication they could afford, all men, even the whealthiest, were condemned to suffer the complications of chemical orchiectomy (loss of libido, ostoporosis, fatigue, depression, diabetes, maybe heart attacks) that would have been largely avoided with the cheaper estrogen.

Somebody sensing whether some personal feelings might make me so critical of Lupron makers would be on the right track. I will never forget the company rep raising his finger at me, like the wand of a witch administering a curse, and telling me, in a menacing voice, echoed by the look in his eyes: "We will see! You will tell the audience that Lupron now is the standard of care, that orchiectomy is obsolete and that estrogens are dangerous!"

This conversation happened many years ago, maybe as long ago as 1984, in my laboratory in the Veterans Hospital of Jackson, Mississippi. At the end of my training in 1979, I had accepted a position in the VA system. That decision was inspired by a combination of factors, including the hope of conducting some basic research. I also wanted to develop my teaching skills, which I considered my forte, and to assure a lifestyle that allowed me to spend time with my infant child and work on my crumbling marriage.

In 1984 my research was at a standstill, my most recent grant proposal had been rejected, and I was desperate to gain some academic visibility. For this reason I literally begged the representative of the new drug to provide me with some speaking opportunities. As a federal employee, I could not accept any honorarium, but my presentations would have allowed me to become known, at least locally, as an expert in the area. His answer shows how much he thought of me, of my credentials and of my board certifications. He felt he did not even have to pretend to be flattered by my offer. It was clear that in his opinion a VA physician could be considered only an unqualified failure undeserving of any formal respect!

So, yes, I do acknowledge that I have never completely been able to overcome my resentment toward a company that manifested its contempt for me through the mouth of its representative. I felt I had to disclose this anecdote, in the name of full disclosure, to explain why I chose to describe the Lupron saga among many forms of pharmaceutical fraud. I could have chosen fifty other examples in its place.

I also want the reader know that I myself might have been for sale. "*Homo sum, nihil humani a me alienum puto.*" "I am human and I don't pretend to be foreign to any human experience," claimed Latin playwright Terentius. It is very possible that I myself might have been among those experts lauding the virtues of Lupron if the company had not wastebasketed me. But I also consider this rejection a blessing, as it opened my eyes to Big Pharma's lies!

Many more frauds may be identified in the design of clinical studies and in the marketing of new drugs, but I will stop here. The Lupron saga is enough of a frame of reference to give the reader a way to interpret Big Pharma's systematic deceptions. Look out for them! I believe that two types of action are in order to overcome the fraud of the medical industrial system. One is political and involves the idea that the government take a more active role in the control of health care. I personally favor a national health care system similar to the one that makes the French patients the best treated in the world (see the movie *Sicko*). But even if this position is too extreme for many Americans, it is only reasonable to ask that the scientists of the National Institutes of Health provide overview of the design of clinical trials so that the results may be meaningful instead of being deceptive, as was the case of Lupron. Likewise, a price analysis of any new drug or device should be submitted to the correct sample of the U.S. population: those who ultimately will be paying for any so-called medical advance. Before Lupron was approved—and its manufacturers were allowed to make the cheaper and probably safer alternative all but disappear—I felt I had a right, as a citizen, to decide whether I wanted to pay through my taxes and insurance premiums for the extra cost of this drug.

Likewise I would like to have been asked whether I wanted to pay $5,000 a month for the drug erlotinib, which promises two extra weeks of survival to patients with pancreatic cancer. At a personal level the patients should ask to be informed of the benefits he or she can expect, of the complications and the cost of each treatment, of the available alternatives and on what type of evidence the treatment was approved. When asking about the latter, find out whether information was gathered in a randomized, controlled study (which represents the best type of evidence) or through some loophole in the approval process. Drugs sailing through the loophole include pralatrexate, which at $400,000 per treatment may not be any better than its older cousin, methotrexate, costing less than a dollar a month.

While it is my intention to protect patients from the deceptions of the medical industrial system, the main goal of this book is to denounce those lies that prevent the discovery of our deeper needs and our adhesion to the supreme form of love, referred to as agape. My approach was never meant as an indictment of the medical-industrial system as an exclusive source of lies. As I am a physician, medicine is the area I have more knowledge of, so it is not surprising if I insist on unmasking medical lies in some detail. But medical lies are nothing more than a manifestation of the mother of all lies; that is, that we can build a world independent from the person, that we can mortgage our human experience to the delusion of building a world that is objectively good. The ultimate dream of this delusion is to build human beings as clones without human weaknesses, clones corresponding to a godly ideal of perfection like the statues of the Greek sculptor Phidias, who made

Olympic athletes resemble gods. Supposedly, the elimination of human weakness will eliminate any form of suffering. But only suffering underlies dependence and interpersonal bonds which are the ultimate source of love. A world without suffering is a world without love and without any other human expressions, including the arts that enlighten our history with beauty, inspiration and living words. Perhaps art is so cherished and permanent because it expresses all the words we are unable to utter.

In the Christian tradition, the centrality of suffering to love is highlighted in the figure of Christ. A God that is self supportive and self sufficient in His and Her presumed glory elected to send his Son to become the most dependent of all men—this, to be able to manifest His and Her love to humankind. In some mysterious way this God tells us that He and She cannot enjoy presumed perfection without being loved by humankind. To gain this assent, this love, maybe even this forgiveness from humankind, God through his only Son becomes dependent up to the point of death. In the Christian tradition it is legitimate to ask whether God redeems humans or is redeemed by humankind. This dependence of the Christian God on humankind is described in a magnificent 1950 French movie: *Dieu A Besoin des Hommes or God Needs Men*. Director Jean Delannoy describes how a priest abandons his parish in a northern island of France because he can no longer tolerate abuse by and incomprehension of his flock. Then the priestless crowd asks the sacristan to stand in for the priest. Reluctant at the beginning, the sacristan becomes more and more involved in the role of substitute priest. In this way he becomes a living proof that God needs humankind to transmit and divulge a message of love and redemption. In one of the first scenes, the sacristan takes his sister-in-law to a hospital by boat because of her difficult pregnancy that may cost her her life. The young woman, facing imminent death, feels the need to confess to him that the child she carries is a product of adultery. "That God may forgive you!" states the sacristan in form of absolution. There are many messages in this movie. The one I wish to underline is that the Christian God has no choice but to manifest His and Her love for humans by being human, by speaking and manifesting himself and herself through the human being.

Even in the classical tradition, gods cherished their mundane clothes that allowed them to be human and to experience those same human feelings that characterize humanity. Troy was destroyed because Hera and Athena were jealous of the beauty of Aphrodite (Venus). Jupiter transformed himself into a bird or a raging bull to be able to copulate with the most beautiful women on earth. And the cuckhold Vulcan (Hephaestus), to console himself over the many betrayals of his spouse, Aphrodite, spent his time blacksmithing to produce arms, intent on destroying the same humankind whose love his goddess spouse was seeking. The gods of classical mythology craved being human.

Yet the aspiration of the mother of all lies is to deprive humanity of those very characteristics that represent the ultimate aspirations of both of the Jewish-Christian God and of the classical gods! This aspiration is well illustrated in the sad history of one of my closest friends, whom I'll call Peter. When I established a relationship with my first girlfriend (a relationship that ended up in disaster, as I will chronicle later), Peter was critical of my decision. "Yours is not a free choice," he stated. "You don't love her. You are only looking for a way to assuage your loneliness and get your rocks off! I would never get involved in a relationship unless I felt I was fully independent from the person I chose, unless I knew that I could live perfectly well without her."

Truthful to his construct of freedom, he became a well known psychiatrist and never married. Eventually he was struck by an unusual disease, pulmonary fibrosis, which compelled him to take high doses of cortisone. At last he became dependent on an oxygen unit. The last time I saw him, at a school reunion, he used a walker and carried an oxygen tank on wheels. He was accompanied by a woman in her late thirties, a teacher he had met at a party and who elected to dedicate her free time to his care. That is not surprising, as Peter knew how to be affectionate and charming, and probably these traits became more prominent and evident during the course of his disease. There is also an interesting message in the fact that as a young man he had been proud of his sexual performances. Yet, the first time he earned the complete devotion of a woman was when he could not perform anymore! Eventually he married his girlfriend in a religious ceremony celebrated at his house a few days before he died. I cannot help but see in that marriage his ultimate reconciliation with a God that craved his love.

The second fraud, interconnected with the first, is related to a test, the Prostate Specific Antigen (PSA), which during the last twenty-five years has increased the human and economic cost of managing prostate cancer. Unlike the case of Lupron, the fraud surrounding PSA did not stem from the greed of a single company intent on deceiving the public for profit. Rather, the PSA fraud stems from the good intentions of several groups of people wishing to stamp out death from prostate cancer. Once again this example demonstrates how the best of intentions may be detrimental to people when advocates try to promote health in ways that bypass the person and his or her own values.

Of course members of the American Urological Associations and the companies that sold the test profited greatly from the promotion of PSA as a form of prostate cancer screening. Profit on the scale of billions of dollars every year has certainly motivated professional associations and pharmaceutical manufacturers to promote the test. But I believe that the initial thrust toward the unwise but mystifyingly universal support of the practice can be found in voluntary organizations such as the American Cancer Society or patient-advocate groups determined to reduce death and illness from cancer. In the case of prostate cancer, unfortunately, they succeeded only in increasing human and economic costs of the disease without saving men's lives. At the same time, they incurred a deleterious effect on quality of life.

The PSA is a chemical substance, an enzyme that allows men to be fertile. Thanks to the PSA, spermatozoa are freed from the glue-like prostatic fluid and can swim toward a woman's uterine cervix to meet and fertilize an egg. The fertilized egg is called a zygote, and once implanted in the uterus, it will evolve to become an embryo, a fetus and a baby. PSA is manufactured exclusively in the prostate. The levels of PSA in the circulation reflect the size of the prostate as well as the velocity with which the prostate cells reproduce themselves. It was a reasonable assumption, confirmed by facts, that increased levels of PSA in the circulation might indicate the presence of prostate cancer, as the reproduction of cancer cells is much more rapid than that of normal cells.

The discovery of PSA fed the hope that one may make a diagnosis of prostate cancer in men who have no symptoms by monitoring their levels of this substance and, further, that early diagnosis might improve chances of cure. The screening of aymptomatic individuals for some forms of cancer definitely saves life. Serial PAP smears of the cervix in sexually active women have reduced by 75 percent deaths from cervical cancer in women younger than 40. Serial mammograms have allowed early detection of breast cancer and improved the chances of a cure by at least 20 percent in women ages 50 to 69 (and probably in older women as well). Screening individuals older than age 50 for colon cancer and individuals affected by hepatitis B and C for liver cancer has also reduced deaths. A recent study showed that serial CT scans of the chest may allow early detection of lung cancer in smokers and ex-smokers and increase the cure rate, though there is some controversy over whether the amount of radiation from CT may be itself a cause of cancer.

The theory underlying the screening of asymptomatic individuals for cancer holds that there is a time in the development of cancer when the cancer is localized to an organ and has not spread via blood to other organs. Screening individuals at risk for these cancers prior to symptoms may improve the diagnosis of localized cancer and thus improve the chances to cure it via surgery. Prostate cancer is the second most common cause of cancer deaths in men. When the cancer metastasizes to the bone, it causes death, pain and disability. It was legitimate to hope that early diagnosis of prostate cancer may prevent death and disability in a substantial portion of men.

The first results were very encouraging. PSA levels higher than four nanograms/dl heralded the presence of prostate cancer in as much as ten percent of unsuspecting men, and in ninety percent of the cases these cancers were localized and potentially curable with surgery or radiation therapy. Definitely, optimism was in order, and many experts started questioning the need for additional data before recommending wholesale screening for prostate cancer with an annual PSA test. Indeed, in 1993 the American Cancer Society issued this recommendation among its cancer screening guidelines despite skepticism and criticisms from prominent population scientists, including those working at the National Cancer Institute. Not surprisingly, the American Urological Association enthusiastically embraced the guidelines, which promised a windfall of unexpected money for its members. And the public was successfully enlisted in the endeavor to recruit more and more subjects to screening, most of whom may now be considered "screening victims."

Every small town in the United States had its own chapter of "man to man" support groups. These included prostate cancer patients who shared their experience with individuals newly diagnosed or with individuals hesitant to undergo screening. From the pulpit of her universal church without walls, influential advice columnist Ann Landers instructed her female readers to coerce their husbands into being screened for prostate cancer the same day the wives were getting their yearly mammograms. Thanks to the discovery of PSA levels, cancer screening appeared ready to become a family activity like a family vacation or the purchase of a new dwelling.

I still remember a social fund-raiser jointly sponsored by the American Cancer Society and the cancer center where I worked. Somebody asked how many of us had been screened for prostate cancer. The center director, the associate director and I, along with the former U.S. senator who chaired our board of directors, dutifully raised our hands. I knew for a fact that neither I nor the center director had had our PSA checked, ever. But we knew too well that to counter the American Cancer Society's recommendation was tantamount to questioning the flag and motherhood. A lot of eyebrows rose when the National Cancer Institute director who attended the event did not raise his hand. When asked why he had not been screened, he ducked the question by saying, "I am not 50 yet." This, instead of providing the candid answer: "Because all this is unqualified, dangerous and expensive bullshit." The National Cancer Institute never endorsed the recommendations for prostate cancer screening, and two of its investigators protested

Ann Landers' advice. After receiving this complaint she retracted, in part, her previous suggestions.

The National Cancer Institute's director was shrewd. He knew only too well that it would not have paid for a government organization dependent on taxpayer money to question the action of a venerable voluntary association such as the American Cancer Society. In the minds and the hearts of many red-blooded Americans, the government is wrong and the private sector is right until proved otherwise. This is true despite the fact that the National Cancer Institute, which never endorsed the recommendation about PSA screening, mentored clinical and basic scientists who are the envy of the free world. And, of course, the National Cancer Institute was ultimately proved right.

In 2011 the bomb exploded. A well done American study demonstrated that years of mass screenings of men for prostate cancer employing PSA tests did not save lives and might even have been detrimental. Patients were divided in two groups: One group received yearly PSA tests and the other group received no screening. Not unexpectedly, the diagnosis of prostate cancer was three times as high in the group given PSA screening. And yet the truth came out: Increased diagnostic yield did not lead to a decreased risk of mortality from any cause, including prostate cancer.

Men were being screened, but no fewer men were dying despite the screening. At the same time, men unnecessarily treated for prostate cancer were forced to suffer the consequences of treatment, which included side effects such as sexual impotence, urinary incontinence and colitis. Some of them even died as a result of unnecessary surgery. A study with a similar design, published at the same time, was conducted in Europe. This study showed a modest reduction in prostate cancer-related mortality in the screened group but no reduction in overall mortality. According to this study, to save a life from prostate cancer, seven men would have to undergo unneeded prostatectomy and 157 man would have to undergo a painful prostate biopsy.

After review of the available evidence, the United State Preventive Service Task Force (USPSTF) recommended against prostate cancer screening for a man of any age because the risk of complications overwhelmed the small potential benefits. Though it is reviled by all medical associations for being a government agency, the USPSTF is the most objective source of evidence-based recommendations for the prevention of all diseases, from cancer to osteoporosis to complications of diabetes. It is the best protection against the propaganda of the medical-industrial complex. Patients would be wise to look to government, not private industry, for their health information. Indeed government-led research in the medical field has been most valuable.

This VACURG's study previously described, established that 1 mg of DES daily was as effective but much less traumatic than orchiectomy in the management of metastatic prostate cancer. The VACURG had become the model for all cancer research cooperative groups in this country and abroad. Despite the reviling of the Veterans Administration by right-wing politicians proclaiming that the free market is the key both to scientific advances and cost control in medicine, the VACURG testifies otherwise. When provided with proper resources, government-sponsored medicine is the source of better care and vital scientific information than research sponsored by the profit-driven private sector.

Another example of well run research is the intergroup study for the management of large cell non-Hodgkin's Lymphoma. Since 1974 more than fifty percent of patients with this previously deadly disease had been cured with a combination of chemotherapy drug called CHOP. In the early eighties a number of young and aggressive investigators roamed that country proposing new and more toxic forms of treatment. Some of these investigators even tried to use the M world (from now on the use of CHOP would be malpractice against physicians using the old fashioned CHOP that in their opinion was dated). More than economic rewards these investigators were looking for academic credibility. They wished to be remembered as the scientist who had cured all forms of large cell lymphoma.

The director of the National Cancer Institute was not impressed or discouraged by these threats. He threatened to withhold the funds for any cooperative group activity until all groups run a randomized controlled study comparing CHOP with the other proposed treatments. Surely enough CHOp turned out to be the most effective and the safest. Dr. Vincent DeVita saved thousands of human lives by imposing this study on recalcitrant and undisciplined investigators. Probably the most influential person in modern cancer treatment, Dr. Devita knew how to be stern and authoritative.

Referring to his Sicilian background some of his many friends joked and many of his detractors complained that he run the National Cancer Institute as a Mafia chieftain. If that is the case the Mafia was instrumental to save thousand of lives in this occasion!

For the record, Dr. DeVita was at that time a conservative republican! He certainly did not believe in big government. He was a visionary man, however that understood that in the modern world the government had an important role in preserving the health and the assets of all citizens by preventing dangerous and costly frauds from the medical industrial complex! Myths surrounding the wonder of privatized medicine are another major lie, where economic interests and corporate power once more choke the voice of the truth.

One may wonder why the early diagnosis of prostate cancer did not save lives. The reason is simple. The screenings uncovered cancer that would have never shown up during a man's lifetime. No matter how long he lived, he would likely have died of something else. In the meantime the diagnosis of prostate cancer involved a painful biopsy that can bring on complications (infections, bleeding, etc.), and the treatments (surgery or radiation therapy) may bring on erectile dysfunction. Surgery has also been associated with incontinence and, occasionally, death.

But there is more to the prostate cancer-screening story. The discovery of PSA levels and the subsequent screening of asymptomatic men for prostate cancer had additional consequences that have been as dreadful as those described so far. After a man was treated for prostate cancer, it became customary to follow him with serial PSA levels being tested every three to six months to detect early recurrence. Of the 250,000 men diagnosed and treated for prostate cancer every year, approximately 30 percent (75,000) will eventually experience an increase in their PSA levels, and most of them will become anxious about what that means. In a few cases the detection of an early rise of PSA levels after surgery is a sign of a local recurrence, which can be treated and cured with radiation of the prostatic bed. In the majority of situations, however, the PSA rise indicates that the patient has a number of cancer cells somewhere in his body whose number is too small to be detected by any form of imaging. (It may take as many as a billion cancer cells to produce a nodule detectable by CT, MRI or bone scan.) Nobody knows what to do with these individuals, because there is no proof that the treatment of early recurrence with castration prolongs the survival of these patients.

There is plenty of prove, instead, that early castration may increase by fifty percent the risk of bone fractures from osteoporosis, by eighty percent the incidence of hot flushes and debilitating fatigue, and by 100 percent the loss of libido. Please remember that people undergoing prostatectomy or radiation of the prostate may be unable to have an erection, but they are still able to achieve a dry orgasm and may benefit from intervention that reinstitutes the erection. After chemical castration, sexual intercourse becomes all but impossible due to loss of desire. Not to mention that, in patients with coronary artery disease, chemical castration is associated with increased risk of heart attacks.

I have already mentioned how costly this unnecessary and possibly detrimental chemical castration is. By a conservative estimate, the cost of castrating (with Lupron and similar agents) half a million men a year at a conservative $50,000 per patient is a whopping $25 billion per year. And this does not take into account the use of bisphosphonate to prevent bone fractures (conservatively $250 million per year), the cost of managing the fractures, the hot flushes, the fatigue, the depression and the hours of work lost due to the symptoms! Nor does it take into account the human cost of this misguided practice.

So why do most physicians, including myself, oblige the patient's desire to suffer the consequences of castration for the satisfaction of seeing their PSA levels drop? In some cases it is greed. In the majority of cases the motivation may be frustration and lack of time. It may take more than an hour of the doctor's time to convince a patient that a simple rise of PSA levels does not warrant castration. Predictably, in some cases the patient will be unconvinced and may look for and find a more complacent practitioner. And here's another possible outcome: If the patient were to abide by my recommendations and then develop metastatic prostate cancer at a later time, I may find myself a defendant in a lawsuit trying to explain to a shrewd trial lawyer and twelve jury members why I did not follow the so called "standard of care." Even if I were to get a judgment in my favor (which is uncertain) I will have spent hundreds of hours in defending myself and in dealing with my angst; I will have deprived my other patients of my service during this time and also robbed myself and my family of legitimate income. If I were to oblige the patient and sign an order for Lupron, my time with the patient would take no more than one minute. Whether I spend one minute or one hour with the patient, the visit is still reimbursed for as much (or as little). In addition, my employer, my institution, pockets a substantial amount of money from the administration of the injection. It sounds like a no brainer, because it is a no brainer, and I am protected from any malpractice law suit because I did follow a fallacious "standard of care.."

Unlike the Lupron-related fraud perpetrated on men and third-party payers, the PSA-related fraud stems from good intentions more than from greed. Yet good intentions are not sufficient to guarantee a favorable outcome when they are founded on a false assumption, on a misconstruction of the reality: in other words, a lie.

Let's stipulate that the majority of us wish to stamp out cancer and all serious diseases. As far as we know, we cannot stamp out death, but we can reduce the duration of pain and disability that precedes death, and cancer is certainly a major cause (maybe the major one) of pain and disability. This desire is more than legitimate. It is a fundamental part of our humanity, an innate aspiration.

These aspirations have been twisted and co-opted by a number of organizations including the American Cancer Society, the Leukemia Society of America, the Susan B. Komen Foundation and others that are largely staffed by individuals wishing to serve their neighbors. Perhaps the majority of these individuals have been touched by cancer in themselves or in a loved one, and they want to put their own experience to the service of other cancer victims. Whether they know it or not, they are trying to put their own suffering to the service of other people who are suffering. They wish to bring about redemption through their own suffering. Even if they are atheists or non-Christians, whether they like it or not, they participate in the redemptive work of Christ, and they deserve the respect due to a divine intervention in world history. The achievements of the American Cancer Society cannot be overstressed. They include the goal of a smoke-free America; millions of lives saved through screening for cervical, breast and colorectal cancer; and money dedicated to clinical and basic research.

Having said that, one should admit that any large organization needs to define its priorities to survive and to focus its actions. This activity may become the limit of any organization claiming to be of service to the people. "We save lives in our free time," sang American Cancer Society volunteers during a national meeting in New York that I attended as president of the Society's Mississippi Division. The performance was an inspiring manifestation of the joy to serve. For a believer like myself, it was a universal proclamation of the love of Christ through the mouths of people of different beliefs, including the belief that God does not exist. It was a practical triumph of the Christian message of service. But sometimes it is not enough to stamp out cancer to save lives.

As meritorious as the goal to cure cancer is, the cure itself may not save lives when the focus is on cancer instead of being on the persons who host the cancer. When one abides by the lie that it is enough to eradicate the disease to heal the patient, the service of the patient may become an egregious disservice. The recommendation that all men fifty and older undergo screening for prostate cancer makes this point. Many more men suffered than were healed as a result of this well meaning recommendation. And consider as well the billions and billions of dollars that were wasted in this vain attempt to stamp out death from prostate cancer.

Let's illustrate this point with a personal experience, the story of Brother Charles.

"Jim, tonight I had a vision: an Angel of God touched my prostate and I was healed. I do not need surgery anymore!" The Rev. Charles Gibson, a Baptist minister of a small church in south Mississippi, was talking to James Travis, the hospital chaplain. Aged 51, Brother Charles had been the first in his community to be screened for prostate cancer. As a religious leader he felt endowed with the responsibility to lead his flock toward the noble goal of health preservation. His PSA levels turned out to be high, and the biopsy revealed a prostate cancer, a nonaggressive one, but definitely a prostate cancer.

Reluctantly he decided to undergo prostatectomy, but the day before surgery he called his colleague Jim to share his religious experience. He assumed that Jim would ratify the miracle and allow him to be discharged without surgery. Jim was an old fox: twenty years of experience as hospital chaplain combined with a keen study of human psychology and equally keen human insight, inspired by faith and love, taught him to be skeptical of medical miracles. He knew that to challenge Brother Charles' statements would achieve nothing. Instead, he sat down with him and asked him to tell his story. After half an hour of prodding the truth came out:

"In two months I am getting married," admitted Charles, who had lost his first wife to cancer. "And she is quite a woman. I would hate to disappoint her if the surgery makes me impotent."

Charles was informed that with a penile implant his newly wedded wife would be made even happier (at the time Viagra had not been developed), and so he let his surgery proceed. Things went well for about five years. Then his PSA levels started rising. Bone and CT scans were negative, but his wife, supported by his urologist, insisted that he start taking Lupron. After the first injection, Brother Charles became irritable and experienced hot flushes, which kept him awake most nights. He lost any sexual desire, and he started feeling too tired for social activities. The family reunion with his and his wife's children, which he formerly cherished during Sunday luncheons, became an intolerable burden for him. After the Sunday service he wished only to be left alone and to lie in bed to revel in his misery. He proved unattentive even to church members' requests for counseling. After he missed a call to pray at the bedside of a church member, the church council met and decided they needed to add an associate pastor. He let them do it without any reaction, and soon the associate pastor found himself endowed with full church responsibilities. One year later Charles and his wife went to marriage counseling and a year after that their marriage did end in divorce. Though he was beloved, church members asked that he retire when he was only 61, as the associate pastor threatened to leave if he were not recognized as the full pastoral authority. I don't know what happened to Charles after that. All I know is that thanks to monitoring his PSA levels and thanks to shots of Lupron that he did not need, he had five years of calvary, and we were still counting. Trying to prevent his death from prostate cancer, he underwent the death of the three things he loved most: his church, the relationships with his children, and his marriage. And we the taxpayers subsidized his unfulfilled passions and his human failure with at least $200,000 dollars worth of mistreatment.

Perhaps the worst corollary of the assumption that we are involved in an ongoing battle with cancer (or other diseases) is that death represents a defeat, that the person who succumbs to the disease is a loser. Since we all are going to die sooner or later, we all are doomed, in this perspective. As I have mentioned, death and diseases are defeated only when we are able to co-opt the experience of death and suffering in our own lives, only when we are able to treasure these experiences as we do any other life experiences, only when we are able to identify the redemptive value of death and suffering.

A more practical negative consequence is that one tries to destroy the patient in order to destroy the cancer. This was the case with the promotion of screening asymptomatic men for prostate cancer. The wish to eliminate prostate cancer made people forget that the majority of men do live in a peaceful symbiosis with their prostate cancers. The majority of men are not even aware of having prostate cancer, and they die without having been bothered by prostate cancer, the way the owner of a mansion lives and dies without being aware of a little mouse in the cellar. Nobody would overturn the fundament of the mansion in an attempt to pursue the mouse. Likewise nobody should cause sexual impotence, incontinence, osteoporosis, fatigue, and sometimes death in the pursuit of a cancer that may never manifest during a man's lifetime.

The enthusiasm for prostate cancer screening delayed for several years any clinical studies that might have revealed how the supposed benefits of this expensive and complication-laden intervention were all but negligible. Year after year, at scientific meetings, I heard prominent scientists claiming that these studies should not be done on grounds that evidence of benefit was overwhelming. It would be unethical to deny men the benefits of screening, they proclaimed. It is remarkable, indeed, that studies were conducted at all. In addition to the scientists who decreed their inutility, prominent medical ethicists claimed that such studies would be immoral. A meeting of the Human Investigation Committee, now called IRB (Institutional Review Board) is still impressed in my memory. The function of the IRB is to decide whether a clinical study should be allowed to proceed based on ethical considerations. Only half of the members of an IRB are medical professionals. All others are lay people whose role is to represent the view of the patient. During that meeting a so-called patient representative thundered that it would have been unethical to ask thousands of patients to forgo life-saving cancer screening just to confirm what was already well known, that prostate cancer screening saved lives. In the name of the protection of human subjects' safety and autonomy, the IRB was ready to condemn millions of men to impotence, disability and sometimes death and to load the country's medical system with billions of dollars of expenses that were, at best, unnecessary and, at worst, detrimental to the majority of patients.

"*Tantum potuit religio suadere malorum.*" "So much evil was caused by superstition." So stated the Latin poet Lucretius in reference to the sacrifice of Iphigenia, the daughter of king Agamemnon. Two thousands year later, medical ethicists create millions of victims owing to their own superstition masked as science.

Another case where well intentioned people supported a major medical fraud and delayed its unveiling exists in the use of high-dose chemotherapy and hemopoietic stem cell rescue (commonly referred to as autologous bone marrow transplant) in breast cancer treatment. Again, the scientific hypothesis made a lot of sense. Since chemotherapy at regular doses cured a few cases of breast cancer, higher doses of the same might cure more, even the majority of cases. This approach had become common clinical practice much before its value could be proven. Again, prominent scientists and medical ethicists objected to the performance of a randomized, controlled study (where half of the patients received high doses and half regular doses of chemotherapy) all in the name of patients' benefits and autonomy. Again patients' advocates, including prominent religious leaders (I can remember the Catholic bishop of Mobile, Alabama, declaring that a woman has a right to the procedure even if it is not included in her insurance plan) crowded the courtroom asking judges that insurance companies be forced to pay for high-dose chemotherapy for all women with breast cancer. Eventually the HMOs bent to popular pressure and agreed to include this form of treatment among their benefits even without evidence of benefit. In the name of more effective advocacy, some patients were shamed as cowards when they decided after soul searching that they did not want the high-dose chemotherapy. Like the biblical character of Job, they were blamed for their own diseases by physicians, families and friends when their cancer recurred—all supposedly because they had refused the help of modern science. Hundred of billions of dollars and thousands of unnecessary deaths later, three studies demonstrated that in no cases was chemotherapy in high doses shown to be more beneficial than at the regular dose.

Though greed may play a major role in medical fraud, the saga of prostate cancer screening and high-dose chemotherapy for breast cancer demonstrates that greed is not always the underlying motive of such deceptions. The real culprit is well meaning advocacy that makes defeat of the disease its main goal, even if conquering the disease may involve the destruction of the patient. This advocacy takes many forms, from professional and volunteer organizations to individual champions, to misguided ethicists. By and large the actors invest their own free time and their own resources in an activity that hurts more than benefits the patients and the public. Many lies support this well intended deception, including blind faith in private enterprise and mistrust of government-run research, blind faith in science and in the physician's commitment to general welfare, in addition to clinical studies flawed by the interests of drug companies and equipment makers and their deceptive marketing. But at the basis of all these common lies one can find the mother of all lies, the pretense of an objective good that tramples personal values, the pretense of helping the person without getting personally engaged, the pretense that the human mystery might be unraveled thanks to an EKG tracing, a radiography report, a laboratory exam or a psychometric test, the pretense that in the name of universal love we can dispense with and dispose of personal love.

I have no expectations that this book will end medical fraud or any form of commercial fraud. To my mind, medical fraud is just an example of how any pretense of helping humanity without heeding the mystery of the person is nothing more than a colossal lie. Only the reader can decide for himself or herself whether the personal mystery is served in full by faith in a personal God that represents a living truth. That is the only antidote to the lie I have just described.

CHAPTER 7

# Doctor-Patient Communication
*More Lies*

IMPOSSIBLE CURES. THAT'S WHAT oncologists in the U.S. medical establishment, including myself, peddle day in, day out, despite our best effort to be candid and to present to the patients a realistic assessment of their outcome. Despite major progresses in the treatment of many forms of cancer, most of the drugs offer at best a tiny subset of cancer patients only a few months of extra survival, with questionable quality of life, for an exorbitant price.

Examples? I have seen many in three decades as an oncologist. One of many examples is a drug that adds, on average, nine months to the life of less than one-third of patients with a rare disease (peripheral T cell lymphoma) at a cost that may reachf $400,000 per patient. I heard that the CEO of the company jokes with people concerned about the cost. To paraphrase his sentiments: "Why be concerned? Only a quarter of the patients will pay the full cost. Everybody else will die, or their cancers will progress and get worse, long before they rack up that big a bill!" To Big Pharma, $400,000 may be nothing; but to most Americans $400,000 is an unheard of sum.

When I look at absurdities in the American medical establishment, sometimes I give them my own personal "grandmother test." For my grandmother, who took care of me as an infant and once crowed about a 100-lira bill in her pocket (about 15 cents in 1947; perhaps $5 in current value), that amount of money could not be imagined. For that old dear woman who worked all her life from age 7 (when she abandoned school because she threw ink at a second grade teacher who slapped her) until age 90 (when she was still able to prepare the best bouillabaisse that the family ever enjoyed) it would have been inconceivable to spend that amount of money for medical care no matter what the outcome was.

No matter what, you just do not handle that amount of money, not in a town where, every day, a fishing rod can provide you with fresh fish for dinner, where the countryside is a generous blanket of savory herbs, where the farmers in the local farmers' market are always willing to give you credit. She singlehandedly raised three children, one of whom, my father, became an established professional, universally lauded. She knew how to give and to receive joy, but the medical expenses for a drug like the one I cite above would have been completely out of her scope. When I try to subject our major medical advances to my "grandma test," very few will prevail. When I prescribe these pharmaceuticals, which grandma would have considered a macabre joke, I am the accomplice of a lie, a lie that tries to rob the person of the person, a lie that puts the goal of the person outside of the person himself. But that theoretical objective good that doctors claim to see so clearly—that "good" is often something of which the actual patient has no part.

But the damages of this lie are not limited to the patients; they equally affect the provider. If health is an absolute good, it is worthy of whatever sacrifice their profession demands, ahead of all other values, including nurturing their own families. It is not surprising that the divorce rate is higher among physicians than among other professionals, and suicide rates are high as well. One of the most prominent cancer researchers, involving thousands of physicians, is now destitute and living in a nursing home. Three families including three spouses and five children are feuding over the division of his $40 million in assets, the same way the Roman soldiers cast die over Christ's tunic. And what does he have to show as a prize for so many disrupted lives? Twenty years of data collected by an army of investigators, research nurses and research coordinators, analyzed by an army of statisticians, demonstrating that several different forms of useless cancer treatments were equivalent in their ineffectiveness! We the taxpayers supported this lie (and its pervasive destructivity) with millions of our hard-earned dollars.

There are many more lies of modern medicine, including those related to the advertisement of drugs and new procedures, the promise of the HMOs and other forms of insurance and medical entities to take full care of you—but these are minor lies, comparatively. These are comparable to the lies we all learn to recognize and tolerate in advertisements, whether they concerns a dream vacation, a resort, an airline, a laptop or a new mattress. There is still an area in medicine, however, in which deception is pervasive and most often unavoidable. I speak of patient-provider communication.

"Dr. Balducci, I want you to know that my husband is alive and well six months after your visit," said an e-mail I received a few years ago. "When we met you, you told us that he had only six months to live! Fortunately we did not heed your medical advice. Otherwise we would have sold our home in Florida, and now we would be without a place to live! Your ill-conceived consultation caused us a lot of unnecessary grief, consternation and worry. For the sake of your future patients I recommend that you discuss the prognosis with the family members and away from the patient presence. . . ."

I had only a vague recollection of this encounter, but I do not believe I made a blanket statement, as this lady implied. The patient had an incurable malignancy. After a lot of prodding by the patient I might have stated that in my opinion he might die in six months, after prefacing such a statement by saying that I don't have a crystal ball allowing me to predict the future and that I made a forecast only because I felt that the patient and his family needed to plan ahead for his death.

"Dr. Balducci, I wish to thank you so much for the care you bestowed on my beloved cousin who just passed away. I will never forget your personal interest, your care, your warmth and your compassion," stated a letter. In this case I was partially responsible for the patient's death, as I recommended that her physician administer the treatment that eventually killed her. I had based my recommendation on a report I received from the local pathologist that turned out to be wrong. The correct pathologist report revealed that the patient had a very indolent form of lymphoma not necessitating any treatment. By then it was too late to disavow my original recommendation. In this case my bedside manner had inspired a trust that I clearly did not deserve and prevented a lawsuit for wrongful death, which likely would have been successful. The regret and the chagrin for this tragic outcome are the most lasting lesson of humility that I will carry with me to the end of my days!

"Nobody tells me anything!" whined Mr. Jones from his filthy bed. Everybody hated this stop in our morning hospital rounds. A man of undefined age, Mr. Jones had been lying for two weeks in the same sheet, wearing the same pajamas, without shaving or shampooing his unkempt hair. The seedy picture was completed by rotten food sitting close to a half full urinal on the night table. But most disturbing of all was the refrain, like a broken record: "Nobody tells me anything." My standard answer had probably been a broken record refrain as well. As far away as possible from the repulsive bed, close to the door, I told him day after day: "Mr. Jones, your stomach cancer has gotten worse. We are waiting to contact your brother to make arrangements to send you home," and walked away. That morning I decided I had had enough. Overcoming my disgust I sat on the bed, grasped his hand layered with dirt and compelled Mr. Jones to look into my eyes: "Mr. Jones, what I have been trying to tell you is that we cannot do anything more for you. Your cancer proved resistant to all forms of chemotherapy, has involved your liver and will cause your death within weeks. My recommendation is that you go home and be cared for by hospice to make sure you will be comfortable, if there is somebody staying with you at home. Otherwise we will probably keep you here until you die!" While holding his hand I felt his muscles relax, and I noticed a smile of some kind among his grimaces. Most important, his eyes were fixed in mine, instead of wandering adrift in space.

The following day we found a different person and a different setting. The room had been cleaned and smelled like fresh air; the bed sheet had been changed, there was no food or urinal on the night table, and Mr. Jones had shaved, cut and washed his hair. A woman half of his age was caressing him and playing with his hands. "Come in, doctors!" He encouraged me and my entourage. "I am going home tomorrow; I just talked with the hospice nurse. My brother is free tomorrow and will take me home with his car. Thank you for caring for me." The young woman at his side remained unnamed, except as the "girl with a grateful smile." He died within a month, assisted by this mysterious friend, we were informed by hospice.

Clearly I had been beating around the bush with Mr. Jones, without being aware of it. He needed to know that he was close to dying, yet he didn't know how to elicit that information from me, and I had skirted the issue with expressions such as "your cancer has progressed"—data that had no relevance in how he might plan his life. No wonder he had looked for two weeks like a man adrift at sea. When I leveled with him he was relieved of his anxiety; he could see the land at the horizon and that gave him option, something to live — and to die — for. The woman by his side? We never knew who she was. She was like a goddess appearing from nowhere at a critical time in Mr. Jones' life, helping him to experience the end of his life with her care. To know more about her, to focus our attention on her historical position, would only have diminished her divine role. The deeper truth was that she represented a divine intervention.

"Mr. Smith," I told him, holding his hand and looking into his eyes, "for you there is no treatment." The staunch old veteran who had done both the great and the Korean wars, and now had a barrel-shaped chest from 60 years of smoking two packs a day, showed no emotion. He thanked me with a nod and left. As I was watching his bent body waning through the clinic door, I kept wondering: "Had I really been truthful to him?" Mr. Smith had small cell lung cancer, a disease that responded very well to chemotherapy. He was going to die in a couple of months, but with chemotherapy he stood a great chance to live an additional year, and there was also a small but definite chance of a cure. There was a problem, however. His two daughters, who represented his only financial and emotional support, made it clear that they had no interest in supporting him throughout the ordeal of chemotherapy. Both were divorced single mothers who could not miss a single day of work needed to put food on the table. Without a caregiver's support, chemotherapy might have killed Mr. Smith quicker than his cancer would. And by no stretch of the imagination could chemotherapy be considered a form of euthanasia! I believed then and I believe now that I did the right thing, but I could not help wondering.

I could go on and on, but these cases offer a broad enough picture to support my assertion that patient-physician communication cannot help but be fraught with deceptions and lies. After all it took more than forty years of marriage for my beloved wife, Claudia, and I to learn how to communicate with each other, and this after endless years of argument when we both felt misunderstood and even contemplated ending our marriage! How can anybody in his or her right mind ever think that two strangers who had at best half an hour to meet, and one of whom is facing physical and emotional losses and potential death, can communicate well? The only somehow truthful communication occurred with Mr. Jones, after we had weeks of time to assess each other, a luxury that patients and physicians seldom enjoy now when the name of the game is to discharge patients from the hospital as quick as possible so as not to lose money with the Disease-Related Group (DRG) reimbursement or managed care payments.

In the 18th century, justice Oliver Wendell Holmes wrote a series titled "The Autocrat of the Breakfast-Table." In one of his articles he mentioned that there are at least six individuals in the conversation between John and Jack. These include what John thinks of himself, what John thinks that Jack thinks of him and who John really is, what Jack thinks he is, what Jack thinks that John thinks of him, and who Jack really is. Now, during a visit a patient is generally accompanied by a spouse (or significant other) and one or more children. By applying the Oliver Wendell Holmes rule, the number of people in that room is difficult to count without a calculator. Again, truthfulness in patient-physician communication as advertised in mainline medical and nursing journals is worse than wishful thinking, is a lie stemming from the mother of all lies, that there is an objective measurable truth that can be accepted and recognized by all persons, separate from who they are, by a simple rational process. In the case of medicine this lie has different components. First it holds that the disease is a well defined entity with a predictable course that can be influenced by treatment in a predictable way. The truth is that a diagnosis is not always certain, and diseases are evolving entities. Medicine itself causes new diseases. The immunesuppression necessary to the survival of transplanted organs has lead to a number of bacterial and fungal infections that in the past were all but unknown. In the meantime, diseases that used to be common have all but disappeared.

When I was a medical student in Italy our hospital wards were filled with cases of rheumatic fever and the inherited blood disorder thalassemia. Thanks to improved treatment of strep infections rheumatic fever has become an oddity. Thalassemia has almost disappeared from the Italian medical scene as prenatal diagnosis has led to the abortion of most thalassemia carriers.

Second, it holds that the disease host has negligible influence on the course of the disease, while the contrary is true. The same flu may manifest itself with minor symptoms in a young person who keeps working and may be rapidly lethal in an old person with a compromised immune system. Rarely, if ever, can the influence of the tumor host on the course of the disease be predicted. My twenty-year-old research in the field of geriatric oncology has been aimed to tease out the influence of physiologic age on the course of cancer and its treatment.

Third, it holds that scientific data may be translated into lay plain language. A common complaint is that doctors use jargon that is comprehensible only in their circles. The truth is that patients wish that doctors would encapsulate years of medical research and education in few words comprehensible by an eigth grader. I am not joking. According to the rules governing experiments and clinical trials, informed consent forms must be written in language that an eight grader can understand. By itself, this statement is ridiculous. Which eight grader are we talking about? The one who attends a seclusive Jesuit school or the one who attends a dilapidated school in a poor neighborhood? Of course the patient is entitled to know his or her prognosis, to have a realistic appreciation of the treatment outcome, and to be informed of the promises of clinical research in the field. This is quite different from expecting the doctor to go into a detailed description of the sequential molecular steps of cellular signal transduction. I choose an airline because of its record of punctuality, convenience, comfort and dependability, but few passengers would expect to have a detailed description of cockpit instruments before beginning a flight.

Fourth, this lie holds that communication is a two-way street where the vehicle that goes in one direction comes back the same in the opposite direction. The fallacy of this assumption is highlighted by Justice Wendell Holmes in the dialogue of Jack and John. Nobody has control of how people perceive the words that one says.

Of course everybody supports truthful communication, just as everybody supports full employment, and everybody abhors lies, just as everybody abhors child abuse. But the cases I described and many others I could add show that truthful communication is possible only when two or more persons share the same language. What one says may be different from what one means to say and from what one hears.

The lady who scolded me for having underestimated her husband's life expectancy assumed a number of lies: that a doctor can predict with accuracy the outcome of a disease, that the disease will take the same course in different persons, that we as physicians have learned what there is to learn about the cancer of her husband, that the term cancer encompasses a real defined entity instead of embracing a gamut of entities that are as poorly defined as the weather forecast in a developing country. In recommending that in the future I discuss the patient's prognosis out of the patient's hearing, she assumed other lies, including that no patient can face his or her imminent death and that family members always have the patient's best interest at heart. Finally she lied to herself when she ignored the part of the conversation where I denounced the unreliability of my own prediction. But in making those predictions, no matter how much I avowed the limitedness of my knowledge and experience, I became nonetheless an accomplice of the same chain of lies. I could not help that the lady and the family listened to me as though I were an expert who rarely was proven at fault. In this case a most truthful answer, more congruent with the language of the lady, would have been: "I don't know, and I have no way to know how long your husband has to live. The only thing I know is that we cannot stop his cancer, and his cancer will almost certainly come back. Unless he dies of a car accident or a heart attack, his cancer will eventually kill him." But even this answer would not have been truthful, as I did know how long, in a ball-park figure, the majority of patients with his form of malignancy typically lived, and I believed that the patient and his family needed to know how much time they might have to take care of business.

Likewise I had been truthful in telling Mr. Smith that there was no cure for him, but I was truthful in conveying a lie. What he did understand is that for patients like him with small cell cancer of the lung, there was no treatment, whereas what I meant to say was that for patients as frail as he is, there is no treatment without the support of a caring family, which in his case was absent. Equally truthful, or maybe more so, would have been to let him know that his daughters did not care enough for him to make a sacrifice and undergo some pain and inconvenience in order to prolong his life and relieve his discomfort and allow the three of them to face and negotiate their family impasse. Yet, I could not have assured either him or his children that the treatment would have worked, as only seventy percent of patients with that type of cancer benefit from chemotherapy.

I could go on and on, but I hope I've made my point. The truth is that there is not such a thing as a disease as there is a patient with a disease. The physical as well as the emotional and social conditions of the patient determine the most appropriate form of treatment and eventually this is determined by the doctor's judgment, which is also influenced by a number of external factors.

More in general there is not truth of any type dissociated from the personal experience. I do believe in God, as the ultimate truth, because I am a person with some unique personal talents that allow me to love God in a unique way. There would be no god if I, too, were not here! The very existence of God cannot be extricated from the experience I have of myself. I am a part not just a spectator, of the living truth.

Of course physicians and patients need to communicate; of course patients need to be informed of their options and take ownerships of their decisions. What I am saying is that current expectations about patient-physician communication are totally unrealistic, are a lie. It is a lie that diseases are well defined entities independent from the patients in whom they occur, simply because medicine has not been able to study the disease-host interaction, simply because it is easier to think of the disease as a foreign body whose elimination will make the patient whole again. And perhaps the worst of all lies is the assumption that the cure of the disease may automatically bring healing. Healing is a personal experience; healing is a spiritual experience.

By the way, nothing less than the ultimate form of science, molecular biology, has recently exposed Western medicine's disease concept as a lie, at least in oncology. Molecular biology has revealed that it does not make any sense to speak of cancer of the breast or of the lung or of any other organs, as there are as many different forms of cancer as there are patients, from a genetic standpoint! And maybe there are as many different forms of cancer cells as there are cells, as all cancer cells appear different from each other. It is a lie to assume that a patient is always ready to accept his or her prognosis and to consider rationally the options available to him or her.

Just recently a close friend of mine, a physician who has spent his life studying the cost-effectiveness of medical interventions, has decided to engage in a $100,000, controversial program for the management of his prostate cancer, which had become resistant to the standard treatment of the disease (medical castration). He did so despite my advice to the contrary. This program that at most will provide him with four additional months of life has virtually no chance to work in a man of his condition.

It is a lie to assume that physicians can discuss in a neutral, objective way the options that the patient has, like a car salesman illustrating the different options available on the dealership lot. (By the way, this is probably a lie, too—the assumption that the car salesman has no feelings toward his buyers. A human being without feelings is not human!) The "aequanimitas" of physicians, first enunciated by Dr. William Osler, is indeed the quintessential lie concerning medicine, the pretense that a physician (or for that matter any professional) can drop his or her humanity at the threshold of the clinics or of the laboratory. In his landmark essay delivered as a valedictory address at the University of Pennsylvania School of Medicine in 1889, Osler preached calmness, coolness and even detachment from patients. Aequanimitas may indeed represent the ultimate dream of an assembly line master!

Paradoxically, the lie that medicine is an objective science prevents or at least discourages the only attitude that might provide effective communication even when communication is impaired by lack of time, different languages and cultures, and mutual suspicion. That attitude is compassion. In terms of communication compassion allows a bidirectional flow of feelings among all people involved in a dialogue. As a silent language it is more meaningful and comprehensive than any uttered words; it overcomes any difficulty of hearing, speech and language; it goes directly to the seat of our emotions, which is where all choices, including the so-called rational choices, are made. Because, let's face it, rationality, not unlike physical fitness, not unlike clothes and make-up, is nothing else but a dress of our inner selves we choose as a way to present ourselves in public. Rationality is nothing other than a way to cover the hapless nudity of our fundamental questions and our fundamental fears: Who are we? What is going to happen to me? Who cares about me?

The pretense of neutrality, the pretense to aequanimitas, inspired by the myth that disease and health are identifiable objective entities, independent from the person to whom they pertain, has killed compassion or at least has relegated it to the role of an accessory health instrument, such as aspirin for an occasional headache, something that medicine could do without. Since the first day of medical school we eager, impressionable students were instructed that the best physician is the one who makes the diagnosis the first time he sees a patient and prescribes timely treatment rather than the one who visits the patient's house daily because is concerned for the patient's emotional health. Though they sound good, these recommendations were made in 1962, when many diseases were unknown, most diseases were misclassified, and the treatments were wrong. At that time it was common to treat hypertension or pulmonary edema with a phlebotomy and to starve patients with diabetes in order to lower their blood sugar. It was also customary to let patients die in pain out of fear that they might become addicted to narcotics or that narcotics hastened the patient's death with respiratory depression. Clearly arrogance fed on ignorance. The least we knew the more we were self assured, the more we felt we had to disdain compassion in the name of science, to abandon the personal truth in the name of an ideal objective truth. I don't know whether it is a joke that the only time between 1910 and 1970 when the average life expectancy of the white American man is increased has been during a physician strike, as some studies purport to be true. What I do know is that in the early '70s we amputated people's limb to cure very indolent sarcoma, we mutilated people's genitals to obtain the mythical five centimeters of tumor-free tissue to cure their melanoma. As we were horrified by female infibulations performed in some Moslem countries, we practiced the same type of mutilation to oblige our scientific superstition. We abandoned compassion to practice a superstition that was all but detrimental.

The disdain of compassion, of personalized care in the name of an objective truth has been a cause of poor medical care on top of everything else, and not just because it prevented personal healing. As we have seen, this approach led to unnecessary pain and to permanent compromise of individual quality of life. Worst of all, lack of compassion shortchanged patients, costing them their lives! A recent randomized, controlled study (the source of the most reliable scientific evidence), published in the New England Journal of Medicine, the most respected medical journal, showed that lung cancer patients who received palliative care (that is, compassionate and personalized care) from the beginning of their disease together with cytotoxic chemotherapy lived longer and cost less to the medical system than those who received chemotherapy only!

The lie that truth may be circumscribed by definitions and situational laws is pervasive in all spheres of life, not just in medicine. I spend time on medicine because it is the area I know best, and it is a good mirror of life in general. The major political conflicts of our time including capitalism and socialism, totalitarian regimes and representative democracies, may not be conflicts at all. When one looks at them from an ideological viewpoint, all ideologies imply that there is an economic or a political system that is objectively the best for the community. But, one may ask, if there is an objective truth reachable by reason, why do we have so much controversy? Why do different systems that proclaim opposite forms of government management claim each to be the best? An objective truth, such as the fact that $2 + 2 = 4$, should not be controversial at all (though a critical mathematician will tell you that $2 + 2$ is equal to almost 4, as no unity is similar to another, but we will ignore this for the moment).

An analysis of all proposed political systems reveals that the only arbiter between different choices is power, not reason! Power is the only objective variable in social and political interactions. In the absence of a law or a will that transcends human beings and comprehends them in a mosaic in which each individual unit is irreplaceable, blind power is the final arbiter of human fate. The only argument concerns who should wield the power.

In a capitalistic system, it is a small group of competitive masters whose goal is to exploit everybody else as slaves; in a socialist system it is the collectivity to which everybody is a slave. In a representative democracy, the majority tries to overpower the minorities; in a totalitarian system a small directory tries to overpower the majority. Where power is the lord, there is no room for human creativity, which expresses unbridled individuality.

I don't try to deny here the advances in technology and science that have been the hallmark of the last 200 years. I am trying to ask: Whom has this progress benefitted? Have these advances bettered our humanity or have they represented a desperate race away from ourselves, a form of addiction aimed to suffocate our intimate voices and aspirations? Until five years ago, renal cell carcinoma was considered an untreatable disease (except for the few lucky people who benefitted from a very toxic treatment involving interleukin 2). Today the majority of patients with metastatic renal cell carcinoma will receive at least one out of five different pills, all of which cost more than $5,000 per month—all for the promise to prolong life for a few months in approximately thirty to forty percent of patients. The majority of patients, both those whose survival is prolonged and those whose survival is not prolonged, will also suffer a plethora of complications including fatigue and malaise that may compromise their quality of life (and in a few cases kill them). Have these medications, or others such us Lupron and its accomplices denounced earlier, bettered the lives of the patients? Or have they coerced patients to invest all of their resources in an impossible dream of a cure that deprives them of the opportunity (the freedom) to divert their resources toward activities that are more meaningful for them?

Even in my one-on-one sessions with the patient, I cannot counteract the powerful message that Medical marketing tells the patient: Give up the dream of a lifetime vacation to Rome or Paris (or to Fulton, Illinois, if that is where you dream to be) and use that money to spend your time in a closet without windows. In the book *Treblinka*, a romanticized history of that Polish concentration camp, the author tells how the prisoners were allowed, in an act of supreme sadism, to chose between two roads: one led to Treblinka, the other to an unknown destination. Most of the Jewish captives selected the unknown destination that provided them with a swifter and more painful death. Sometimes I have the impression that this is the freedom of choice scientific advances offers to patients with all types of serious diseases. The British medical system denied the approval of any of these five pills that may prolong the life of a few patients with renal cell carcinoma. The American medical industrial system reviled the British government's decision as an undue suppression of individual freedom. I look at it as the prevention of the freedom to travel to Treblinka.

Today we have the power to terminate a life through abortion because we have made a prenatal diagnosis of a congenital disorder. That means that we have the power to abort people such as Beethoven, Van Gogh, Lincoln and Saul of Tarsus (all of whom could justifiably have been aborted for medical reasons), while we would allow Hitler, Stalin, Idi Amin and Sadam Hussein to be born. Likewise, by cloning we may prevent the birth of a host of artists, philosophers, and saints who have enriched our cultural endowments since the beginning of time.

A medicine that privileges the cure of the disease over the healing of the patient is not different from any other industry (food, travel, entertainment) that tries to create human needs instead of fulfilling existing needs. This process of estrangement is referred to as addiction, in medical terms. It is the search for artificial paradises in order to forget one's daily pain.

A number of myths of the ancient pre-Christian worlds have crystallized these human needs that modern technology tries to quench. Technological advances go arm in arm with the mother of all lies, that there is a definite, well defined good to which all human beings are supposed to subject their will and with which they should identify all their values. In this way human beings may be able to ignore the pain deriving from their innate contradictions. But this pain is what make them human. The elimination of the pain is tantamount to the renounce to one's own humanity. This process was called "disincarnation" by Michael R Tobin, a student of George Bernanos theology. According to Prof Tobin the common theme underlying Bernanos' novels and essays is the human pretence to escape pain by escaping their own humanity. In the promise of artifical paradises where all discomforts and all controversie underlying those discomforts are eliminated, science and technology have justified and fostered this pretence.

CHAPTER 8

# A Girl Named Grace

HER PARENTS NAMED HER Grace, after the grace of God. The history of her birth sounded like a rerun of the Christmas narrative, in Mississippi and in the 20th century. The mother thought herself to be in labor of her first child, but an Asian doctor, whose English she could not understand, was of different thinking and dismissed her from the emergency room. His first duty was to keep the hospital profitable, and this lady had no insurance.

Like most of the working poor, the pregnant woman and her husband could not afford health insurance and did not qualify for Medicaid. Back in their spare apartment, the husband turned on the heat for the first time that winter. Then he went out to buy some milk for supper. When he came back, he found the wife on the floor in a pool of blood.

"I doubt we can save the child," the midwife scolded them. "Why did you not come earlier?"

Alone in the delivery suite, with a blood transfusion running full speed in her veins, waiting for the obstetrician on call, she and her husband held hands and started praying. Grace was born alive, and after spending a week in the pediatric ICU, was discharged in full health. Six years later, hospital bills were still arriving in the mail.

We heard the story from Grace's mother on a leisurely Saturday afternoon as the husband was building a doghouse for our Saint Bernard. The $100 we agreed to pay would have bought groceries for the week. Grace and her little sister were playing in the back yard, wondering at the toys our child had neglected in the grass. It took Grace fifteen minutes to finish the piece of Swiss chocolate my wife gave her. Clearly she wished the pleasure of that unusual taste could last forever.

Grace's mother was a tall woman, pear shaped, the way a woman should look, according to the medical textbooks. Her bones must have been big, like those of a workhorse. She wore a blue dress that hit her legs midway between knee and ankle and, above the waist, did not allow even a hint of a glimpse of her breasts. Her long hair was fair and her face was clean of makeup.

I found her unusual and yet familiar. Eventually I realized why. I used to see her type in movies like *Tobacco Road* or *Hud* and in the cartoons of Dick Tracy and Li'l Abner. She was the prototype of the white woman working in Southern farms in the '50s and '60s. The appearance of her husband was much less distinctive. Had I met him behind a counter of a country fair or among the maintenance workers at my office, I would have ignored him as one of the people my Southern friends referred to as "white trash." But nobody, even the most cynical, could have used that or any other epithet on him. His spouse's dignity covered him as well, an invisible but certain veil protecting him from insult. I was reminded of Paul's letter to the Corinthians: The Christian wife sanctifies the unbelieving husband.

"Thanks for your hospitality," she said. "I hope my children did not misbehave. You have to understand, it is the first time they visit a neighborhood like yours. God bless you," she added by way of farewell.

More than thirty years ago this brief encounter represented a turning point in my attitude toward life. It was a revelation. I came face to face with wisdom. In Grace's mother, life and wisdom were one and the same.

I would not be surprised to learn that Grace's parents believed the world had been created in seven days (without questioning how you could distinguish day from night before there was a sun). They may even have believed that the sun turns around the earth, because it is so stated in the Bible, and they had never had the opportunity to learn otherwise at school. If they ever heard of Darwin's theory they would have rejected it as blasphemy for contradicting the biblical account of creation. Who cares? In the scheme of things such details are negligible.

They knew how to enjoy every minute of their lives as a gift that occurs once and cannot be experienced again. No fear, doubt or resentment could spoil their joy. They did not seek the truth with an intellectual process because they lived the truth.

They did not fear the future's uncertainty. Thankful for a job opportunity that had assured them of next week's livelihood, they did not see the need to worry about the future. Well aware that life is transient, they elected not to worry about death, disease or dangers that could be lurking everywhere at all times. Worries would have not removed the danger but would have robbed them of a joy-filled present, would have occulted the living truth. The ongoing development of their lives was beyond their control.

But, with rare skill, they understood that they could control their attitudes. Without having read Kierkegaard or even heard his name, they had learned that the fear of fear is the source of universal anguish, an emotional paralysis that confines a person to the borders of life, preventing any step into the potentially menacing but enjoyable land of the living. Grace had been born and grown healthy, despite their poverty and the carelessness of the emergency room doctor. They did not see any reason to doubt that life was a prerogative of a loving deity who knows what is best for each of us. Learned in the family, this message was confirmed every Sunday in the statement of the congregation assembled in the same church where many generations had worshipped and thanked the same God. As each life was precious in the eyes of God, why debate whether life begins at conception?

A gift from God may be accepted only with awe. To reject a gift of God because it appears flawed, or because it comes at an inconvenient time, is inconceivable, a recipe for disaster. Do humans know better than God? Of course not. Endowed with the ability to maintain the gift of life, humans are charged by God as stewards of life. It is their duty to take care of themselves, to help each other, to tell each other the truth, to be compassionate. The goal of medicine in their view is to restore health, relieve suffering and prolong life, not to destroy life or manipulate the genome of a zygote. Those actions had always been a prerogative of God.

Assuming that everybody was doing his or her best to be of help, Grace's parents did not resent the incompetence of the doctor with a foreign accent that confused l's and r's nor the greed of the hospital that almost caused the loss of three lives: that of Grace, her mother and the girl who came after Grace. Nor did they resent our mansion, the expensive toys our child could afford to toss aside with indifference, the Swiss chocolate Grace spent minutes savoring, our big dog whose monthly food, grooming and vet bills cost more than their entire family's livelihood. Like anguish, like doubt, resentment would only have deprived them of the present they cherished. As I said, I had a revelation; I found myself face to face with wisdom.

Wisdom's revelation was like an unexpected invitation to a banquet for an exhausted, hungry and thirsty drifter. Fear, doubt and resentment had haunted my life without a truce, like the demons of an ancient Greek tragedy.

I feared so many things.

I feared that I would lose my status, fail to succeed in my profession, drive away or otherwise shed the few affections I had been able to gather after many years of solitude, like solitary flowers in a cave.

And what of faith? Doubt never allowed me to commit myself fully to God. What if God was a construction of our mind, a social construction, an excuse for justifying my cowardice toward life? Did I beseech the help of God because I was not able to approach on my own the difficulty of everyday's life? I could not afford to believe in God unless I believed in myself. (It never occurred to me until then that I might never be able to believe in myself without believing in God, that trying to define myself without the intervention of God might be just an attempt to maintain a plant without roots.)

Most of all, I had been a prisoner of my resentments since I could remember. Memories of resentments dating back even to childhood were fierce. A child of Italian privilege, I grew up in the same hometown that produced the great filmmaker Frederico Fellini, but I was never happy. I felt as if I had spent my entire life waiting to get rid of somebody who was in my way: my fusty grandparents, my bullying father, occasionally cruel friends, my girlfriends once I was finished with them, the overbearing priests of the church. In my mind somebody else was always responsible for my melancholy, my inability to enjoy life and to be proud of myself.

I lived my life as if it were the Kafkaesque castle, where each room leads to another, to a litany of new but all similar rooms without an exit in sight. When finally facing facts, I knew that I didn't sail proudly to America; I fled to America. The transfer in geography was more to escape demons, less in search of a more solid medical training, as I had announced. And though 5,000 miles of water, plants, forests and mountains lay between Italy and America, I was still prisoner of the castle. The exit was no more in sight on this side of the Atlantic Ocean than in the Old Country. In spite of my medical credentials and my fully developed body, I was not much different from the sad teenaged boy who twenty years earlier had locked himself into his room during the Carnival festivity in his hometown. Scared and at the same time resentful of the rowdy celebrations in the street, I wrote poems asking myself why I could not take part in the common joy, why I had never learned to enjoy life. Meanwhile, I disdained the pretense of joy, reflected in the paper steamers left in the street at night.

Of course, after meeting Grace I did not fool myself into believing that I could then and there start living one day after the other, moment by moment, the same way Grace's mother did, by an act of free will. I knew very well that free will, if such exists, cannot influence the way a person feels. Just around that same time, I had discovered that medications might be necessary to uplift a depressed mood, because depression can be traced to a scarcity of certain neurotransmitters, the same way diabetes is due to a scarcity of insulin. The wisdom of Grace's mother provided something more important than a sudden change of attitudes or mood: It provided a glimpse of hope.

Though I had not yet discovered an exit from my castle, I had learned with certainty that there was a different world outside the castle, a world that charmed me and motivated me to find an exit.

Even more, I began considering the possibility of engrafting my whole vision of life on the beliefs of Grace's family. Could I believe what they believed simply because I trusted them, because I was attracted by their beliefs and by the certainty with which they embraced them? Though I might never be capable of manufacturing their brand of joy by myself, maybe I could in some way borrow it. You don't need to be an engineer to enjoy a train ride; you only need to trust the engineer. It dawned on me that trust was the very nature of the faith that gave us 2,000 years of Christianity. Jesus's disciples had only a confusing and imperfect idea of what he was talking about, but they trusted him as the engineer who drove them through the ride to which they had committed their lives. Generation after generation of Christians borrowed joy and trust from the previous generation.

I had discovered the act of faith. I had learned to accept something I could not fully understand because the persons carrying the message had given me reason to trust them.

Does it sound like voyeurism? Of course it does, but is that wrong? Why not delight in the faith-based joy of other people? Don't many parents revel in the sight of their children's zest-filled discovery of life? It turns out that spiritual voyeurism has been a main access, for me, to faith. Basking in this woman's wisdom the way a shipwreck survivor basks in the sun after reaching shore, I became able to unearth some pearls of the same wisdom buried in my own history. I had once known a young nurse's aide, impregnated by a medical student after they both got drunk on cheap tequila. She had refused to get an abortion. Disowned by her mother, shunned by the floor nurses, she had depended on a friend during the pregnancy and afterward in taking care of the baby. She had gotten on my nerves as she begged for money or when she asked me and other acquaintances on short notice to keep her child when she had to work a night shift. But thanks to Grace's mother I could now see in her another incarnation of wisdom.

Against all odds, she decided to carry her pregnancy to term, as she believed that life was a gift of God, even when it had been generated through the obliviousness of alcohol. In her heart of hearts she had known that a derelict life, the most miserable of lives, is better than no life. Furthermore she trusted her friends. She knew better than many of us understood then that to help her raise her child was a privilege, nothing less than helping the Virgin Mary to raise Jesus.

And I recall a character of another generation in another land:

In our high school our professor of religion, an old priest who had been the butt of many cruel jokes, asked one day with a tone of disappointment: "None of you has ever seen your mother helping your father into his jacket before going to work? In what kind of household are you growing up?" He had grown up in the country, seventh of eight children. The family shared two rooms. There was a single toilet in an outhouse shared with five other families. His father had worked as a field hand for forty years before a heart attack had downed him in the middle of the field during the June harvest.

"His mother must have loved to be a sex slave. I bet she wore a chastity belt!" one of the girls had murmured, and the other schoolchildren chuckled.

That same girl's parents had separated after a spate of affairs of which the whole town had been aware. After a broken marriage and an abortion, the girl herself committed suicide via a drug overdose. As for the priest, up until his last days he pastored one of the suburban parishes, inhabited mainly by immigrants who lived off small thefts and were likely to use violence against each other after Saturday-night drinking binges. His wisdom never abandoned him. He never lost his welcoming smile even when the pantry was empty and the house cold.

And still another character, this one an old woman:

"Do you know what it means to have been married forty years to a person and never have heard a bad word from him, a comment that was less than kind? Do you still remember how to pray?" she asked. She was not the sort of person to be taken seriously in elite medical circles. She was an illiterate African-American woman, and she was addressing the chief of nephrology, who had stirred up a tempest in her family. The day before, he had walked into the room of her husband, who had just developed renal failure from multiple myeloma, and without introducing himself said: "You have one of two choices: either die in a few days without pain or die in a few months with a lot of pain."

This physician was very proud of his bluntness and cynicism, but he could summon only a few grunts in response to the wisdom of the old woman as he left, moving on to the next case. "Just tell your children, don't ask questions if they don't want to know the answer!" His shout back to the woman was a lame attempt to have the last word. To no avail. Her words, "Do you still remember how to pray?" hung in the air. The faith of an illiterate

African-American woman had KO'd the world heavyweight champion of skepticism in the jury's unanimous judgment as word of the incident spread around the hospital.

And one more person, one more incident, this one from postwar Italy.

At the time, most people were jobless, most houses little more than heaps of rubble. Roads and railroads were in disarray, and every week a forgotten minefield harvested lives and body parts. My young aunt walked ten miles each way every weekend to reach her assignment in the mountains. She held her classes in an empty stable where she also spent the nights on a makeshift bed, her dreams accented by the noise of rats looking for food and mating in the dark. When she developed a chronic cough that did not abate, even with home remedies, my father kept us away from her out of concern about TB, still rampant and deadly in Italy in the days before streptomycin. Her smile never left her face. She knew she was providing a necessary service to the poorest of the poor by teaching them how to write and read and count, and no price seemed to her too high for this privilege.

These and many other examples of wisdom returned to enlighten my internal vision after meeting Grace's mother. More than an occasional oasis in the desert, as I might have looked at them before, now they seemed milestones of a journey or maybe restoration points in a race that brought me to interact with Grace's mother. That journey, that race, that interaction allowed me to discover the supreme and final form of wisdom: the acceptance of life as a mystery! These people had in common the unshakable conviction that life was worth living as each one of us is endowed with unique talents to share with our neighbor. Then our neighbor becomes a brother or a sister because our ability to donate ourselves to each other makes of us the human family. They are the poor of whom the Gospel talks, the ones who are blessed in the Sermon on the Mount, the ones who will always be with us. The poor who may wait for a birthday or for Christmas to buy a $15 T-shirt or a new pair of shoes, because they are endowed with the sense of sacredness and know that every small luxury is a gift of love. They are the poor that faith made rich. They were a revelation. They revealed to me that I and my colleagues were full of means and resources and yet our lack of faith or our disregard of faith made us poor!

For me they brought an old childhood parable to life. A child was allowed a visit to heaven and to hell. In hell he found a number of people provided with chopsticks too long to bring the rice to their mouths, and they all were starving and becoming angrier by the minute. In heaven people were provided with the same size chopsticks, but they were happy and well fed. They had learned to use the chopsticks to feed one another.

CHAPTER 9

# Life as a Mystery

LIFE IS A MYSTERY. A mystery! That is, a full experience of reality, something that cannot be circumscribed by words or defined by thoughts, an experience that can only be lived. Yes, I am trying to say that life can only be lived; the reality of life consists in being a living reality. Any attempt to describe life takes life away from life, kills life.

A few years ago I attended a reception at the Museum of Natural History in a major American city. Scenes of wildlife were showcased behind glass in a tableau that tried to reproduce the environment where the animals had lived prior to being killed (pardon, "harvested") and stuffed. My guts churned as I was faced with a family of elephants (a bull, three cows and two cubs) standing close to an artificial pond. Proudly the museum staff explained that the family had being playing, washing and drinking in a pond exactly like this the evening before they were shot by the museum expedition. The architects had taken painstaking measures to make the exhibit as close as possible to the habitat of the elephants in the African savannah for the enjoyment and the relaxation of museum visitors. I was offended by the killing of highly developed and sensitive animals with intelligence comparable to that of an eight-year-old child for entertainment, even in the guise of education. But even more I found offensive the pretense of showcasing life by destroying life.

Similarly, even the most thorough description of a living experience replete with the most accurate choice of words can never approximate the experience any more than could the big-city museum capture life in the wild!

Of course we need to communicate our experiences. Communication is the venue of love (and of hatred that is its counter face). Yet the most effective form of communication is nonverbal because it preserves the mystery of life; it is a communication made of living words. Christian art has expressed this silent dialogue hundreds of times in the depiction of the annunciation of the angel to the Virgin Mary. Even more than the German, Flemish or French paintings where the authors generally add the words of the Gospel in the background, I love the southern European ones where the communication is completely entrusted to the expressions of the characters.

The greatness of a painter of human figures is gauged by the ability to convey a message more complete than words alone ever could. Perhaps the supreme manifestation of this art is Leonardo's Last Supper that one can admire in Milan in the convent adjoining the church of Santa Maria delle Grazie. The apostles' surprise after Christ has revealed that one of them will betray him that night is contrasted with the fear of Judas, who did not expect that his betrayal was known, and recoiling from the table he hits and overturns the salt container (which in Italian superstitious tradition means bad luck). In addition, each apostle is expressing his own reaction, which ranges from anger to disappointment to fear. The countenance of each one of them expresses their individual messages, defines them as persons, states the mystery of their individuality more than a dictionary full of words could. And the most expressive silence of all is the loneliness of Christ, aware that he alone must endure his passion. He is overwhelmed by the anticipation of his suffering, indifferent to the protestations of his friends, and still unaware perhaps of being the son of the living God. Leonardo's Christ expresses all the pain of human loneliness aware of the mystery of life but without a clue to guide interpretation of this mystery. More than the triumphant pantocrator (the Western Christian image of Christ seated on a throne as ruler of the world) of the byzantine mosaics, Leonardo's Christ is a reincarnation of Job, prior to God's revelation, or of the author of the Qoleteh (the main speaker in the Hebrew Book of Ecclesiastes) that proclaims the vanity of human life and recognizes human suffering as inescapable.

How many times does our look or our tone of voice mean exactly the opposite of what our words say? This scenario was crystallized in Gabriel Garcia Marquez's masterpiece, *One Hundred Years of Solitude*, when a teenager, Amaranta Úrsula, comes back from a hot date and tells her mother and her grandaunt, "How much I love you!" More perceptive than the mother, the grandaunt understands that she means, "If I just could, I would kill you right away! I hate you and our whole family!" Biblical literature is filled with looks and demeanor that mean more than words. Think of the image of the seal as a metaphor of unconditional love; think about the women behind the window (Jezebel and Michal) signifying supreme contempt for their respective husbands; think of the look of Jesus toward the young rich man reluctant to leave his riches or of the look of Jesus toward Peter after his denial, a look that meant encouragement and love despite disappointment. The Nobel Prize-winning masterpiece of 1950, *Barabbas* by Pär Lagerkvist, stems from a look, not a word, of Jesus.

Mystery derives from the Latin word *mysterium* that signifies an intercourse with the deity, a physical experience of the deity. The deity stands for the reality in its wholeness. Reality has a meaning that escapes our rational definition.

The mystery, the union with a deity, guarantees that human activity is congruent with the meaning of the reality because, through the mystery, humans are united with the deity, partaking of the life of God. The situation is not unlike that of a child who feels confident in working toward his parents' goals when he obeys their directions, even if he is not privy to those goals. St. Augustine best described the role of mystery in human life: "*Credo ut intelligam.*" I can understand the meaning of the reality and my own role only through faith; that is, through acceptance of the mystery. Mystery subsists in modern religious practice. The Catholic and Orthodox communion, where the faithful are allowed to eat the body and drink the blood of the Lord, is definitely a form of *mysterium*. In the writing of some mystics such as Teresa of Avila and John of the Cross, the physical interaction with God in the communion had heavy sensual connotations, became in fact a form of oral sex with God! The abandonment of oneself to God's will preached by Islam (which means unconditional submission to God) also closely reflects the mystery.

Even outside a specific religious persuasion, mystery is an everyday experience for thoughtful individuals. Mystery is the sense of safety and self-confidence experienced by a child growing in a nurturing family where love is the final arbiter of all disputes and dissensions. Mystery is the sense of awe inspired by a masterpiece or a landscape. Mystery is the trepidation and respect elicited during the initial revelation of the intimacy of another person, when sex is lived as a free mutual donation, as the seal of an everlasting commitment and communion. Whether birth is an occasion of joy or concern, whether the proximity of death suggests fear or relief, whether success is a cause of self-fulfillment or self-rejection, all these experiences are life; that is, are mystery.

Am I talking about emotions? You bet! Can one conceive of a life devoid of emotions? The most rational of decisions is rational only when inspired by an emotion; otherwise it is not rational at all. What is the rationale of deciphering the genetic code or of interpreting galactic laws were it not to satisfy a human emotion, were it not a desire for health, power or knowledge? What is the rationale of improving our appearance when we go on a date, were it not to inspire a sense of confidence and attraction in a person whose affection we are determined to conquer? I must say that in my life I have met only two types of individuals: those who think they are emotional and those who do not think at all!

Emotions, not reason, are the fundament of our understanding of ourselves. Our emotions tell us that we are here for a purpose that is certain, because without a purpose our life would not make sense. It is our own sense of dignity (from the Latin *dignus,* or "worthy") that tells us we are worthy in a unique way, that no other person can live our life for us, that we have a unique role in the world. The emotion that gives us our sense of dignity is our own essence—the emotions are ourselves. Emotions do not lie; logic divorced from the guidance of emotions is just a chain of lies.

In his first book, *Sous le Soleil de Satan (Under Satan's Sun)*, Georges Bernanos defines the devil, the incarnation of lie, as "*le raisonneur incomparable*" ("the unsurpassable logic"); that is, the logic left to itself, logic devoid of life, the logic that only deceives. Facing a personal failure (such as the loss of trust or affection by another person, being fired from our job, an economic collapse), logic may tell us that we are dispensable and disposable, that we are a heap of garbage to be incinerated. But as long as we live, our sense of dignity will allow us to keep living even if we are unable to discover our own utility and role. His sense of dignity allowed Van Gogh to keep living and give us some of the greatest masterpieces of all time, though he sold only one painting during his life. Suspicious of his novel form of art, his well-intentioned friends and relatives recommended that he quit painting, and other more malignant ones such as Paul Gauguin recommended that he even destroy himself, as his life had no use.

Paradoxically, the centrality of human dignity to human survival is stated every time some person or group plans to subjugate or destroy another. This attempt is always preceded by a denial of dignity, of the right of independent survival.

The ancient Romans called barbarians, uncivilized, unworthy of freedom, the individuals they conquered as slaves or exhibited as gladiators in the arenas where they were asked to kill each other for the populace's entertainment. The slave traders considered their human merchandise subhuman, a feeling that persisted for a century in America during Jim Crow even after the abolition of slavery. The Nazis created the myth of racial purity to justify the slaughter of Jews, Catholics, Gypsies and handicapped individuals. The Jacobins during the French revolution (and later the communists in Russia, China, Vietnam, Cambodia and North Korea) justified the elimination of millions of the supposedly nonenlightened because they represented a danger to the triumph of their rational truth.

In present-day America we deny the dignity that all human beings deserve to millions of illegal immigrants whose only fault is that they provide cheap labor as they attempt to better the living conditions of their families. Not long ago, at a party, one of my neighbors, holding a tumbler of Scotch, bragged about having compelled a team of illegal Mexicans to care for his yard free, under the threat of reporting them to immigration. This gentleman is a self-proclaimed church-going Christian who feels that people without a visa can be used as merchandise; that is, they have no human dignity. To illegal immigrants one should add ghetto dwellers, whom conservative politicians try to confine to the ghetto as if it were a wild animal sanctuary, in the hope that they will destroy each other, without access to voting booths, good schools, or even to law enforcement and basic medical care.

Human dignity is the recognized basis of human rights and civil liberties, and the only way to deprive people of their rights and their liberties involves depriving them of their dignity!

The other basic emotion that is a corollary of our sense of dignity is the desire for personal immortality, as Miguel de Unamuno underlined in his book *The Tragic Sense of Life*. As he pointed out, it is the human aspiration to immortality that generates the desire for a god and for a relationship with an eternal god that supports our own eternity. The aspiration to immortality might have generated religion, but certainly it was not—as the rationalists and the materialists argue—religion's goal to create a delusion of immortality. Marx's claim that "religion is the opiate of the masses" should be reversed: "Pure reason is the opiate of the masses." Opium is a substance that assuages one's pain. Blind faith in rationality is the opium that prevents some people from feeling the pain of the human drama, the aspiration to personal immortality in a world of finitudes. Religion keeps that drama active, allows us to endure the pain of living.

Today the idea of one's personal immortality may appear absurd after science has shown us that specific lesions in our brains may alter our own perceptions as well as our own moods. How can we keep being ourselves as our brain starts liquefying a few minutes after we cease breathing? It is this irreconcilable incongruence between the limited evidence of our own eyes (which suggests our permanent and total dissolution) and the aspiration to immortality that keeps us living that defines "the tragedy of human living."

"*Credo quia absurdum.*" Translation: "I believe because it is absurd," as stated by the Latin father of the church and founder of Western theology, Tertullian. In view of the modern scientific evidence that decrees the limitedness of the whole universe, let alone our temporal life, this statement could not be more timely! Perhaps a modern translation of Tertullian would say, "I am asked to choose between my aspirations (emotions) and the limited scientific evidence that I can manage to grasp. There is no doubt that I have to choose my aspirations, if I have to live, because I would not be alive at all without them. The so-called scientific evidence is very limited, and scientific discoveries are ongoing. New scientific discoveries quite often contradict the interpretation of previous data. But I have only one life to live. I can't wait the thousands of years of investigations it will take to define who we are (something that may be all but impossible). I have to know who I am and what my goals are right now. The internal revelation of my emotions is the only truth I can really trust for this purpose. The real absurdity, then, is to ask an ever-evolving ever-changing science to tell me who am I!"

In *Le Mystere Frontenac* Francois Mauriac describes human freedom (or, better said, the absence of freedom) when human mystery is neglected and ignored:

"You are free to drag though this world a heart I have not created for this world; free to look on this earth for a food that is not destined to you, free to try to placate a hunger that cannot be satisfied." Life without mystery is a tragedy of desperation and self-destruction. Properly, in his book *Amor y pedagogia, (Love and Pedagogy)*, Miguel de Unamuno asserts that the rational truth is the worst of all lies. The main character of the book tries to organize his own life according to rational principles, unencumbered by emotions, and as expected his life is an unconditional failure that culminates in the suicide of the son he had tried to raise in obeisance to pure reason as the source of perpetual happiness. It was Blaise Pascal who said, "The heart has its reasons which reason knows not." When emotions and reason are at odds, emotions should prevail.

Last but not least, the mystery and underlying emotions are the source of human bondage. The mystery of life is a shared adventure, whether a person is aware of it or not. The emotions with which we approach the mystery of life—including awe, fear, confidence, love, hatred, rejection—are individual in the sense that nobody can live them for us; they bring our imprint. Yet they are somehow shared. Whether we describe them with words, or communicate them nonverbally, we are able to recognize passion, fear, love, hatred, confidence, attachment or annoyance in another person's words or demeanor.

Emotions define us as individuals capable of the same type of emotions, reveal somehow a common root of our humanity. The fruit grown on different branches may have different sizes and nuances of color, but ultimately they all have a similar shape and a similar taste. Though lived differently in different cultures, this communal consciousness is universally acknowledged. We are human because we partake of the same adventure through the mystery of life. We are humans because we engage in this adventure with the same provisions; that is, the same emotions, though the distribution of these provisions, the use of these provisions and the experience of these provisions is different for each one of us.

Perhaps the early times of my marriage to Claudia (and I believe this is true of many marriages, at least of my generation, for whom living together prior to marriage was not an option) best showed this communality of emotions with different expressions. When we had to make plans together, such as organizing a weekend outing or buying furniture for our living room, usually our discussion ended up with me shouting and Claudia crying. Eventually we almost always made up by hugging and insisting that we loved each other, and we completed our pacification in bed, as a way to manifest that we belonged to each other. Our initial confrontation, the shouting and crying, revealed our mutual frustration at being unable to convey our desires to each other. We both felt frustrated, but we expressed it in different ways. We acknowledged that different emotions underlay our differences in plans, and we were frustrated by not partaking of those emotions, though we recognized each other's emotions. In my desire to save money by passing up pricy furniture, Claudia recognized her father's obsession with the fear of being left without resources. In Claudia's wish for an expensive living room, I recognized her need to make our living environment personal, different from a hotel room or a bus station lobby. Eventually, in our statement of mutual belonging through cuddling and sex, we declared to each other that emotional misunderstanding did not erase the deeper feeling of mutuality that had inspired our marriage. It took us a long time to learn how to communicate without conflicts, but the conflicts played an important role in identifying each other as unique human beings by expression of our own emotions.

In *The Labyrinth of Solitude*, Octavio Paz describes how in the meso-American culture, the opening of oneself to another person is a form of death. The worst offense for Mexicans is not *hico de puta* (son of a whore) as it is in Spain and in most Western countries, but *hico de la chingada* (son of a woman who has been violated). The worst personal fault is to let somebody else penetrate your own mystery, because once the mystery has been penetrated the person penetrated has been dissolved. This conviction underlies at least in part the association that poets of all times have established between love and death (think of Giacomo Leopardi's 1832 canto "Love and Death," where death is considered a corollary of love: You can only love when you die to yourself).

The cultural attitude of meso-Americans highlights how the loss of the mystery can only be associated with the loss of one's life. Yet I believe you can love and still be faithful to your own mystery. Love is a voluntary donation of oneself rather than total submission into slavery to another person. As the mystery of life involves an ongoing self-discovery, the gifts that two people in love can share are more varied and unexhausted if each person preserves his or her own mystery. The characters I have mentioned in this book—Grace's mother, the old priest who grew up in a peasant farm and pastored a destitute parish, the illiterate African-American woman who put the obnoxious professor in his place, my wandering aunt who walked miles in the snow to teach a few mountain children—they did not renounce their mystery as they shared their lives with others. As well-managed reservoirs, they were able to irrigate cultivated fields, satisfy the drinking needs of the city and serve as home to different varieties of edible fish without compromising water levels or purity.

Even Claudia's and my initial marital confrontations I now see as a way to share our love without renouncing our decision to be ourselves.

Sadly, life is full of examples of reservoirs of love that have flooded the surrounding countryside or have turned dry or become poisoned by hatred. The emotional world is full of Katrinas! The current epidemic of suicides by young veterans of the Afghan and Iraq wars, the epidemic of hatred that pervades the extreme groups of virtually every religious denomination, the spousal hostility that gnaws as an inner worm at so many marriages—these are just a few examples of love reservoirs turned bad. They have exterminated life around themselves and produced a social desert comparable to what colonial powers have done to most of Africa or India where drought is a perpetual cause of starvation and disease.

How can such reservoirs be well managed, then? The answer once more goes to Grace's mother—through the freedom that faith produces; that is, freedom from fear, freedom from doubt, freedom from resentment.

Christian faith is clearly relational: It is learned, is it practiced, it is shared, and it is witnessed in the community. The community then cannot be neutral to one's faith. It can either reinforce or threaten it.

CHAPTER 10

# The Death of Betsy

A WOMAN I'LL CALL Betsy was, at first, far from joy, then full of joy.

After a weekend binge of drunkenness and masturbation ("the only thing I did not do that weekend was go out in the street and invite the first passerby to fuck me," she confessed), Betsy decided she needed help to break the vicious cycle of her addiction. Monday morning she called Alcoholics Anonymous.

As a marriage agreement, she and her husband abandoned the heavy stuff, but they still smoked pot. After her husband died of lung cancer, alcohol remained her solace and her prison. A cultivated woman who knew Latin, spoke both German and French and traveled extensively throughout five continents, Betsy had visited a number of unusual places including Ethiopia and Afghanistan. In the '70s she took a driving tour with a boyfriend from Copenhagen to Tibet.

Betsy was a respected and renowned writer for a major U.S. newspaper. Her professional behavior was impeccable, her conversation rich and meaningful. Still considered very attractive in her late forties, she received frequent propositions and proposals, routinely rebuked. She did not seek male companionship.

More than a form of allegiance and devotion to her late husband, her lack of interest in men stemmed from the multiple and often casual sexual experiences she had engaged in, in her youth, as a dutiful flower child of the make-love-not-war '60s. Eventually I learned that alcohol and drugs had been the basis of all her indiscretions. She had few good memories of these experiences. The main reason she slept with men was to oblige them. Indeed

## The Death of Betsy

she had been able to achieve orgasm only though oral sex (something many men shy away from) or masturbation, which she best carried out on her own.

At that particular time of her life she did not need the additional complication of a relationship, of the anxiety to prove adequate to the needs and wants of a companion. A number of men had complained that in bed "she was good but not very good," and they had tried to subject her to a heavy course in the loving arts that she had found both boring and demeaning. At the same time she was trying to reach out to her father, who had disowned her during her marijuana-peace-free-love period. A new man in her life would have complicated the achievement of this goal that she saw as a major priority.

Throughout her life her partners had always represented a rebellion against her parents, especially her father. She had willfully chosen individuals her family would disapprove of. Her late husband had been a truck driver and a college dropout. It had been fun for a few months but eventually as expected they drew apart. She gained weight and started drinking heavily. Divorce was on the horizon had he not developed lung cancer. I share these details that I learned over five years because I believe it would be impossible to understand the joy of her conversion without this background.

Betsy started emailing me after I read some of my poetry during the annual Memorial Day at the cancer center where I worked. She attended the memorial in honor of her spouse, who had rapidly succumbed to lung cancer.

Initially I humored her, but a tinge of self-interest contaminated our relationship. First of all I cannot help but acknowledge the interest that any woman has for me, even if my mind could not be further away from thoughts of an affair. It is an instinctive reaction that has its root, I believe, in my lonely youth when I felt disdained by all women. Just as a man who has suffered starvation will not refuse a free meal, even when he is already full, I feel I should not miss my chance when a woman shows interest in me. In addition, it's always helpful to have a journalist on one's side. A journalist can be a source of visibility essential to the career of an ambitious professional; a journalist can also help repair one's image should one fall from grace. At that particular time Claudia was less than appreciated by her chief of staff. A journalist could have seen in their conflict a great case of sex discrimination. But soon I forgot Betsy's occupation. Rather, I became aware of the privilege of partaking in the joy of a human being who was wondering at her own sacredness. I was witnessing the work of the Spirit. Our face-to-face meetings were infrequent, and yet I came to know her more than I know any other close friend.

Alcoholics Anonymous, or AA, emphasizes that two conditions are necessary to overcoming alcoholism and other forms of addiction. The first is faith in a benign deity to whom one can relinquish both human will and decisions. The second is the support of a community of individuals sharing the same goal to overcome addiction—a community of faith. Indeed AA is structured as a church (from the Greek *ecclesia* that means an assembly of individuals sharing the same convictions and the same goals, even if they may not always be like-minded). During the five years between Betsy's commitment to AA and her death she did not touch a single drop of alcohol, though many of her other friends still indulged. Perhaps more important, in AA she discovered her call, her own sacredness. Her great intelligence, her worldly experience as a cultured woman—those aspects gave her a credibility that established her as a leader within AA, even though she had not sought nor desired such a role. Soon she became a sponsor of new members and became, almost to her own surprise, a powerful advocate for the weakest members.

I cannot help seeing a form of poetic justice or maybe a divine sense of humor in the fact that a former hippie who smoked pot, did heavy drugs and professed free love as the supreme form of freedom had decided to surrender her will and her decision to a higher power. She wanted to believe because without such power her life would not have made much sense. More than that, she had become a master of spirituality the same way she had once been a master of vice. But perhaps it is not so surprising. What would have happened to Saul of Tarsus had he not fallen from his donkey on the way to Antioch? Had he not remained blind for three days from the vision of God—or from a post-seizure episode (it really does not make any difference; the only thing that matters is the faith that lead Paul's life thereafter)?

It is not farfetched to think that he might have been one of the more ferocious and unyielding persecutors of the Christian faith. The same passion may lead to a great evil or a great good, according to the circumstances. Is not the hatred of God a manifestation of a deceived love for God, a manifestation of the pain of not being able to believe?

The weekend Betsy spent drunk on the floor may represent a modern-day example set by Saul with his three days of blindness.

To have overcome her addiction did not bring peace to Betsy, though it brought joy. Like Moses in the burning bush she wanted to know the name of the God that delivered her from slavery. When you love somebody you want and need to recognize the person you love. Her immense capacity for love would never have been fulfilled by an idea: She wanted a physical presence; she needed intercourse. Like the blue prince of Cinderella, Betsy believed she could not find peace until she ended up in the arms of her beloved, even if she had to overturn the whole kingdom in order to find the foot that would fit the glass shoe in her hand.

For the first time in her life she felt able to make a free gift of herself, whereas in all of her past relationships she had felt cheap and disposable; she had made her body available to anyone who would reassure her, give her a sense of belonging in the comfort of a temporary intimacy at the price of her self-esteem.

Her restless and indefatigable search led her to the threshold of a Catholic parish. There, with the help of a sensitive pastor, Betsy recognized the spouse she had longed for, for a lifetime, in a young Jewish carpenter who explained to her that love is very simple. As he had done 2,000 years earlier to an illiterate Samaritan woman, Jesus showed to Betsy that love for the world sprouts from the love of oneself as a precious unique instrument of a loving plan aimed to heal all afflictions that make of human life a vortex of desperation and self destruction.

As Jesus had asked the Samaritan woman to call the husband she did not have (after five husbands the woman was living with a man to whom she was not wed), Jesus appeared to Betsy as a divorced alcoholic deadbeat father of two asking her for water to placate his thirst and bail him out of his prison. To her surprise, thanks to the encouragement of her sponsor, who asked her to get involved in a situation that common sense gave up for lost, Betsy discovered herself to have access to a fount of perennial life. At the very moment she had asked for help for herself, she discovered the source of help for all humanity.

Her words, her actions now spoke on behalf of the whole of humanity—prisoners of all forms of addiction, even prisoners of self-centeredness, preoccupied with their own feelings and reactions. The self-centered have no time nor sight to discover their own potential to give life and freedom to their neighbors.

A colleague of mine had succeeded in wooing and marrying a nurse after a lot of begging; eventually they had a little girl who for many years was the apple of their eye. He completed his training in obstetrics and gynecology and after many trials his wife got pregnant again, as they had both desired. But a few months before the baby was born, he told her he did not want the child. He wanted out of the marriage.

While moonlighting at an abortion clinic, he met a divorced nurse with two children. He had decided to start a new life with this woman. No reason given. This is what he felt like doing at that point in his life.

I will never know why his wife agreed to defer to his will and undergo an abortion. The last I heard his little girl pretended that her daddy had never left and that she was playing with her daddy every day. This colleague of mine epitomizes the prison of self-centeredness that is both the cause and the consequence of addiction. Blindsided by his own self-centeredness, he has spent his life in a monologue, talking to himself about himself. The others mattered only inasmuch as they influenced his appreciation of himself. He was the only character in his ongoing stage play. When he got tired of the script the only recourse he had was to change the other players. He never looked for a new play, just for a change of scenery. Inflicting unimaginable pain on his daughter, his wife, his unborn baby and his friends, he was nevertheless the first and ultimate victim of his own imprisonment. In ignoring the pleas of his little daughter he really ignored his only way to freedom. When one has no other recourse nor resource outside of his own feelings to assess his life, all he can hope for is either a condition of permanent orgasm or a condition of permanent oblivion. Or a condition of permanent orgasm leading to permanent oblivion, as was the case with another friend of mine from medical school. During high school, he had spent every day petting with a girl he did not care for, just to drown the existential confusion that had made his life unbearable. Any outside intervention that may disturb these conditions will be rejected and ignored. Any outside contact is a threat to the prison of self-centeredness and addiction.

When she discovered AA, Betsy broke loose from these chains, but she did much more than that. She also became a model of hope for anybody who desired to get loose the way she did. When I heard her story I could not help seeing a parallel with the resurrection of Christ who broke the prison of death for anybody who believed in him.

Thanks to the instruction of the Roman Catholic Church, Betsy could finally learn the name of the people who started crowding her doorstep looking for the living water she had discovered upon surrender of her will to a higher power. The alcoholic deadbeat father of two, the single mother who tried to drown her remorse in alcohol over the violent death of her youngster, the lesbian reporter who could not forgive herself for the abortion she had when worrying over her sexual identity, and many more lost souls—all of them were opportunities to care for the wounded Christ. The joy Betsy encountered in ministering to them was the joy of a loving spouse responding to pressing requests of love from her new partner. In witnessing her undefatigable activity I was reminded of what a mystic of the fourth century, the Saint Macarius of Egypt, wrote about spreading the Spirit — that we should allow the Spirit to work in us.

As she fully joined the Catholic community the requests for love by her wounded spouse became more insistent and assumed the varied faces of humanity!

In addition to prisoners of alcoholism, she had the opportunity to care for those addicted to drugs, sex and work as well as to the poor, the sick, ex-convicts nobody wished to befriend and undocumented aliens who would otherwise have passed by unnoticed. She also became privy to the secret life of well established parish families and, surprisingly, these were the ones more difficult to help. She learned that a respected teacher had had a long-time affair with a married physician, and she had become intolerant of both her spouse and her children. In another case, a respected professional and family man had been carrying on a homosexual relationship. Betsy learned of children who hated their parents and vice versa, of priests who had lost their faith and on and on. Her first step in dealing with this array of different people was always to relieve guilt and to reinstitute self esteem, the recipe that had restored her freedom to her. The problems that crowded her life did not interrupt her joy: In any new experience she recognized an act of trust from her spouse, an opportunity to soothe the physical and moral wounds of the Christ, and she learned to appreciate the deepest meaning of the transfiguration. In each of these individuals coming to her for a sip of living water she could see what God had seen in each one of them, as the apostles saw Jesus on Mount Tabor, when he appeared in full glory, radiating light, conversing with Moses and Elijah. This vision was a source of undefeatable hope.

By then she was writing me almost daily, communicating a joy that overwhelmed all expectations. Her favorite reading was Thérèse de Lisieux, Sister Teresa of the Child Jesus, the saint of simplicity and innocence. In the Catholic saint also known as the Little Flower of Jesus, Betsy had found a form of reincarnation, as if she was being born again. From time to time I felt like warning her that suffering is often also part of the faith experience, but she did not appear disturbed. "Maybe I already paid my price of suffering with the suffering of my early life, when I lived in the darkness without God," she wrote to me once.

Unfortunately suffering was, indeed, lurking behind her joy. Physical suffering, it turned out.

Betsy's best friend called me while I was in a conference in Denver. "Betsy's had a terrible headache for three days; she can't see and she's had an episode of urinary incontinence." I referred her to a neurologist friend who in twenty-four hours came out with the diagnosis: Betsy had a malignant brain tumor. She needed emergency surgery. She was at risk of dying any minute because of increased pressure within her skull. This occurred approximately three years after her confirmation in the Catholic Church.

After surgery and other treatments, she enjoyed approximately fourteen months free of the disease. During this period she went back to her work. She even informed her newspaper readers of the tumor that she called "a nuisance." The miracle was that not even severe physical suffering interfered with her joy.

She traded on her experience by reaching out to readers with cancer, advising them, from a consumer standpoint, how to get help. She continued her mission work in the parish as well.

She took a two-week break to go to Rome. Thirty-five years earlier she had been briefly jailed in Rome after she and four schoolmates escaped at night from a dormitory where her parents had stashed her. She wanted to go back to the Spanish square where she had been arrested to have a picture taken with a Roman cop. For her it was a sign of reconciliation.

Shortly thereafter her tumor returned with a vengeance and her eleven-month passion began. As she told me when I went to visit her in the hospital, this was also the opportunity for new discovery. A fiercely independent woman who had left her family at 18 when her mother discovered a collection of condoms in her chest of drawers, she had never asked for help from anyone. When a crisis occurred, as in the disease and death of her mother, she had been the one who took charge of the family. She had also been the responsible one in the communes where she had lived. For the first time she was helpless, and being helpless allowed her to recognize how many people were eager to care for her. "I needed to learn how to be cared for," she confided in me. "Without my disease I would have never discovered the depth of love by which I was surrounded, but even more important I would have never discovered that it is a form of love to allow people to take care of you."

Knowing she would appreciate the works, I took her a replica of Michelangelo's Pieta and a copy of the almost equally famous painting by Cosimo Tura representing the pious women holding Christ's body. The peace of the Virgin Mary in Michelangelo's sculpture and the expression of uncontained grief in Tura's masterpiece reflected the feeling that the people around Betsy were experiencing. She had the privilege of learning in her own flesh that the supreme act of the love of God was to allow humans to care for Him by caring for his son!

Soon her left arm gave up, then her right leg, then the right arm. We would never be able to write the book we had planned: a doctor-patient book. Before her voice would wane forever she summoned enough breath to tell me: "Qu'est que cela fait? Tout est grace!" "No matter what, everything is grace!" as Thérèse de Lisieux had said on her deathbed. I am grateful that, the night before she died, I was able to talk on the phone with her to thank her for having reinvigorated my own faith. I was privileged to serve as a pallbearer at the funeral where the full parochial community turned out to see her to her final rest.

I dwell so much on Betsy's joy because her experience is similar to mine in vital ways. Though my early sexual experiences had been neither as numerous nor as colorful as Betsy's, though I never did indulge in drugs, I had lost my innocence in an act of intellectual contempt of myself. I had disdained my desire for God because I had felt that everything belonging to me was inspired by weakness, was cheap and disposable.

I thought I was seeking God because I was unable to fend for myself.

CHAPTER 11

# I Almost Lost Claudia!

My beloved spouse is my unique friend of more than forty years. Was the better half of me, in fact, lost somewhere on the 3,000-feet west wall of the *Corno Grande* (Great Horn), the tallest peak of the Gran Sasso D'Italia chain of mountains? A network of iced channels and precipices, the wall was intimidating at any time of the day. Close to sunset, at 6 p.m., it towered over my head as a mortal trap, a potential tomb, where a wrong step might have led to a hundred-foot fatal fall, and a body might have remained buried by rocks and ice until the end of time. These questions haunted me after I waited for her hour after hour at the base of the wall, on a mountain path surrounded by stones, snow patches and a few spurts of grass.

In the twilight a wrong step and a fall were only too real a possibility. Any stone rolling down the wall ignited the fear that Claudia would soon follow tumbling in a rough descent. At the very best we could hope that she could find a cave in which to survive a bone-chilling night without food or water. Our last contact by cell phone had been disheartening. Prey to exhaustion, fear and discouragement, her voice had become feebler than usual, and she had begged me to leave her alone. My growing anxiety only worsened her own sense of impotence.

What a way to conclude a day that could not have begun better! The first day of the first vacation we had been able to spend together in more than two years had greeted us with a glorious cloudless dawn. We had been determined to celebrate our time together by climbing a mountain that had overlooked, almost like a trusted friend, the unfolding of our love forty-two years earlier. Excited and happy, we had left our apartment in Rome early in the morning. After two hours of a scenic drive among fields, forests, rivers and rocks that all seemed to welcome our homecoming, we had reached Campo Imperatore, the base of all ascensions to the Corno Grande. No other car was in sight. Instead of finding that fact disconcerting, the solitude awed us. It seemed that on this day the Corno Grande was reserved just for us.

As I am much heavier than in my youth and suffer from arthritis and other ailments, we elected to reach the top via the easier of two paths. But even that venue proved too tough for me. After a few hundred yards I decided to renounce the climb and vicariously enjoy the enthusiasm of my wife, who kept climbing oblivious of her age. She arrived at the top in the early afternoon, then decided to come down via the more rapid but more challenging west wall that we had braved without any problem together when we were carefree twentysomethings. This decision proved foolhardy.

The hours of not knowing whether Claudia would survive were agony. As painful as was the idea of losing the most important part of my past, the future concerned me even more. Besides being the only lover with whom I had felt fulfilled, in our marriage Claudia had been variously a reference, a reproach, a rock and an inspiration. With her skill and charm she had dissolved the protective cocoon I had fashioned to secrete myself.

I owed her any sense of being able to embrace life unrestrained by fears. I owed to her the ability to see in other people an opportunity instead of a threat.

In the last few years she had been the mainstay, the soul of my discoveries. I had borrowed her joy, her curiosity, her sensitivity, her common sense. Only through her could I fully enjoy the visit to a new city, the sight of a new landscape, the interaction with a new friend, the understanding of a new painting or a piece of music. And our grandchildren have been the most important shared discovery of all.

Less than one month earlier Helena, this first granddaughter, had been born. Together we had threaded years of plans for Helena and Luca, our two-year-old grandson. Without Claudia that beautiful carpet would have dissolved in multicolored and meaningless fibers. Only Claudia could keep the tapestry whole. Without Claudia I might not have treasured my grandchildren to the fullest, I feared.

Yes, I am not ashamed to say that Claudia has been my guide! Without her strong and clear-headed advice, I often would not have known what to do in time of critical decisions, despite the fact that we are both medical doctors and that my education is equal to hers. If this sounds like dependency, it is, and it is a freely chosen one.

Claudia possesses a contagious capacity to enjoy new experiences. I am all but devoid of this talent on my own, but I know I can share in her zest for living because she loves me and is happy and proud to share her assets. There is no shame in being dependent on someone we love who is possessed of a particular capacity necessary for survival that we ourselves lack. Aren't we all at some time dependent on the expertise of a physician, a mechanic, a pilot, a cook?

And now, for who knows how long, I could do nothing as my own precious love suffered from an exhaustion she had never exhibited before. Fatigue threatened to paralyze her. She could have succumbed to the frigid weather or even been trapped or dashed by a rock.

After the phone call, listening in panic to her diminishing voice, I stood up from my resting place and tried to run. I wanted to reach her, to help her. But my efforts to move were fruitless. After two hundred feet I had to sit again, prey to chest pain. I soothed it with a few ounces of dirty snow melting in my mouth.

The only thing I could do was to pray. And pray I did!

I vowed to honor my wife more than ever before if she came back to me intact, and I recited a rosary to the Virgin Mary. Thereafter words started accumulating in my mind quicker than my mouth or even my internal speech could pronounce them. It felt like my whole history was melting into a river whose currents were carrying fragments of my past colliding from different directions before they could be identified and defined by words.

After being adrift on this flooding prayer for about half an hour, as the twilight was moving closer and closer to the darkness of night, I thought I saw a shadow walking toward me. A young man (young for me at least; it turned out he was in his early fifties) was readying for a night ascension of the west wall. Hearing my story, he promptly decided to renounce his original plan and start looking for Claudia. Equipped with a hard hat and a headlight, well familiar with the terrain of the Gran Sasso, he found Claudia in less than an hour as she was trying to negotiate an icy channel, and he led her safely to the mountain's base. From there he accompanied us on our two-hour hike back to the car, making sure neither of us suffered any bone fractures or joint dislocations during the steep descent in the dark. He gave us his name. He said he was an engineer from Rome who had moved with his family to L'Aquila, a town at the feet of the Gran Sasso, in order to be close to his beloved mountain. Yet we have been unable to find him in the telephone directory or even in the municipal list of the L'Aquila, to thank him. Who was he really?

Driving back to Rome with Claudia sleeping on the passenger seat at my side, I could not help thinking of a song of my youth. In "Meraviglioso"

("Marvelous"), Domenico Modugno narrates how a passerby prevented his suicide by showing him that life is indeed marvelous. The singer asks himself whether that person was not really an angel (*un angelo vestito da passante*). This has been the latest of many experiences in which I felt (and recognized as I felt!) a direct divine intervention in my temporal life.

What are the chances in early June, when the Gran Sasso is still snow-capped and the hotels of Campo Imperatore still closed for the season, of finding an experienced climber preparing for a night climb at the very time my beloved spouse is risking her life at that spot? From a logical viewpoint, from a mathematical viewpoint, the odds are so slim that belief in outside intervention becomes a distinct possibility!

Was he a response to my prayers? I don't know, I will never know, and I really don't care. As St. Augustine says in *The City of God (De Civitate Dei)* the main function of prayer is to make us aware of God's design for us, to participate in God's consciousness while maintaining our own consciousness. Unlike the state of nirvana described by some practitioners of Buddhism, in which human consciousness dissolves into God's consciousness the same way a small river dissolves its waters in a larger river or in the sea; unlike a karmic view that consists of a liberation from the vicious circle of reincarnation, the Christian relation with God comports a preservation rather than an annihilation of human self-awareness. As suggested by the Bible, as suggested by some mystic saints such as Saint Teresa of Avila, sexual intercourse is the most meaningful metaphor of the relationship of God and the human person. In the ideal sexual intercourse, man and woman receive from each other pleasure and a sense of belonging that can be generated exclusively through their union, and while uniting their bodies and their consciousness they maintain their self-awareness, their cognizance of the unique experience of being together.

Today the metaphor of sexual intercourse may be at least controversial. For many young individuals in the Christian world, sexual intercourse has become a social interaction, a way to get to know each other, hardly more personal than a meal consumed together. No sense of sacredness, of uniqueness is preserved in these casual encounters. The *Unmarried Woman* in a forty-year-old movie of the same title claimed she was seeking experience in matters of sex after her husband ditched her. Yes, some experience sex as if experiencing ethnic food. "No man would buy a car without first testing it," said her fiancé to a reluctant woman who wanted to preserve her virginity prior to marriage. For married couples sex may be mainly a means to engender children; for older singles a desire to break their solitude, to feel that they still belong to the human consortium. In this ever changing perspective it would be difficult to recognize the special unique relationship of each person with God, though I still hope that this special relationship may widely exist and remain the model of the highest expression of sexual intercourse.

Perhaps the closest metaphor of the human-God relationship is the one of a baby with the mother, the wordless communication made of smiles that are more comprehensive and meaningful than any words. From the mother's side it expresses unconditional affection, from the baby's unconditional trust. I have been privileged to witness such a relationship twice, more than thirty years apart.

I remember as if it were yesterday Claudia smiling at our son sitting in the highchair. Last year I experienced the same sense of transport into a world of undefeatable trust as I caught sight of our daughter-in-law and our grandson smiling at each other as they were lying close in bed during a pause in Christmas activities. In both cases the child abandoned himself to the limitless joy of being loved for himself. He abandoned himself to his mother without strings attached, aware of his total dependence—and yet the child remained aware of himself. Mother's love filled him with loving energy the way a fire turns on another fire: The two fires are separate but partake of the same fire (this metaphor is from Miguel de Unamuno in *The Tragic Sense of Life*).

Life of faith is to become that child talking with a smile to that God-mother. Without faith the same events of one's life may unfold, but those events are lived with suspicion, even when they bring joy, because they are the results of a capricious destiny instead of gifts from a loving God. Faith may provide joy even in suffering, while lack of faith prevents joy even in the absence of suffering, unless one considers joy the desperate search for pleasure through all forms of addiction (drug, sex, work, material success, etc.).

Of course nobody can prove that the coincidence on the mountain, and other coincidences in life, are the result of a mysterious plan rather than of chance alone. Faith makes me feel part of a unique plan designed for me alone, makes me feel endowed with a unique task that I and only I can perform. In other words faith makes me feel sacred (from the Latin *sacrum*, "reserved"); that is, reserved for a unique function. The only control I have over this plan is to accept or reject it, and reject it I did for most of my youth.

Prior to meeting Claudia I had felt dispensable and disposable, ready to stoop to any level of human degradation, ready to deny what was true about myself many times if that could gain me some transient intimacy or some degree of human approval. More and more I became my own Judas. With a kiss promising a few minutes of intimacy, a fading orgasm, I consigned myself body and soul to my own enemies, for my own scourging and crucifixion. In Claudia I felt validated. I had obtained a glimpse of my unique function and a belief that my awareness would mature through years of marriage. I started recognizing and fulfilling those aspirations that had always been the essence of my mystery but that I had sacrificed in trying to belong to a world that had rejected me because it recognized my bluff, my lack of substance. In Claudia I started being who I was supposed to be.

CHAPTER 12

# Sex without Love

MORE THAN ONCE I have experienced direct divine intervention in my life. Of two notable episodes, one occurred in 1960; the other ten years later.

I was walking with Don Oreste Benzi toward the small port of my hometown, Rimini. As usual I was hoping that the words of a charismatic priest might soothe the pain of the doubts that prevented my joyful adhesion to God's love. At 16 that pain had led me to the threshold of suicide. The priest was on his way to bless a new fishing boat and I tagged along. After the ceremony he confided: "This morning a desperate woman came to see me. She needed 6,000 liras to admit her husband to the hospital, and the only way to obtain that money was to go to bed with her employer (the head of a family where she performed domestic work). I asked her to wait until tonight. The owner of the boat just compensated my blessing with 6,000 liras!" Don Oreste had no trouble recognizing this as divine intervention and neither did I.

In April 1970 I drove from Rimini back to Rome after attending my cousin's wedding. During eight long driving hours in the Italian mountains in my old Fiat 500, which gasped at any steep ascension, I had the opportunity to deepen into my solitude, made more acutely painful by the contrast with the conviviality and gregariousness that all but exploded in the joyful wedding of my younger relative. At 26 I had had only one relationship of any significance—and this was hardly successful. Memories of exploitation and lies persisted from those two suffocating years. (In addition, of course, to increased shyness as well as suspicion toward women and more crippling self doubt.)

After a number of stormy relationships with other men, my girlfriend wanted only one thing: to get married. Toward this goal she provided to me a limited and expensive access to her genital organs, even though her comments revealed her true underlying feelings. She despised me. On my side, after many years of sexual deprivation I felt so dependent on that sex administered rarely and in small drops that I did not mind paying any price she named and resort to whatever lies necessary just to be able to stick my hand between her thighs or to massage my aching body over her still body. I depleted my bank account converting loans into lavish presents. Daily I made claims of everlasting devotion that she never did believe and that I myself had ceased to believe. At best our relationship had been an abortive attempt at love. Neither of us dared to recognize this painful truth.

I had gained my place in the society to which I craved belonging. Like the perfect bourgeois of turn-of-the-century Italy described by Fellini movies, I had rejected my Christian faith as superstition. So now I was given the opportunity to enjoy the marvels of free love. The castle of lies I created around the relationship made me feel like a peer among my friends, even though this, too, was a lie because I later learned that most of them knew or suspected that she had been cheating on me all along. Hypocrisy made me a legitimate member of that society, provided a valid ID as citizen of an enlightened country. Things came to a breaking point after her last betrayal, which she decided to confess to me, underlining that it had been a "superb sexual experience."

Our farewell was far from peaceful: for six months I had to endure a number of angry encounters and phone calls during which I was called everything from a worm to a varmint. "If there is a woman in this world who will ever be able to love you, and I doubt it, make sure to learn how to please her. Try to graduate from the University of the Passeggiata Archeologica (at that time the area where the Roman prostitutes congregated), though I doubt you will be getting passing grades." With these whipping words she exited the night we broke off our engagement. Of course that I had endured a relationship such as this for two years showed how low my self-esteem had sunk.

I did not blame her then, nor do I blame her now. She had made a business decision: to feign love for me in order to obtain bourgeois legitimacy, or in the language of that place and time acquire a respected name for her future children. Eventually she made the reasonable decision that I was not worthy of the effort. Her affairs were too frequent and too well known for me not to have noticed. She could not possibly have survived in a relationship with me without going to bed with other men. And I really could not say she was wrong to do it! I was incapable of loving anyone and this was my real liability in the bedroom. The more I tried to please her the more I succeeded in distancing her from me. I was desperate to seek the delusion to be loved and to be in love. She had seen through me, and at the end had decided that she could not continue to support this delusion any longer

After the breakup, I was the one drifting without a goal. I had abandoned the faith that I had concluded was a hindrance to the discovery of love. I had become only more alone and more dissatisfied. But despite this emotional failure I did not want to give up a relationship I equated with my newly found freedom. Bernanos described my situation in *Under Satan's Sun* better than any other commentator when he said, describing the genius of the devil: "The peerless sophist disdains to contradict us and delights in *drawing out of his victims their own death sentence.*"

During this long solitary drive loneliness loomed as my final destiny. Maybe my loneliness represented a privileged sign that marked me with the tasks of a Prometheus, a Nietzsche, a Robespierre or a Cromwell and preordained me to suffer in ways only few elected spirits were privileged to recognize and afford. But despite my delusions, this time I could not revel in any supposed nobility of my soul. I did crave intimacy.

As disastrous as my engagement had been, it had nonetheless provided a reference or at least a hint of how fulfilling intimacy might be. I needed to feel desired for myself. I craved meeting some other being on this earth who would consider it a privilege to learn, along with me, how we might speak to each other through lovemaking. The disastrous affair had dropped my self-esteem to a new nadir, had increased my insecurity as well as my suspicion—but nonetheless it had given me a taste of intimacy.

The affair taught me that sex is a special language, a unique way to communicate, in some ways like but not unlike any other human activity. Like a child exposed to adult conversation, I did not understand the meaning of the words, but I learned that words are tools of communication. I had simply been using the wrong words, I came to believe. I needed to learn how to speak. Words embedded in my body needed to find expression or die.

Solitude submerged me like a low-level unceasing flood; yet from time to time a transient sunray seemed to cross the clouded sky. More than a silver lining, it was a soft voice trying to overcome the hammering sound of the rain. (The still small voice famously referred to in the Bible? I was not sufficiently spiritually developed to have made that association.)

In that sunray came an image. The image was strong but poorly defined. There was a face, a sympathetic human face, and on that face was a smile of acceptance. More and more that face came to reflect that of my friend Claudia. This was the clean face of an adolescent with long fair hair and an overwhelming ability to love; that is, to accept. She appeared eager to engage with me in the discovery of a common language, one that was reserved for the two of us, and with sexuality defined not as a mere contact sport, as had marked my experiences so far. Claudia worked in my ward as a medical student. She was the only child of an authoritarian single father, and she had embraced the practice of medicine as a way to establish herself as an independent human being.

That smile that should have been an inspiration presented itself to me as a siren song, a dangerous and distracting temptation. My plans were clear, and I would not brook any interference, I told myself. First; I had to abandon the painful memories of Italy. Second, I had to be free to start a new life in America. All types of emotions and especially a new love would have represented a burden on a journey I intended make free of baggage. I must endure the flood of my solitude while steering clear of any deceptively alluring stretch of dry land, I told myself. Until I became able to build my own boat, I could not afford to leave the water that covered my feet. And if I never arrived to build the boat, so be it; I would just drown. Never before I had been so determined and so clear in my determinations.

All I wanted that night was physical intimacy, and I knew at least three women willing to have sex without strings attached. I can see now how delusional that desire was. It amounted to no more than a sexual monologue, a faint counterfeit of lovemaking, a new lie to add to the mosaic of deceptions and lies that had made up my life so far.

One was an older single friend of the family who had always been happy to oblige when I was in need. The other two were colleagues. Like me they had just broken free of relationships that had left them emotionally drained. Like me they did not care to make any lasting commitments. We had an unspoken agreement to use each other like time-share apartments.

As soon as I arrived at my lodge in Rome I grabbed the phone and made, one after the other, three increasingly urgent calls.

But my sexual partners had already gone or made plans for that evening. I let the phone ring until the operator disconnected the calls—there were no cell phones and no voicemail at that time. The flood of my solitude threatened to drown me that night. I had to do something right away. I needed to act. Against my better judgment I grabbed the telephone one more time and called Claudia. She was at home.

I asked her if she would mind joining me and my parents for a visit to a Benedictine monastery during the coming weekend. She agreed. That phone call was the beginning of my recovery; I am not ashamed to say, of my resurrection.

The next day, one of my sexual friends called me for a date! Too late. Even though at this point we had shared only a phone call, on some level I knew that my half-century of travel with Claudia through the unexplored world of marriage had just begun, and I was not willing to relinquish it for any reason. My emotional intelligence had won. I was on the way to recovery; that is, to learn the language of intimacy; that is, to learn the language of love.

Of course our marriage has experienced peaks and valleys, and, like many strong-willed couples, more than once we have been close to divorce. Like all successful human relationships, we had to rediscover each other every moment of every day, and we were forced to readjust our goals as our journey proceeded. What was different in my relationship with Claudia was that we soon learned to be open to each other.

We each started with an agenda. I was looking for peaceful companionship where sex was a part but not the focus of the communication, though I expected it to be available on demand. For her part Claudia was looking for an opportunity to start her own household, according to her specific dictates, with a person over whom she felt comfortable she could prevail. And yet we soon learned to modify our agendas when they interfered with our common discovery. We learned that you cannot possess another person, that misunderstanding is part of a deeper and more complete understanding, that argument is the source of a more durable and well rooted peace. The basis of a relationship is never to completely comprehend each other but to continuously strive to comprehend. And love finds its highest expression in this ongoing mutuality. We lived what a young priest had once preached during the Holy Family Sunday Solemnity: the foundation of a good marriage is not the absence of dissent, is not the avoidance of skirmishes (as my mother believed). It is the ability to make up (something my parents never learned, at least as long as I lived with them). Making up means to continue working toward being a couple, to develop and perfect one's ability to love.

I still shake in my boots when I think of that eventful night. The life I cherish has developed thanks to the coordination and concomitance of a number of small details with little significance of their own: the marriage of my cousin that made my craving for intimacy more acute, a solitary drive that allowed me to experience the depths of my loneliness and realize that no escape or professional affirmation would have satisfied my desire for companionship, an old used car that delayed my return to Rome, the absence of all three partners and Claudia's presence.

That night I went down a tricky and perilous mountain slope where each step might have meant losing my life in a fall into a precipice or a crevasse. Who led me to the end of the slope? Fortuity, blind destiny or a love that had saved for me a unique function, that was aware of my sacredness long before I became aware of it? Did the prayer of people who cared for me, my aunts, my parents, my grandparents, the priests I had met, entice that love on my behalf?

Forty years later I almost lost Claudia during a night descent from a perilous mountain wall of rocks and ice. She too was saved by a totally unexpected intervention. One more time I felt the work of God in our daily life.

CHAPTER 13

# My Mother's Grief

It might have been a form of poetic justice that at 83 my mother's back was bent by Parkinson's disease as my grandmother's had been by osteoporosis. When urinary incontinence struck a few years later the resemblance of my mother and her old nemesis had become complete. We had come 360 degrees! The hostility of these two women, which many times had been anything but silent, had tarnished my infancy and my early youth, and it may still underlie my insecurity and fear of conflicts. I had loved both of them, as at different times they had been the only reference of my affection. I could not help asking whether it was some form of punishment, or a mysterious act of God's grace, that these two pillars of my life who had resented each other so deeply and for so long became so similar in their appearance with age!

What was my mother thinking at my father's funeral? Half paralyzed by Parkinson's disease, her face in a perpetual grimace, she had followed on foot as the coffin was carried into the church, as straight as her disease allowed her to be.

Was it relief at the end of a fifty-year nightmare or a sad farewell to her intimate companion of half a century? In her last public appearances in town, she showed herself as others knew her: the fearsome teacher who had not been bent by prayers or threats, the incarnation of a strict form of judicial fairness that had gained her the grumbling respect of the hordes of professionals who had been her pupils even if more than once they had grumbled murderously when they saw their end-of-the-year report cards.

She had been the impeccable socialite in front of whom all off-color talk came to an end when she accompanied my father to any civic function. One of her colleagues, a very liberated woman active in the communist party, used to say to her male friends on the few occasions that their crudeness was too much even for her: "Unless you quit right now I am going to tell Fanny Balducci." Believe it or not all the dirty comments and conversations stopped at once under the influence of her threatened enforcement. With her presence at the funeral she had performed her spousal duty to the very end. But what did she feel?

The reason I pose this question is that what the townspeople didn't see was the tone and tenor of my mother's home life. She had been the victim of fifty years of emotional abuse, neglect and derision, at least to my eye. She had been used by my father and his family as a faithful servant that nobody felt the need to thank or even acknowledge for her loyalty and dependability. Worst of all she had been denied virtually any breathing space. She had to go where my father wanted and do what my father asked her to do even if that meant renouncing her own long made plans. I remember her silent disappointment when my father decreed that they would visit the south of France to celebrate the New Year after depositing the children with her father and sisters in the countryside. For my mother the few days she could dedicate to her own family were sacred, and since I could remember we had always spent the end of the year at her father's house. Without a second thought my father overruled her deepest desires for solace, for temporary respite from a family where she felt like a prisoner and a stranger!

One may say that our family life hinged on not making my father angry, which was an impossible task as his anger simply reflected the way he felt that particular day. If he had a bad day at school everything was annoying—from the taste of the food to the color of the wall. If he had a good day he would insist that my mother accompany him to a movie or a visit with neighbors or shopping, whether she wanted to go or not.

A few months before I departed for America, I happened to read a letter to the editor of "La Famiglia Cristiana," a Catholic magazine for families. The letter was from a woman asking the editor what he thought of her situation. She had been married almost thirty years to a man who passed for one of the pillars of the local society and the local church, a highly respected professional considered thoughtful and compassionate. And yet this paragon of a man had shown her only disdain and neglect throughout their married life. Their sexual encounters had been rare and completely impersonal; she used the word "forgettable." They had two children who had learned from their father to disregard their mother: to her they were foreigners. Recently an old flame had contacted her, but despite the dissatisfaction of her marriage she would never have considered betraying her husband. I don't know whether my mother wrote that letter, but she could have. That was my mother's life as I had seen it. She was always ready to perform her duty to the end at whatever price, always resentful because her commitment to the cause (work, family) had been disregarded or belittled.

All in all she had been incapable of letting her feelings rule her behavior. She had been the woman whose love I tried all my life to turn in my direction, and yet I never succeeded in extracting from her a compliment or an expression of praise. In her last few years, to her credit, my mother had done her best to ask for understanding and forgiveness, something I had already conceded a long time before. When her friend Fedra died, she wrote me: "I envy Fedra: she knew to show her love to the people she had loved, something I have never learned to do. Believe me: I had and I have plenty of love in my heart." Talking about an old priest whose mass she attended every Sunday, she admitted to having confessed to him that she had been too severe with her children. With her grandchildren she managed to prove the most affectionate grandmother. I have always admired my mother, especially the hard-won insight she showed in her last years.

And yet I remember my childhood and adolescence as painful. I share details here not to indict my parents but to show how—without the redeeming presence of God—even the best intentions may be marred by misunderstanding and result in unwanted consequences.

At age 10 I had survived a serious disease but nonetheless passed the exam—first in my class—that decided admission to middle school. As I gave her the news, I was filled with joy and pride. Mother reminded me that my scores could have been much higher and that I should have striven to obtain better marks.

At age 12 I got a less than stellar mark in math. That Christmas I was reminded that I did not deserve the presents I was going to receive. To each group of relatives visiting us for the holidays, I was indicated as the child who had fallen short of his mother's expectations, who had spoiled the immaculate school record of our family, which had never before received a negative mark in any matter. (Eventually I learned that this was not true, that both my mother and my aunts had received negative marks in scientific subjects in high school, but the truth was not allowed to intrude upon the myth to which I was forced to conform.) All this was happening while my schoolmates were getting presents, including travel and expensive toys, as rewards for barely passing their classes.

I learned that failure was not an option if I wanted my mother's love. Instead of indulging in my personal inclinations toward literature, poetry or philosophy, I felt charged with obtaining the best marks in every subject by all possible means. And surely enough I used all possible means even if they were demeaning to everybody's eyes including mine.

Throughout my high school years I regularly copied the math homework from a more capable friend. I also devoted myself to futile efforts, such as memorizing pages and pages of Latin and Greek, in order to not forget the proper translation when questioned. My fear of failing prompted me to secure the benevolence of my teachers (both in high school and medical school), though I paid a price in terms of sacrificing my dignity and earning the dislike and disdain of my schoolmates who witnessed my toadying. "Do you realize how much he humiliated you?" asked a good friend, a lay nun who felt sorry for me after the professor of dermatology bestowed on me a high mark I had not deserved. To describe how humiliating that experience had been, one must see the 1959 French-language movie *Les Liaisons Dangereuses*, precursor to the famous 1988 English-language movie *Dangerous Liaisons*. In prerevolutionary France during a garden party, male aristocrats who needed to pee would call a valet to bring them a silver container where they relieved themselves while continuing their conversation. At the end they threw a coin in their own pee as a tip for the valet. But I was deaf to the concerns of the few people who did still care for me. I was focused on only one aim: never to disappoint mother's expectations.

I also started nurturing dreams of grandeur, imagining myself obtaining a double Nobel Prize or being elected to the highest national office. (This, though my low popularity precluded my election even to the student council!) In this mirage of outstanding achievements I was finally able to savor the love that I was craving and that appeared out of reach in my real life. Like a form of artificial rain, these dreams prevented the irreversible drought of my emotional life.

One of the many consequences of my subservient behavior is that I could never appreciate my own successes. Did I graduate second in my class in medical school because I was the best of the best or because I prostituted myself and brownnosed my teachers, as my colleagues implied? Seemingly, the need to answer this question prompted at least in part my emigration to the United States. I wanted to prove myself in a new situation, unimpeded by my emotional baggage. Of course that baggage remained with me across the ocean, and I still don't know the answer to some of these questions.

One may wonder why I was so willing to be robbed of dignity, why I did not stand up for myself, why I endured these years of shame. Without trying to justify my weak character, I believe my history provides insight. I did not rebel because I perceived my mother as a victim of spousal abuse, and somehow I felt I had to protect her, and my only way to protect her was to live up to her expectations.

A banal occurrence may demonstrate. It occurred at the end of one of our usually contentious dinners, during which all conversations were suppressed by the voice of the radio, as my father valued the daily news more than any family conversation—this to my mother's enduring chagrin. For dessert my father grabbed an orange and, after finding it rotten, dropped it onto my mother's plate. "It is rotten!"

With fire in her eyes, mother halved the orange and dropped half of it on my plate and the other half on my sister's: "Give the rotten food to your children rather than to your wife!" she shouted.

As horrible as it may seem, my father's behavior sprang from lack of manners rather than from a disdain for my mother. The only child to study at a university from a very poor family, he had always been considered a prodigy, worthy of being put on a pedestal. In the large and informal family where he grew up, and where it was common for family members to share plates, his action reflected no more than the complaint of a spoiled brat to his understanding mother. The interpretation of my mother's reaction is much more complex and disturbing. Her fury toward my father was understandable. He had never made an effort to outgrow his upbringing, to give his spouse the respect a partner who was also a successful professional deserved. When they were still dating they went for a vacation in the mountains. It was 1941 in fascist Italy and at that time it was inconceivable for an unmarried couple to spend a vacation together. My mother took this initiative despite the wrath of her own mother. To quench any possible murmurings she had booked her hotel two miles from her fiance's. The last day of the vacation after a long hike my father claimed to be too tired to accompany her home. The following day he admitted, without a hint of shame, to have spent the night playing cards with friends!

Her behavior toward us, however, had deeper and fearsome, albeit poorly expressed, implications. It certainly signified a jealousy over the fact that we as children seemed to draw more respect than she did from her husband and her mother-in-law, who lived with us. It also meant that her children were not as much her children as his children, as she had lost all control of our upbringing, and ultimately implied that it was OK with her if her children were treated as garbage disposals.

We were not what she had envisioned. This resentment toward us colored one way or another most of my infancy and adolescence. How many times did I hear her saying "you" with that "you" including, in addition to my father and grandmother, also me and my sister, as if our family were polarized into two parties: her own minority party and a majority party including everybody else, one that had no consideration or respect for her. How many times did my mother hint with her friends in front of me that

I was destined to grow up like my father, a self-centered schoolteacher, enchanted with his own words and oblivious of the practical world outside himself? How many times did her frequent reproaches to me contain an indirect reference to my father or my grandmother?

One time, at age 16, I visited a friend of hers in Liguria, and she stunned me with the abrupt declaration: "I don't think your mother likes you too much."

I had deceived myself that the month of vacation in the mountains we spent every summer as a family and without the intrusion of my grandmother was a happy time when everybody was at peace as we shared the daily hikes and the saying of the rosary in the evening. Only later did I realize that she had lived that experience that I had treasured as another burdensome duty of a family from which she felt estranged. As soon as I opted out of the family vacation, she started going on vacation on her own in trips around the world (England, Scotland, Russia, etc.). Clearly her deepest wish was to stay away from, rather than with, the family.

Mother was born at the beginning of the past century in a very strict family in a small country town in northern Italy. Her father was the local doctor of veterinary medicine, and her mother was an elementary school teacher. Her grandmother used to tell her children that no matter what grades they received at school they were not good enough: Only when graded "maxima cum laude" had they accomplished their duty and nothing more. Mother and her two twin sisters were raised in the belief that life was a God's gift to be approached with gratitude, awe, humility and most of all discretion. Earth's resources were to be used sparingly and with the exclusive goal to sustain life. Any extra comfort, any extra pleasure was to be considered a luxury and ultimately a vice.

Though my grandfather was affectionate and could have not been more generous toward us, he was also very strict. I still remember that in the summer of 1960 my sister, then 13 year old, had invited a friend to watch the Rome Olympics on television. When he found out, my grandfather asked her: "Do you have the money to pay for the electricy to run the television?"

"Of course not," answered my sister, astounded.

"Nor do I, so turn the television off!" he commanded.

"I want to raise her according to my methods," he confided in me later. I am not sure today whether he was looking for my support, as I had become my mother's and her family's informal champion by that time, or whether he was trying to apologize for an action that he himself came to recognize as excessively strict.

In her old age my mother once reminisced that as children they were instructed never to eat a piece of candy offered to them on the rare occasions when they made some social visit. Rather, they should hold it in their hands and play with it as if they were uninterested in it, to make sure that their host did not offer candy again a second time. Going through some old pictures we found one of the elementary school class of my aunts, where my mother was present as well, though she was a year younger and belonged to a different class. "In that way your grandmother could see all of her children in a single picture and would have not have had to pay twice for it. Wasn't she provident?" asked my mother. I don't know whether she spoke with bitter sarcasm or sincere devotion. I know that to be able to participate in some extracurricular activities at the university, my mother found the money by skipping evening meals, using the school library instead of buying her textbooks, and delaying the purchase of needed clothes or a new pair of shoes.

I heard from other sources that there had been dramas as well in this well oiled family, as when my grandmother discovered one of her daughters writing a message to a boy late at night. I was not provided the details, but I understood that this indiscretion was punished with the utmost severity, and only after begging forgiveness and promising never to take this type of initiative again was the rebellious daughter readmitted to the family consortium. The disciplinary Old Testament God, rather than the Christian God of the prodigal son, appeared to rule the Christian life of this family. Love was to be earned; unconditional love was all but unheard of.

Though she had always referred to her parents as exemplary saintly persons, I do know that as a young woman she put distance between herself and her family and claimed her independence both of action and judgment. Proud of the autonomy she gained through her own effort, I believe my mother resented the fact that our generation and in particular my sister and me seemed to be offered on a silver platter the same opportunities she was forced to fight hard for. For example, she was outraged when the Italian high schools started offering international study-abroad travels (to Greece, to Israel) to their pupils. "What have these spoiled brats done to deserve these privileges?" she would ask with resentment and bitterness.

After graduating in humanities at 23, she went on to teach middle school as far as possible from home. When a position in the middle school of her hometown became available, she avoided it. She took and passed a test to teach high school, and this is how she moved to Rimini and met my father. Prior to that she had studied German and French on her own and had taken trips to both France and Germany. I heard that in Germany she had been charmed by the Lutheran celebrations and considered the possibility of converting to Lutheranism, which she saw as a form of religion more accessible to modern people than Catholicism. She probably would have been disowned by her family if she had taken such initiative.

How my mother and my father got married remains a puzzle. I remember that as a boy, I must have been 9 or 10, I was repeating at home what I had learned from an older friend. He had claimed that young women were looking for beauty and charm, but when the time came to get married they were looking for status and money. "Than why do you think that mother married me?" asked my father. "Because she felt that she could not do any better," was my heartfelt answer. My father laughed as if it were cute. Thinking of it sixty years later I am disheartened. I had included in my despising of myself despisement of the whole family. My parents did not realize, or pretended they did not, that even as a young child I knew their marriage was unhappy.

There must have been a time when my parents liked each other. My first memory is joyful: I was sitting at the dinner table in my high chair. Though I could not understand what they were saying, they looked happy as they smiled at each other, and I used to add my laughter to their conversations. Perhaps the problems started when my father's mother came to live with us, but my recollection of a change is connected with the death of my mother's mother. My mother confessed that she flunked more students than usual that year because she was angry with the doctors who had taken care of my grandmother and whom she judged incompetent, besides being indifferent to the anguish of the family. She transferred the anger she had accumulated toward the doctors to her students. "These boys better straighten up!" she thought. "If I pass them now they will never learn how to be responsible. They will graduate and go on to become incompetent and arrogant, just like those doctors."

One October as we were threading our way through mountain roads back to Rimini, after my grandmother's interment, she declared to my father in front of my sister and me: "From now on things are going to change. I will take charge of our children's rearing, and no longer will you or your mother interfere with my methods or my goals!" With that declaration of war my Prague spring ended and my nightmare began.

Having had no successful combat training in her own family, my mother was doomed from the start. In all discussions my father triumphed because she could not counteract his verbal and emotional violence. Very soon I started perceiving my father as a bully, and this perception did not abandon me, to my chagrin, until I saw him dead. In his last few years he had become a kind of larva spending most of his time in bed, smoking in front of television and reading his old diary. I always denied him, to my lasting regret, the sympathy he was looking for because he never quit being in my eyes the capricious master whose shouts ruled our family life, evoking only fear and guilt.

"Damn this shitty family that compels us to stay together," he would shout every time the family radio was on a channel he didn't like or he could not find a fork close to his plate. More than once he told my mother's father, a respected old man who had gained the whole village's admiration as an elder, to shut up because his talk disturbed the television watching. One might say that he made a particular effort to be disagreeable when we visited my mother's family to assert that he was still the master. "I cannot eat this shit. Why can't we buy some decent grapes?" he snapped once, knowing very well that the grapes from the family garden were one of the major sources of pride for the family. Not to mention that this garden had been a source of survival for him during the war, when the food in the marketplace became scarce. "You don't seem to care at all for your husband and your children," he would shout at my mother any time she would leave home to visit her ailing father. These verbal fights had become so common and frequent that I was scared to ring the doorbell coming back from school. "What might have happened" or "What will happen today?" was my silent daily fearful question.

This impression of bullying was all but confirmed by my father's statements. Once I hinted that I desired to manage my own family in quite a different way than he did. He said: "For the love I have for you, I hope you realize soon enough that in life you only have two choices, to prevail or to be prevailed upon!"

My whole life I had suffered from insomnia, so as a teen-ager I had the opportunity to overhear the pillow talk of my parents. It was not pretty! The leitmotiv was the imploration of my mother to my father to have regard for her feelings and the response of my father that the only way to assert her feelings was to engage in their ongoing battle and beat him. Eventually the witnessing became so painful that when I overheard a conversation I wrapped my head in a pillow and tried to think about something else or to cry so loud that I could not hear.

I remember a repeated nightmare or dream of those times. I had discovered that my father had a lover that he used to receive at home in his office, and anybody trying to enter the office while he was entertaining this woman was rejected with shouts, the only type of communication my father was able to muster. I remember that I killed this woman whose face I never could identify, and I was condemned to life in prison for murder.

I believe that nobody who had met him, except perhaps my mother, would recognize my father in the picture I draw of him here. Most people knew him as a warm and congenial man ready to help his neighbor even at the cost of serious personal inconvenience, and he had remarkable successes as an advocate for the poor and destitute. Once he singlehandedly succeeded in obtaining the release of an Italian laborer who had been imprisoned in Germany for homicide. More than once he helped me out of difficult legal or professional situations. And he certainly tried to reach out to me. When in a good mood he could be very affectionate. He insisted that I go to medical school in Rome, away from the family, even if that choice was expensive and barely affordable for a family like mine. Shortly before I left for America he wrote me a letter asking to talk. He wanted to know why we could not talk to each other. I answered his letter in a very impersonal and hurtful way, stating that I had found my own way of life and did not feel any particular need to communicate with him.

I probably better understood my father's attitude toward the family after watching the Godfather movies, especially parts two and three. My father was convinced that he could never lose his family, as Mrs. Corelone told Mike when he started nurturing some doubts about his relationship with Kay. After all, my father had witnessed his own father bullying his mother, not only with words but even with physical violence. And in spite of it he never felt that there was any lack of love in his own family. In one of the more moving Godfather scenes, Mike asks Kay what he was supposed to do. He had been determined to grow up different from his father, but he loved his father, and his father's life had been in danger. So Mike had followed in the footsteps.

Likewise, in my home, it never occurred to my father that he could lose his family. When he did realize that he had driven us off, it was too late to mend fences and build bridges. (This is not an indictment of my father but rather a report of my own emotional experience. I couldn't bring myself to be part of any fence-mending.)

My mother's tenure with her mother-in-law had been a long one. She came to live with us when I was 3 and my sister was a newborn. A rowdy woman who had been expelled from elementary school at age 7 for having thrown ink on a teacher who had slapped her, she was vocal in defending her offspring in all family disputes. In addition she did not hold back negative comments about my mother's family. For example, she voiced a number of misgivings about the apartment where we lived, though that had been a generous gift from my maternal grandfather, a gift that allowed us to own a residence for the first time. Though my parents supported her, including my mother's income, she never uttered a word of thanks. She felt that the gift of her son to my mother entitled her to be considered a queen. I remember one night coming home from a movie and finding my mother baking cookies. "Why are you doing it in the silence of the night, like a monk?" I joked. "Because I don't care to be harassed by your grandmother!" she retorted. "I have to hide myself in my own house to be able to send some cookies to my father!"

Of course she paid my grandmother back in devious ways. For example, she refused to buy a television that would have been entertainment for my homebound grandmother, who on some evenings would try to entertain herself by watching our neighbors' television sets from our balcony.

I was very attached to my grandmother. Before I went to school she was my trusted companion. We used to leave our dwelling each afternoon with some table scraps to feed a wild cat we had adopted. My grandmother had called him Moschin. That means "little fly" because of a spot on his nose. From there we would reach the railroad and watch the trains go by for hours. I did bask in her affections, and she was satisfied in contemplating my happiness. That bond of love was never broken—not even when I started resenting her presence and blaming her for my mother's unhappiness.

Anybody reading this account who has known my family will be stunned and probably scandalized. Both my parents were well established professionals who touched many lives and elicited the gratitude of generations of students. Each of them contributed to society with passion and personal commitment. After his retirement my father became a powerful advocate for prisoners and the homeless, my mother a supporter of children with incurable diseases and of retired nuns.

Toward me they could not have been more generous. Not only did they support me through medical school, but they also allowed me to waste a lot of money in a number of entertainments, including the support of my girlfriend, without ever asking for an account. But maybe the greatest gift of all I received from both of them has been the insight into my situation, the ability to write these very pages. In a way my comments are meant to be praise rather than accusation. My parents allowed me to look at them critically, to use my intelligence, to reject any form of myth. I would like it if my son could one day say this of me.

Yet, despite their generosity and good intention, despite the respect and the admiration I have now for both of them, they left me with very few sweet memories. I am very thankful for my mother's heroic effort to survive so many years of an abusive marriage. I have no problems in accepting that a broken family would have been much more destructive for my sister and me than a dysfunctional marriage. Their union provided support to our growth in many ways, including the expensive education we received, the emotional security in times of serious crises, and maybe most of all the capacity to survive in difficult conditions and to utilize a critical mind. These are no small achievements and perhaps more than many children might have expected from their upbringing.

But in revisiting the emotional desert of those years, I cannot help asking some questions. I wonder about the personal insecurity that emerged from it and that caused the almost universal rejection by my peers. Underneath the jolliness I feigned in vain, they easily perceived my own rejection of myself. I am trying to gain a scope of my l early life, not to pronounce any indictments.

Why could not mother vanquish her preconceived ideas about child rearing and show us the affection we craved even if we were different from what she had planned? Her marriage might have represented a unique opportunity to show her children how love may overcome the limitations of one's vision and make us partners with creation, utilizing the material we hold in our hands, not the material we would like to have. Her reserves of anger, accumulated at a high interest rate over twenty years, trickled on us, creating a chronic disabling infection that estranged us from our family and made us afraid of personal relationships the way arthritis makes people scared to run or chronic TB brings on shortness of breath with exercise. We did not perceive her sacrifice in swallowing our father's abuse in silence as inspired by love but as inspired by a burdensome sense of duty. Witnessing my mother's suffering made me a staunch supporter of divorce in my earlier years. I remember saying more than once, "Blessed Henry the Eighth who sent the pope to fuck off when he tried to impede his divorce!" (Of course I ignored that the British king also had a habit of beheading his divorced wives.)

In the same way I cannot help asking why my father could not perceive the distress his outbursts created in our family. Why could he not muster some act of kindness toward mother or express his emotional support in her diatribes with his own mother? Why did he seem to put his immediate comfort ahead of participating in family events? The very night we moved to our new dwelling, a generous present from my mother's father, he elected to join his friends at the civic club for a game of bridge, instead of staying home and expressing his gratitude and his allegiance with a family celebration. This attitude is even more astonishing when you consider that this man was prompt in responding to a request for help from his pupils, even at great personal discomfort. He had lived his profession as a high school teacher as a mission, and he had been true to it up to the time of his retirement. Clearly he saw his family as a haven, an energy generator, a gas tank rather than as a mission requiring his daily commitment! The affection of his wife and his children were taken for granted, and he never became aware, until too late, that they were dissipating under his own eyes. As intelligent and as cultured and as caring as my parents were, they could have become role models for how to build a new life together. They could have represented what a living marriage is supposed to be, a reflection of the creation. If this ever happened, it happened too late to have any effect on me.

Of course better communication techniques, including the use of the "I messages" taught in modern marriage counseling instead of the accusatory ones, might have helped. But marriage counseling was all but unheard of then. Better psychological insight might also have facilitated a dialogue. But in post-fascist Italy, psychoanalysis was unknown and psychology was taught based on nineteen-century animal observations. (Examples: cats cover their excrement so as not to inform other cats of their movements, while dogs leave them uncovered to be tracked by their packs.) Psychology was rooted in the myth that animals are instinctive and only humans are intelligent creatures, able to suppress their instinct with the power of reason. Even Pavlov's classical experiments on learned reactions were known only in sophisticated circles. But all these stratagems would at best have led to more civil behavior; they might even have led to what is called "a friendly divorce," if there is such a thing. I don't believe they would have fostered more understanding. My parents acted like two shipwrecked individuals quarreling to no end on how to preserve their area of comfort in the island where they landed, instead of putting their efforts together to build a new ship and reach the mainland. They were too concerned about losing their relative daily safety to abandon themselves to the safety of love that does not betray, that does not wane, no matter what the circumstances were. Basically it was a scarcity of faith.

Both my parents professed the Catholic faith (my father had even spent five years in the seminary). Like the majority of their peers in the Italian middle class rebounding from the ruins of war and the fall of fascism, they saw religion as a set of rules that are good for the functioning of society and that should be accepted with a number of exemptions. Birth control and tax cheating, for example, were widely accepted and even encouraged. Religion might also have been used as a form of temporary comfort on the occasion of stressful events such as a death or disaster.

They never learned, as I later did, that the faith in the Christian God is empowerment to love. That is, to overcome one's limitedness in the commitment to love one's spouse, one's children, or, in the case of a pastor, one's flock. Had they been able to see this face of God, they would have been able to face their shortcomings instead of protecting their cocoon of prejudices and false certainties. Lacking awareness of God's love, they spent their married life defending themselves from mutual accusations instead of taking each other's criticisms as an opportunity to grow together with the assistance of God. God had committed Himself and Herself to help them to build a new life together, to explore an unknown land together, with the guidance of faith. But they never learned this sacramental aspect of their union. They saw only a threat instead of an opportunity in each other. Awareness of a mission that transcends each individual player, of a destiny beyond ourselves, of a unique role as unique pebbles in God's own mosaic, is the foundation of unconditional love, the common aspiration of all humanity. Because of deficiency of faith, my parents could never overcome their "fear of flying." They never allowed themselves to love each other and their children to their full potential.

This deficiency of faith was also founded on the mother of all lies. The culture they absorbed in their schools and in their relationships held that humankind should be able on its own to build a life consistent with each one's values. While in words this culture honors love, it has lost the sense of sacrifice that is the seal of love. It sees love as mutual attraction that under the best circumstances survives for a lifetime, under most circumstances may be disposed of like old clothes. Since humankind is unable to practice unconditional love, this culture has decided that unconditional love does not exist and that the human aspiration for unconditional love is a dangerous delusion. To try to satisfy this aspiration with faith in God is an act of ignorance to be discouraged.

I cannot help finding it ironic that the same culture that pretends to use science as the only gauge of truth loves fairy tales in which the protagonists live happily ever after.

CHAPTER 14

# 'Empty Bed Syndrome' and Other Lessons from Medical School

IN THAT HUMAN DESERT that was the University of Mississippi Medical Center, Claudia and I passed ninety percent of our time succoring dying individuals, all the while anticipating the criticism of our supervisors and our colleagues hinting that it was time for us to sail back home on a banana boat. In reality people could not have been more supportive, but their support did not relieve our fear of the unknown and the different. A humorous episode that happened at the end of our internships will illustrate the way we felt.

Claudia was managing a patient with congestive heart failure, and she called for the help of the senior resident, who said, "You should catheterize the coronary sinus." He meant that a complex intervention, which could be executed only in a specialty lab and by a properly trained professional, would be required to determine the depth of the patient's heart disease. Claudia did not pick up on his sense of irony. She believed that he was, in fact, telling her to catheterize the coronary sinus. She called me at home asking me how to do it. We both spent the evening embarrassed, worried that somebody would find out that we could not perform a procedure that probably any third-year American medical student was able to do!

In the wake of my birthday Claudia had arranged a special meal. At 5 p.m., the time I normally should have left work, I informed her that I would not be able to come home for dinner. One of my patients had had a stroke, and I wanted to wait for the result of the angiogram the neurologist had scheduled for 8 p.m. My presence at the hospital was not necessary at all, but I wanted to provide proof that I cared for my patients more than I did for a candlelight dinner with my wife. When Claudia came to pick me up at the hospital we did not exchange a word; we did not even kiss each other goodnight. When I woke up in the night looking for a sandwich, I found in the garbage my favorite pasta: a collection of tortellini that Claudia had handmade the previous night as I was sleeping. I could not help thinking that those tortellini seemed a metaphor for our marriage: prepared with hard work, supported by a joyful commitment and yet ready to rot.

The working demands that challenged our marriage were all but an expression of a life philosophy opposed to that we had embraced when we married. Our vision in getting married was to revel in each other's affection. Our love for each other was supposed to be the sun around which our work and other activities would rotate. We learned during medical training that personal time was a luxury. We were poised to pay any price including the dissolution of our union to succeed in our profession. And success was defined as the ability to endure long working hours, to withstand any form of emotional abuse and to be as intrusive as possible in a patient's body—not, as popular images of doctoring would have it, as the ability to relieve the suffering of which we were surrounded. This feeling was crystallized by the words of a former chief resident who stated during a student-evaluation session: "I could not care less if the students hate the patient, as long as they learn how to do their job."

A few years later, a college student named Libby Zion famously died in New York under the care of sleep-deprived residents and interns. Shortly thereafter a resident interviewed after a twenty-four hour ER shift horrified the nation by stating on national television, "If you think that I give a damn about the patients after having been on call for twenty-four hours, you are really full of shit!" He could not have learned his lessons better!

During the surgical rotation students were divided into teams and each team was responsible for performing surgical interventions on stray dogs. The contest was won by the team that succeeded in performing the highest number of interventions prior to their victim's succumbing to death. That team was also the least sensitive to the mute pleading of the tortured animal, whose vocal cords had been severed so that he could not complain or plea for compassion. That was the anticipation of the type of medicine one was encouraged to practice.

Perhaps the signature program of this philosophy of life was a pervasive sexuality that you could breath everywhere against your will, just as one cannot escape from the smell of dead fish in a seaside resort on a windless day.

"What does it feel like to be screwed by an Italian man?" a colleague of mine, a mother of two, would ask during the sleepless nights in the ICU over a coffee break. She was embroiled in an affair with a resident, also a father of two. A few days earlier both were called for a Code 99 (a patient suffering from cardiac arrest), and his face was streaked with lipstick. Her skin showed signs of being abundantly sucked, and she clearly had no bra under her scrub suit. Our conversation took place as we both watched a young mother who had lost her highest brain functions after a car accident wane in the night, her lungs requiring more and more pressure to be filled with air.

"I only date married men. They are much more fun," said another woman. She was a resident from New Orleans whose father owned a race-horse breeding farm. With her deep brown eyes and her long dark hair, she resembled a mix of the scheming Scarlett O'Hara in *Gone with the Wind* and the mischievous Miriam in *Hush . . . Hush, Sweet Charlotte*. She made these confidences to me and a nurse while suturing the face of a comatose man who had been shot by his wife, who had caught him in bed with another woman.

"Do you like my new perfume?" asked a young ER nurse, clinging to me. She managed, as many women did in that ER, to rub her crotch against mine while standing as if we were dancing cheek to cheek. All this happened while medics were carrying in two gunshot victims. I learned later that this woman, popular among the residents because of her double vagina, had bet with a colleague that she could sleep with me within a month. "We fucked our brains out," announced an ER nurse arriving at a party where the head nurse had challenged me to show that I was the best lover in the world. "Your wife will never know of it," promised an African-American housekeeper, begging me to make love to her and not easily dissuaded.

Most of the medical staff's trysts took place in the penthouse where the residents had their sleeping quarters. One day I went there during daytime hours to catch up on sleep after a night's work. I crossed a well known lady in her forties, the wife of a prominent lawyer who had just been laid by a resident half her age. Other favorite places for clandestine encounters were the laboratories to which secretaries and technicians held the keys. I will never forget the day that the chairman of the Department of Medicine, with an entourage of fellows and faculty, led a visiting professor to see the newly developed pulmonary lab. There, they startled a resident, a father of two, down on the floor with a technician, also married. Believe it or not, the same chairman who a few days earlier had fired a resident for taking a beer to work felt that the incident was funny! My colleague was rewarded for his indiscretion by a division director who called him a few days later to say, "Listen, I am at the Holiday Inn with three women. I know I can handle two but I am not sure about three. Would you mind coming to help me out?" Camaraderie was born over recreational sex more strongly than over the solution of a clinical problem.

Perhaps the most representative symbol of that time was a well known resident bragging about extracting forty orgasms from his girlfriend in a single night. At the end of his residency we knew of at least three women in his life. One was his wife. The second was his impregnated girlfriend, and the third was the mother of his child.

I probably have indulged too much in the description of these episodes, which in fact are just a few of what I witnessed and represent small fish in a pond rich with big fish thriving on dirt. The psychiatrist and author of the 1978 book *The House of God* did a much better job than I in reporting the sexual indiscretions of an overworked and confused house staff in a major Boston hospital (Beth Israel, indeed the "house of God"). My aim is to highlight that these experiences were as monotonous as the melody of a broken record and expressed most of all a desire for self-destruction. The goal of the actors in this tedious play was to despoil the sexual act and with it obliterate in themselves all sacredness, all uniqueness. The sexual ritual was an initiation ceremony destined to make well-oiled cogwheels in the hospital factory out of each and every hospital worker.

We were divorced from the reality of the lives of our patients. I still remember the case of an illiterate African-American farmer with renal failure resulting from uncontrolled high blood pressure. When we approached him with the offer of a kidney transplant he had a big laugh. It took a few moments for me to realize that he thought we were joking. He found it all but unbelievable that anybody could harvest a fresh kidney from a corpse and engraft it into a living human being. He felt very witty in not falling for the fairy tales a group of young doctors had concocted to have some fun at the expense of an ignorant black man. He saw in us the heirs of those planters who used to sip mint julep on their front porch in the Mississippi Delta and for their own amusement whip the legs of his ancestors, ordering with a big laugh: "Sing, you happy nigger."

In fact, the desensitization process had begun even before I left Italian soil.

As a medical student and a young physician I trained in the Agostino Gemelli General Hospital in Rome, arguably the largest and most modern hospital in Italy, at least at the time. One of the most disconcerting experiences was to receive patients from the Southern part of the country, who reached us after a perilous trip from some lost village without paved roads and running water. As the hospital was affiliated with the Catholic University, the local pastor, who presided over the annual fundraising for our institution, might have convinced them that cure was at hand if only they could reach our Mecca. Many of them gave up all their resources, including their poor dwellings, to underwrite a pilgrimage of hope and faith. The national health care system enabled them to receive free care but did not pay for the trip nor for the lodging of their families. Access to the most modern medical care turned out to be access to the worst of nightmares!

One case speaks for all innumerable cases that I witnessed, to my present chagrin, with insensitive indifference or even amusement. A young man from Calabria, Southern Italy, was taken to Rome by his parents looking for an impossible cure for acute leukemia. During my morning rounds I repeated the promise that a new and miraculous medicine might arrive the following day. "Hurrah, Doctor!" he used to exclaim at the end of the visit, with his mouth and his tongue more swollen every day and his eyes more opaque from internal bleeding.

His parents and three small brothers camped in the waiting room. The parents were sleeping on the floor, wrapped by a cover of unrefined wool that shepherds used for sleeping together with the flock in the mountain outdoors. For the softer backs of the children they had bought three inflatable rubber mattresses. Most of the time the night nurse supervisor, a nun, allowed them to stay, as long as they agreed to retreat to the darkest side of the room to avoid being conspicuous. Occasionally a particularly strict nun forced them to leave in the name of preserving the hygiene of the ward. Rules and regulations were an excuse, I believe, to inflict punishment on people they disliked. Those women from Northern Italy in immaculate uniforms, with skin paled by unceasing smog and long sunless winters, felt suspicious of and threatened by a lifestyle so different from their own. I would not have been surprised if they expected to find urine and feces on the floor together with the chicken bones, orange peels and the remains of a campfire at the end of the night.

The father, a short ruddy man, had a face burned by the sun from innumerable outdoor scorching summers and pierced by the needles of a dark beard, which gave it the appearance of a porcupine's butt. The eyes, reddened by sleeplessness and tears, gave the impression of two furnaces ready to torch the hospital. I am sure the nuns read as anger and destructive impulses the fear of the big city and his angst over being unable to vocalize his pain. The mother had long oily hair and mostly missing teeth. An overexpanded belly covered the tops of her thighs and compelled her to walk with the oscillating gait of a duck. An unbiased medical observer would have recognized the combination of multiple pregnancies with a diet poor in proteins and vitamins. In that body, consumed by the effort to give and protect life, the nuns preferred to read feminine subjection and lack of self discipline, instead of heeding their own vocation and recognizing the wounds of the suffering Christ calling for healing.

Nuns are people, too, and they, too, enjoy power! Because they could not relate to it, they considered that family a disease in itself, to be eradicated like the leukemia of the son. One night while on call, I witnessed the eviction of this caravan fading in the dark. They didn't look back as they dragged their few belongings along the floor, like oxen dragging a plowshare. The bent backs had been broken by centuries of oppression and could not straighten.

"Sister Giovanna must have been on call last night," I joked with a colleague the morning that I found the waiting room empty. Sister Giovanna was known as the strictest and the meanest among the nuns. All student nurses were terrified by her face, which seemed incapable of a smile, and by her voice, which might have been programmed by a computer. She might have been a precursor of Sister Aloysius, the suspicious nun impersonated by Meryl Streep in *Doubt*. In the movie the nun causes the downfall of Father Flynn on the unfounded suspicion of child abuse. Minutes later I realized that the son's bed was empty as well. Instead of my emotions and better self being stirred, I came up with another lame joke. We referred to patients who had died during the night as having succumbed to "the empty bed syndrome," a parody of the "empty sella syndrome," a disease of the skull.

CHAPTER 15

# Tempted by Icy Waters, Saved by a Priest

FOR A NUMBER OF reasons, the most important being intellectual contempt, I kept my distance from the church during my young adulthood. I was the child of two renowned teachers of humanities; I had little to learn, in my view, from ministers drawn from the farthest Italian countryside and who had entered the ministry as an escape from poverty and starvation. The Italian middle class, though it still attended mass on Sundays and so-called days of the obligation, was harboring toward the Catholic Church the same type of suspicion and contempt that the early American colonists expressed toward the Irish, Italian and Polish communities: unenlightened people who had sworn their allegiance to a Roman tyrant instead of a duly elected representative government.

Despite my ambivalence toward the Catholic Church, my eventual leaps of faith rest on the testimony of two Catholic priests who at different times of my life proved to know—much more clearly than I or my parents or siblings and friends did—what was good for me.

At age 16 my desperation had brought me to the doorstep of suicide. After deserting my religious practices, which I considered founded on specious self-serving reasoning, I had completely lost any sense of my belonging to the human consortium. During the summer of 1960 I spent long nights terrified by the emptiness of my life, unable to feel anything for anybody, asking myself repeatedly what reason I had to keep on living. Any window, any riverbank, any staircase prompted the same leitmotiv of the same broken record: should I throw myself down?

I avoided friends (or acquaintances; I am not sure I had any real friends then), because their talk, their interests, their activities were foreign to my inner turmoil. In their company I would have felt like a patient invited to a banquet while receiving intravenous doses of a drug that causes violent nausea. My parents were all but oblivious. They had too much drama in their strained relations to be aware of mine. Mostly they were in total denial—or at least so I thought by then—of the fact that one of their children might be affected by mental or emotional illness.

As different as they were, as disagreeable as they had managed to be to each other at times, as disparate and antagonistic were their life goals, they both succeeded in suffocating any recrimination, any spurt of rebellion, even any question that might have distracted them from their ongoing cold war with each other. And both of them used guilt as the most practical way to prevent any type of confrontation with me. If I dared to express my discontent I was reminded that my life had been much easier and enriched than theirs, from the expensive toys I enjoyed as a child to the yearly summer vacations, to my rich mess where food was never missing, to the entertainment I could enjoy. My discontent, my desperation were just the expressions of an ungrateful brat who had been too pampered for his own good.

If I tried to explain my intellectual doubt about God's existence and the veracity of the Catholic message, I was dismissed as a lazy intellectual who had too much free time. "Look at your grandfather," my mother would insist while organizing her desk and cleaning her office. "At age 86 he still does not have a free moment. When he does not work as a veterinarian, he takes care of the vegetable garden, he repairs the house. Faith is his support. He does not have time to waste in doubts."

My father was equally unhelpful. "Why must you revisit the reason for which you believe?" he would echo between puffs of his favorite cigarette while scanning the daily newspaper. "When you have doubts the only solution is to abandon yourself to God." Of course the message I received from both of them was that they had no idea what I was talking about and they definitely did not care. A more benign explanation, the one I would choose today, is that they were scared of the very issues I tried to discuss and hoped to disperse their fear by ignoring the problem. Feeling inadequate for parents of their generation was tantamount to acknowledge role failure. Successful parenthood was founded on the lie that parents should always be in charge, and to that end they could not afford to be wrong, even to have doubts or questions. In other words, being a parent required a divorce from your own humanity.

Even though my parents didn't seem to notice, I did feel guilt on several fronts. I felt guilty for being unhappy, for having abandoned my religious practices, for being (I thought) ostracized by my peers, for the fact that girls were not flattered by my courtship, for being unable to get in touch with my feelings, for thinking of killing myself. Perhaps more than any other emotion it was this guilt that made my life unbearable, and maybe it was the same guilt that paralyzed my will and kept me from taking definitive action. While some of my peers were cavorting on the seashore or indulging in sexual petting under cover of the tides, and others were enjoying camping in the great outdoors, I passed my summer days in long walks, thin and unkempt, like a ghost of myself, trying to drown my solitude and my desperation in physical exhaustion.

I survived that terrible summer only thanks to Don Oreste, a Catholic priest who at that time was dedicated to youth ministry. My hometown was a small provincial town trying to recover from the wounds and the loss of World War II. Twenty thousand deaths, a hundred thousand wounded, disabled and homeless—all were perceived as ghosts of the past. The establishment, the professionals, were only too eager to go back to their way of life without even questioning if the destruction and the displacement of the war mandated a second look at that lifestyle. The old civic club was rebuilt much sooner than the schools and the cathedral. That way the elders of the city could start back up with their card games, their gossip and their lies.

Count Ricasoli had come back from the countryside with his mistress, in whose name he had registered all of his possessions. The only novelty: She was sporting a new assortment of wigs from Florence after the count's wife had scalped her during a catfight. The hospital's director's wife resumed her serial love affairs after the self-imposed moratorium of the war, during which she had worked selflessly to assist the wounded. Her husband was still threatening to strangle her from time to time. Back from Russia where he had been imprisoned three years, Mr. Bonardi had resumed his practice of law and in the meantime was rekindling the passions of wealthy housewives as was his prior practice. He was also planning yearly vacations without the family in esoteric places "not to lose my training again," he claimed. Father Belfanti, too old now for womanizing, as he had done as a young priest and preceptor moving about freely in aristocratic families, graced the civic club with his culture, jokes and poems that had been gathered in a book titled *Bocciouli* (*Tree Gems*). These and many other stories were repeated day after day, games after game, smoke after smoke, drink after drink, to reassure the town elderly that nothing had changed, despite fifty million deaths worldwide, the explosion of the first atomic bomb, the attempted extermination of the Jewish people, the continuing crisis of colonial power and the division of the world in two major blocs. Likewise, in our high schools the teaching occurred according the same educational principles of the fascist period. Nobody questioned that students should be stuffed with notions the way a Thanksgiving turkey is stuffed with dressing, that critical learning is optional and to be used with extreme caution, that a student's good will and hard work are the only ways of learning.

Defying the skepticism and derision of the establishment of my hometown, Don Oreste had introduced new advances in psychology into his ministry, and for that he underwent unanimous criticism. I still remember the scandal that resonated through the smoky walls of our civic club when he recommended a young man who had finished high school consult a psychologist to help discover which profession best matched his inclinations. A crowd that did not hesitate to smoke 5,000 liras worth of American cigarettes to be exhausted in a couple of leisurely afternoons found it scandalous that a young man might pay 5,000 liras to find out what to do with the rest of his life! How could a priest born on a farm, raised in the rigid culture of the local seminary since his infancy, pretend to teach highly educated professionals who were fluent in Latin, ancient Greek and the humanities how to raise their children? He probably did not even understand what he had read in those books of psychology! There should be a law to keep priests chained to the altar and the confessional and prevent them from mingling with world affairs! So went the town talk.

Don Oreste received me in his office, carved in a niche of the palace that hosted the local seminary, just on the side of our majestic cathedral. The office had two small rooms where Don Oreste and Don Luigi received their visitors. Wooden banks lined the waiting area.. The office room contained a wooden table, two wooden chairs and a crucifix on the wall: no bookcases, no linen, no painting. An old woman's bike was parked outside the building. That bike was Don Oreste's only property (the car he drove belonged to the diocese) and was so old and unappealing that it had never been stolen, despite the fact that it was left unattended night after night.

When I first had an opportunity to unravel what I understood of my desperation, he looked me directly in the eye, and from that look I learned that he had understood much more than I knew of myself. I never had been looked at in that way before. Occasionally my grandmothers had looked at me with pride. Of my mother, her father and her sisters, I remembered only that they used to look at me shaking their heads in disapproval for the way I had been raised. I remember my father looking at me with a sense of disappointment and reproach, my friends looking at me with pity, and some of the girls with disgust.

Maybe Don Oreste's was the look by which Jesus convinced Nathaniel to follow him and quit his "siesta" under the sycamore. My parents seldom looked me in the eye when talking to me. Usually when I tried talking to them, they were busy doing something else and acted as if more important issues demanded their attention. The only time I remembered them looking me in the eye was when they meant to make a point, and that point was accompanied by a negative comment meant to stir up guilt.

Don Oreste's look was a look of unconditional love, of agape, something I fully understood only decades later. But despite my inexperience and lack of knowledge of agape, I felt in that look a hint at a different world, an invitation to healing and blessing. Healing: There is not a word in Italian (or for that matter in any Latin language) for healing or "making whole." In all Latin languages, healing is equivalent to curing, restoring health after a specific disease. These languages seem to ignore that one may be made whole even when affected by an incurable disease, even on the threshold of death. Or that people need healing even when they carry no disease. I learned about healing in Don Oreste's look decades before I even learned the term!

His first words underlined the message I had gleaned from his eyes: "Remember, you have no responsibility for the way you feel: You are hurt and you need to soothe your pain. Like a disease that confines a man to his bed, your pain keeps you from entering life. I feel privileged by the fact you entrust your care to me, and I will do my best to deserve your trust. You are not more responsible for your emotional pain than you would be from the pain of an ulcer or a heart attack. Though you may not be able to understand it now, Jesus feels your pain; if you would only allow him, he would be happy to carry your pain for you. That is the reason he took on flesh and came down from heaven to meet you. He knew that neither you nor any other human being can get rid of this pain on his own, and only he could soothe your pain by taking it on himself." Don Oreste repeated that same message two months later before I left for my summer vacation. This message, which he backed with action, summarized the content of our relationship.

It took me fifty years to completely grasp the sense of his words, but even at the beginning, they gave me a glimpse of a world where I could make a difference, where my survival would bring benefit to somebody, sometime. This possibility put at least a temporary halt to my obsession with suicide. Some of his words were particularly striking, as when he said it was his "privilege" to take care of me and that he hoped to be worthy of this calling. This was the opposite of what I had heard from my parents, grandparents, teachers and other priests. They had all agreed that I was privileged in being cared for by them, and I had to prove myself worthy of their care. Any behaviors or expressions I exhibited as a result of my mental and emotional discomfort were rebuked and classified as a form of ingratitude.

Don Oreste's view was radically different. I was not to feel guilty about my pain: my pain was a disease of the soul just like diseases of the body. I needed healing, not punishment. I needed a physician, not a taskmaster. In the meantime, I could not simply outgrow the pain, just as a heart-attack victim often needs a physician's help. I learned from Don Oreste that I need not add to the pain of the disease the self-inflicted pain of feeling guilt.

But the most striking and innovative, albeit then poorly understood, concept was the description of Jesus. Though I did not know how to unload my pain onto his shoulders, I learned that he was here to help me, not to judge me. Learning this gave a new sense to the words of John, "For God so loved the world, that he gave his only begotten Son, that whosoever believeth on him should not perish, but have eternal life." Jesus was a physician rather than a judge who came to condemn; I could trust him, rather than fearing him. I could look at him for protection and support, rather than seeking haven from his judgment and his punishment. For the first time I learned that confession of sin (today called "reconciliation") was aimed to receive a declaration of love, rather than an absolution, from God.

And from his message emerged the figure of Christ as a "wounded healer" that became critical both to my personal life and my professional practice. From the wounded healer I learned to show the bottle of my antidepressant medications that I carry in my pockets to patients reluctant to accept help for their cancer-disrupted emotions: "Look, without these I would not even be able to come to work!" From the wounded healer I learned to share with my smoking patients that I myself used to smoke. They don't need to feel guilty about it; I am well aware how hard their struggle is to quit. They don't have to fear my judgment if they don't succeed. From the wounded healer I learned to communicate to the spouses of my patients who feel unable to support any longer the care of a dying partner how Claudia and I had marital problems, how our lifestyle had to be adapted to each other's needs that might have interfered with our individual plans and desires and yet enduring these difficulties allowed us a more complete discovery of our own assets. From the wounded healer I learned to share my chagrin at missing the deaths of my parents, who lived across the Atlantic Ocean, with my patients' children living afar and experiencing guilt because their own families and their businesses keep them apart from their dying parents. From the wounded healer I learned to hug my patients after delivering bad news, which signals that I share their pain and know how disconcerting this information must be. Mostly from the wounded healer I learned that the loneliness Claudia and I experienced when we seemed unable to understand each other was a divine experience, was nothing less than the worldly incomprehension Christ experienced in the olive garden.

This view was critical twenty-five years later to the restoration of my faith and the preservation of my marriage. Just when I felt that I had failed once more, that my marriage was likely to dissolve and I would be unable to be loved by anyone, the vision of Jesus the physician took a very realistic form. My prayers in those desperate moments established a lasting relationship with Jesus as the centerpiece of my human mystery.

Even before the blessing of the boat and the appearance of 6,000 liras that allowed a poor woman to admit her husband to the hospital without prostituting herself at the lustful insistence of a "good Christian family man," I had faith in Don Oreste and his healing power. Suffice it to say that I took seriously his invitation to call him anytime and that I became a pest. Sometimes I visited him many times a day to unload my fears and my anger. The only thing I did not do was wake him up in the middle of the night, and this only because my use of the family phone would have made my parents aware of my problem and compelled me to face their unwanted comments and advice.

Don Oreste never once shut me out or dismissed me. Unlike everybody else he recognized that my internal pressure owed to the fact that I could not love because I had not felt loved—and that I couldn't overcome this predicament until I could feel loved for myself, loved unconditionally. He could not provide me with parental love, but he could and did provide me with an attentive ear; he gave me the assurance that what I was enduring deserved the highest attention and concern.

Once he failed to keep an evening appointment, and I was very angry at him. I was too anxious to sleep. For an hour I walked up and down our little city port, as the lights of the nearby restaurant were cutting off, considering throwing myself in the icy water. I actually came close to doing the deed that night, and if I am honest I will admit less of a desire to quell my anxiety and more of an aim to punish Don Oreste.

When I finally arrived home I learned that Don Oreste had called from the hospital's Emergency Room. I ran there. He had had a car accident trying to keep our appointment. He was rushing from a function in a distant village that had lasted longer than predicted due to the number of people who wanted to talk to him. He took a curve so quickly that the car went down a precipice, hit a tree and crashed. It was a miracle that it did not go up in flames. As he arrived at the ER, before letting the nurse and the physician take care of him, he called my home to make sure I knew he had not forgotten me.

It was the first time I had visited the ER of my hometown hospital, which was hosted in a 17th century monastery taken from the church after the unification of Italy. Most of our public buildings at that time(hospitals, schools, government offices, municipalities, barracks) were hosted in churches and monasteries. The lay Italian government, corrupted and incompetent, had found it convenient to feast on the munificence and wisdom of the Catholic Church while pretending to free the country from the tyranny of the clergy and to educate the populace away from religious superstition. This is another egregious example of public lies the people of Europe have been fed over the past two hundred years. In revolutionary France, in the name of religious freedom, Catholics who preserved their obedience to the pope were beheaded, and that unique masterpiece of Middle Ages architecture that is the Church of Notre Dame in Paris was transformed to become powder storage. I can't help believing that it is an example of God's love for his people if Notre Dame were to be preserved to the awe of future generations!

The ER was located in the previous refectory of the monks, a large room with a central desk where the nurses and doctors were sitting with patient beds nearby. As soon as I entered, the smell of disinfectant and blood churned my stomach, and as I turned to hide my grimace I noticed a basin full of blood close to the bed of a patient who had just died; the discharge was from his lung.

"Get out of here," shouted an old nurse, overweight, with a raspy voice and quite a few hairs on her chin and her cheeks. "Can't you see we are busy? You are in the way!" She ran toward the door with a gurney to receive a patient having a heart attack and almost slid on a spot of blood that had not yet been washed out of the floor. Somewhere close by a baby screamed as a doctor was trying to draw blood from its scalp; the mother expressed all her impatience and fury at the doctor: "You are killing my child!" I had almost decided to leave when I identified a smiling man waving his hands. From the torn and muddy cassock on the chair I understood it was Don Oreste. As I saw him on the gurney, all my disgust and fear waned. I started crying for joy that he had remembered me, not out of sympathy for him. He embraced me and asked the ER physician to keep me there while he was being medicated and sutured. That night I learned that Christ may die in many ways, including in a car accident, to express his love for people! I also had a glimpse of what it meant for Christ to carry our pain. The concern about my pain motivated Don Oreste to speed, causing the car accident. Now my pain was in his wounds, in the stitches that the doctor was putting in his skin without anesthesia, in his flesh mortified by the weight of the car.

As we walked home together I forgot all of my anxiety. His accident, and the sacrifice he made in the aftermath, had made me whole.

Of all the wise men and women who surrounded me, of all relatives professing their love and care for me in an extended and overbearing Italian family, only Don Oreste had understood what I needed. Only he had been able to face my pain. With his indefatigable attention and support he helped me to live with it. He wasn't necessarily smarter or more cultivated than anybody else, and he certainly hadn't discovered in me sources of charm that nobody else had recognized. He knew what I needed and was able to fulfill my needs because his faith had provided him with a unique vision, a unique capacity of love, in the form of agape. His faith also enabled him to face the enemy in me that was responsible for my pain. Everybody else, including my parents, had been skirting my pain, had been fearful of it, because they did not have the faith to deal with it, nor the faith to face their own shortcomings that was in part responsible of my pain. They feigned an interest in my health, but all they wished for was to be reassured. As it is common among polite societies in the United States, when they asked how I was doing, the last thing they wanted to learn was the truth!

How close I had come to throwing myself into the icy waters the night of his car accident! Don Oreste's faith had saved my life.

I decided that I could keep living if his faith became mine. Only through this logic could I make sense of my life. This is what I mean by "act of faith."

## CHAPTER 16

# Father Serra

BEFORE I MET CLAUDIA I was involved in a long-term relationship, barely aware that my girlfriend and I were mutually abusive. Deluding myself with the fact that I finally had what most people would call a "normal" relationship, that I had joined the rest of happily attached society, I decided it was time to re-establish my relationship with the Lord. I made an appointment with Father Angelo Serra, a Jesuit who was our professor of genetics in medical school.

Father Serra was waiting for me on the threshold of his office, the way the father went to meet the prodigal son. The image of Father Serra waiting for me came first to my mind when I had the opportunity to admire Rembrandt's masterpiece "The retour of the Prodigal Son" at the Hermitage in ST Petersburg. He did not want me to have to go through his two assistants, as his professional visitors had to do. He knew I asked for the priest and he wanted me to meet the priest, not the professor. His office was spacious, with a large walnut desk and a small round table with three comfortable chairs.

At the center of the desk a mahogany crucifix expressed the primacy of faith over science. At the farther extremity of the desk one could find a binocular microscope (a novelty for those times and for Italy). The walls were entirely lined with bookcases, and a large wool carpet occupied most of the floor. The office was connected to an antechamber where a receptionist and a typist were sitting. In addition, four armchairs surrounded a small desk loaded with the most recent issues of the journals Science, Nature,

Experientia and Medical Genetics. The walls were decorated with reproductions of chromosomes, cells in division, the DNA structure and Gregory Mendel.

When I arrived at his office and sat down in front of him around the circular table, I had very little time to make an account of the environment. I recognized the look that Don Oreste had fixed on me, the look of Jesus calling his disciples, the look expressing his everlasting love for Peter despite his betrayal, the look that Judas avoided in the olive garden. In no time he realized that I was seeking a validation of my relationship rather than a theoretical certitude of the existence of God. The more I pretended that my relationship with my girlfriend was inspired by love, the more I pretended at having a satisfactory sexual life, the quicker my net of lies got unraveled, like a roll of wool in the hands of a playful kitten. At the end of the conversation I realized that I was haunted by fears: fear of losing the scanty intimacy on which I was pretending to rest, fear of facing my inadequacies, fear of my own lack of self-esteem, fear of acknowledging my inability to find and give love. All I wanted was a seal of approval to affirm my normality, just as the main character in the Fellini movie *The White Sheik (Lo Sceicco Bianco)* was concerned more with maintaining the family's papal audience than in gaining the affection of his newlywed wife who was off dallying with a soap-opera heartthrob during their very honeymoon. Despite the fact that Father Serra was extremely preoccupied with cutting-edge molecular research, he asked to meet my girlfriend and, more than forty years later, he is still a trusted counselor for both of us, though the romance ended long ago.

Thanks to his masterful intervention, inspired by a faith that had given him a knowledge of people that no psychologist could achieve, I did realize that I had never learned the language of love because I did not know how to love myself. I could have learned to love in the relationship with my girlfriend if we had broken the cycle of abuse that kept us bound together in a sunless cave. My urgency to have sex with her was inspired by a desire of possession even more than a physical demand (which, in fact, I could have satisfied as well on my own). Rather, my access to the female body was proof in my eyes that I was normal, a man like any other man who had been able to conquer and command the love of a woman, as a real man should be able to do. She had recognized my dependence on her body and had taken part in this humiliating pact because I gave her money for her immediate needs and implied the promise of an honorable marriage. If the pact was unfulfilling for her, it was more so for me, because the source of my sexual urge was that old unfulfilled need to feel loved. As she was doing her best to deprive me of this feeling, all I was left to do was exhaust myself in peaks and solitary orgasms over a body that I penetrated without the owner's full-fledged consent.

After months and months of vain trials to develop and express respect for each other and to communicate with our souls, Father Serra empowered my girlfriend to confess her last indiscretion and to allow both of us to face the reality that we resented each other. Despite his frequent travel to international conventions, his obligation to mentor three trainees, write papers, lecture, participate in the governance of the university and prepare grant applications, he was available to both of us on demand to help us through the difficult breaking-up process. He even invested time in home visits with my girlfriend, soothing her anger and encouraging her to get on with life and allow me to do the same. No matter how busy he was with cutting-edge research, with a worldwide education effort aimed to substantiate biological research with Christian priniciples and with mentoring young people, he made us feel that we were his first priority. He knew that Jesus had conquered souls one at the time. Books, publications and conferences were not a substitute for a personal interaction for a person who had elected first of all to be a minister of God. We learned later that he was the supervisor of worldwide Jesuit biologic research as well.

As I became involved with Claudia, Father Serra played an even more important role in directing my life. Despite that Claudia never gave me any reason to doubt her affection and commitment, I had many unconfessed misgivings about marriage. Partly, the trauma of my previous relationship had left me suspicious of every woman. Partly I did not feel sure about myself because I did not know how to love myself. Partly I was concerned about her difficult family situation.

Her mother, with whom Claudia had had only scanty interactions, lived in Germany and expressed no inclination to participate in our wedding. Her authoritarian father had ruled her life with an iron fist and appeared positioned to rule our marriage as well. As usual, my insecurity prevented me from defining much less voicing my worries. I expressed my uneasiness by throwing a monkey wrench at any step of the process. For example, when we went to see Claudia's pastor to receive the authorization to get married, I stated that I was not a practicing Catholic and I had no intention of becoming one, a declaration that precluded marriage in the church. A civil marriage would have been difficult for Claudia's father and my parents to accept. That was when Father Serra intervened and, by explaining our situation to the diocesan vicar, succeeded in obtaining approval for a church wedding. Likewise he used his influence to allow us to bypass the six-month waiting period that was normally required in Italy between the announcement of intention to marry and the actual wedding. One may say he was in a rush to see us married, which is absolutely true, because he had realized (twenty years before I did) that marriage to Claudia was the most promising way for me to return to my faith. He loved both of us much more than we were able to love ourselves. Through this form of agape he was able to see in us what God had planned for us.

When Claudia's father became seriously ill during our first year of residency in the United States, Father Serra himself took over the old man's care, which included daily home visits. This prevented Claudia from being forced to interrupt her training and putting an additional pressure on our marriage, already strained by the exacting residency schedule. Other pressures threatened our contentment as well. We had felt the initial isolation of being in a new country whose idioms we were just learning to master. Still tethered to the medical-education establishment and not yet completely independent as doctors, we also felt a sense of professional inadequacy. But by far our most profound difference came in our conflict over how to manage our family. After a miscarriage Claudia wanted more than anything else to have a child, while I wished to delay. A baby, I thought, would interfere with our training. Claudia's foiled hopes for a child were a major cause of hostility between us. For fear of an unwanted pregnancy I avoided not only sexual intercourse but also every form of intimacy that could have led to sexual intercourse. Claudia felt deserted and I felt forsaken.

Even though I refrained from sexual escapades, our marriage was nevertheless strained when Father Serra stopped by to see us after a convention in San Francisco. His visit was designed to help support what might have been a relationship on its last legs. We spent two nights talking, and the main result of that talk was to feel permeated again with the spirit that had originally inspired our marriage. These talks brought us back to our roots. We acknowledged once more that we were made for each other, albeit I must confess I lacked the enthusiasm that led me to declare myself to Claudia coming back from the abbey we had visited with my parents in the Apennine Mountains.

Father Serra did not have any more occasions to visit the United States, but he remained available by mail and by telephone, and in every conversation we were able to breathe, at least for a time, the pure oxygen of our love even when it had felt irremediably polluted. Claudia and I had lived with festering conflicts for years, and at that point he had been the Good Samaritan at every turn.

During his visit I'm sorry to say we did not even give him the satisfaction of participating in a common celebration of prayer. When he proposed to celebrate a mass just for us in our house, we used our work schedule as an excuse. When he asked where he could find a church to celebrate the mass of his faith, we had to confess that we had no idea where a Catholic Church could be found in Jackson, Mississippi. And yet the image of that small-sized priest who made a long journey just to talk to us about ourselves, who went looking for a church in a foreign city always with a smile on his lips, would never be cancelled from our hearts. That manifestation of agape was unearthed like a treasure map concealed in an old chest when the time came to face God's love for us. That image more than any theoretical consideration remained my blueprint to the house of the father.

When I think of Jesus walking on earth I always think of Father Serra and his paternal smile walking through the unknown roads of Jackson looking for a church, not holding onto any bitterness for our emotional and personal desertion. How many times I had seen him like that: when he ran in the rain to reach a medical student who had problems with his thesis, when he received me and my girlfriend before an important Hungarian meeting he had to chair the morning after, when he drove his car (an old beaten-up 500 Fiat) off the road going to visit a sick student nurse in the hospital prior to returning to his community late at night. And he was one of the more prominent geneticists of our time. I cannot help thinking of Paul's words: Even if he had assumed the form of God, Jesus never claimed equality to God. Father Serra's modesty, his insights contained in his fulsome love, represent for me another living experience of Jesus among us.

Later I came to appreciate my marriage to Claudia as the centerpiece of my recovery, for providing the venue that taught me how to love myself and how to express love. Many years before we made this discovery, Father Serra knew it, and he did whatever was in his power even at great personal discomfort and inconvenience to bring our relationship to fruition and make it last. As in the case of Don Oreste, he knew what was good for us much before we had learned it, and he felt committed to supporting us in a way in which none of our relatives, including our parents, would have ever been available or able to do. The source of his vision and his commitment? His faith. His faith had made me whole. Once again I felt the need to make his faith my faith.

CHAPTER 17

# Redemption

ALMOST TWENTY YEARS AGO I learned that a couple of my closest friends had dissolved their marriage after twenty-four years together and four children. The news was particularly distressing and surprising because the wife had been the one who asked to be out of the marriage. When I first met her, in medical school, this young woman had very seriously considered dedicating herself to religious life. At the wedding ceremony, where I participated as witness for the groom, we heard much talk of how their marriage would become a model, a counterpoint to the troubled story of marriage in our society. How this exemplary couple could separate and eventually divorce is beyond me. I have never had an occasion to speak to the wife. Though I do not condone divorce I hope against all hope that her move was inspired by faith, by a greater love of her husband and her children. A situation like this where a marriage was dissolved in the name of a greater good was portrayed in an old Elizabeth Taylor movie, *The Sandpiper*.

The discovery of one's sacredness is linked to redemption, because our ultimate call is to redeem the debts contracted by our parents and our predecessors. This was the next discovery I made after re-embracing faith in Christ. The awareness of how my parents' shortcomings influenced my own behavior gave me a new appreciation of the deep veracity of the biblical legend of original sin. Appropriately, in *The City of God (De Civitate Dei)* St. Augustine refers to it as "original" not as "initial" sin, implying that disobedience to God is not just a beginner's mistake but also a characteristic embedded in human nature, something we could not eliminate without quitting being human. Before then, when I wanted to believe that each of us could be arbiter of his or her own destiny, I had a hard time understanding how God could impute the guilt of fathers on their children. Now everything became clear. It was not God's doing; we were doing it to ourselves! We are programmed to mortgage our children's future. On this aspect politicians of all parties are right, though they do speak a truth they don't understand, as did Caiaphas, the Roman-appointed Jewish high priest who is said to have organized the plot to kill Jesus, when he claimed that it would have been better if only one man died for the salvation of Israel. God's intervention consisted in giving us a second chance. After paying our own debt, He and She gave us a chance to become a partner in the work of redemption.

Practically the only choice we have is to accept or to refuse this partnership, to work toward making this world more livable or instead seeking refuge in the ridiculous question: Who owns the problem? And ignoring the suffering around us as long as we can obtain some personal delusion of peace of mind. More than fifty years ago, a friend of mine, a teen-ager, committed suicide because he could not gain the affections of a Greek girl he had been courting for a year. When interviewed by the local newspaper about her feelings, the girl answered: "I am sorry for him, but it is his problem, not mine." It is this attitude, I believe, that kills marriage, that almost killed mine — when a person refuses to take ownership of a common problem or more important refuses to acknowledge that every problem is common. I don't mean to imply that the girl was responsible for my friend's suicide, of course; but I found her answer disheartening. Did she not feel the burden of having been the involuntary cause of a lost life? Had she learned anything from this experience besides protecting her own feelings?

The concept of redemption hinges on the figure of the redeemer. In ancient Israel, this was the man who redeemed the unpaid debts of a family member and in that way prevented the enslavement of the debtor and his family. There are at least four ways in which we can redeem the debts left unpaid by our predecessors, and all four are inspired by Christ's sacrifice.

The first is by refusing to propagate the evil we have inherited. An example of this propagation came in how I penalized my father-in-law, as well as the soldiers and the patients trusted to my care, with the pain that had been inflicted on me by my mother. To try to unload our pain on another is a common reaction, probably as original as the sin described in the Bible. I have known plenty of women and men, including myself, who bestow on new partners the pain that has been caused by previous partners.

So the first form of redemption is to state, "The buck stops here. I will become a dam that stops the flowing of this river of pain." This is what Christ did as he accepted his crucifixion as a "lamb led to the slaughter" and refused to allow his friends to take up arms in his defense. This is what the Italian Carabiniere Salvo D'Acquisto did in 1943. The young man sacrificed his own life so that two dozen others could go free. He assumed responsibility for a bombing that killed at least one German soldier so that the Germans would halt their planned execution of innocent farmers rounded up from the countryside as reprisal.

As I will further explain, this form of redemption is available to whomever has been wronged. By sparing the life of the murderer, the relatives of murder victims have the power to redeem the murderer, and themselves, instead of becoming accomplices to a chain of killing that causes even more pain and spawns more crimes! Unfortunately forfeiting retribution is not a popular message in a society that has enshrined retribution to a ridiculous degree. One may be sympathetic to the murder victim's relatives who ask for the execution of the murderer; to the child victims of sexual abuse seeking punishment of the perpetrator; to people injured in traffic, labor or medical accidents. But I must confess I have a hard time mustering any sympathy for smokers who claim to have been misled by cigarette companies.

And I also disagree with the claims of the woman who received millions of dollars from Merck, the pharmaceutical company, in compensation for her husband's death, ascribed without any clear proof to the Cox-2 inhibitor drug Vioxx. She claimed she filed the lawsuit to prevent anybody else from going through what she did, as if death were a preventable occurrence. I confess I would have respected her more if she had been bluntly honest and said: "I saw in my husband's death a unique opportunity to take a powerful and cash-loaded drug company to the cleaners." The lawsuit caused withdrawal from the market a medication that had helped relieve arthritis pain in individuals with gastritis and kidney problems. The lawsuit might also have stopped the development of an agent that showed promise in preventing cancer of the large bowel. Lawsuits like these can do widespread damage—not to mention that every sanctimonious claim for retribution is a step away from redemption.

The second form of redemption consists in providing a lightning rod for hatred and to ameliorate in that way the hatred that poisons the world and fuels the propagation of evil.

The culminating scene of *The Diary of a Country Priest* both in Georges Bernanos' novel and in the movie version by Robert Bresson is the priest's confrontation with the countess. Despite her devotion to all Catholic practices, including weekly mass and yearly confession and communion, the countess had nursed a progressive hatred for God, whom she blamed for the loss of her infant boy. Prompted by the priest to reveal her feelings, she states: "If there were any place in this or in any other world where my child and I could be taken away even for a single moment from the control of God, I would not hesitate to enter that place." To which the priest responds: "If our God were the almighty one painted by the renaissance artists or in the Byzantine mosaics, our own misery would be sufficient to draw him down to earth from his sky of glory. But our God willingly took our own flesh, to be derided, smited, spat upon, tortured and at the end crucified. He died so that our hatred could die with him. Let your hatred be crucified with him. Give to him the gift of your hatred."

These words have been particularly meaningful for me, as I had been a prisoner of my own hatred, like Bernanos' countess. When I left for America I hated everything Italian, including myself, my family, my wife's family, the Catholic Church, my medical schools, Italian politicians, the relaxed Italian lifestyle. Yet my transfer did not do anything to quash my hatred, which paralyzed me because it did not allow me to see what I really could do with myself. I was intent on the vain effort to suppress my hatred. Like characters in Greek tragedies, I did not know how to get out of my prison. The country priest of Bernanos' imagination provided the answer: I could elect not to act on my hatred if I allowed it to be dead with Christ. Likewise, irrespective of whether we deserve the hatred directed at us, we all can act as lightning rods for hatred by declining to react to the hatred. We can let it die in the death that it wished on us or, even better, engraft our suffering in the suffering and death of Christ, as he himself invited us to do in the Gospels, not least in the Beatitudes when he declares blessed those who suffer in his name.

Though I might not have deserved being called "hateful" or a "monster"—two of the epithets that girls bestowed on me in my teen and young adult years—I nevertheless behaved in ways that cemented my unpopularity. Today the behavior might be termed "inappropriate"; it included unwanted touching, off color comments and disregard for other people's feelings of privacy. I can see all of that now. It was widely felt that my school marks were inflated because I was the son of two respected school teachers; plus I did successfully brownnose my teachers. Did I mention that on top of all this I had an unkempt appearance? I think now that it must have been at least mildly revolting. Once a girl in my class asked me not to sit close to her at school lunchtime because she could not tolerate my presence.

Whether these complains were justified, I wished to believe that the hatred poured over me helped to free those people from hatreds that otherwise might have been directed toward other targets such as their own families or close friends. The common disdain toward me might even have helped keep together my schoolmates' cliques, which without a common target might otherwise have split. Like the capacity of love, the capacity of hatred is also limited. Once it was exhausted on me, not enough would have been left to affect other relationships. I thought that nothing bad would happen in my little world as long as I did not react to this shower of hatred but kept silent as "a lamb led to the slaughter," according to the description of the suffering servant by Isaiah.

The world is filled with suffering servants, with lightning rods of hatred. The most visible perhaps are death row inmates whose executions may temporarily quell the hatred of a populace that still misses public lynching. The poor are definitely the most common lightning rods. Ronald Reagan was savvy in use of terms that suggested justice but inspired enmity. When he talked about "the truly needy" he implied that a lot of welfare recipients were lowlifes and freeloaders who deserved only contempt and rejection. He opened a hunting season on the poor that is yet to close.

Once, when I was working at a VA hospital, the chaplain succeeded in letting a patient with lung cancer have a glass of Scotch to celebrate Christmas. One of my medical students was indignant: "Can you believe this, Doctor?" he asked me. "Not only are taxpayers forced to pay for the care of his self-inflicted disease, but they also have to buy him a Christmas present!" Likewise, in southern Europe one can witness the daily martyrdom of immigrants from impoverished countries such as Albania or the African or Latin American continents. In addition to being the objects of actual violence, they experience a martyrdom that consists of living in conditions of perpetual fear, far away from their spouses and their children in makeshift accommodations.

The third path to redemption is to transform the suffering bestowed upon us in currency to redeem the debts left unpaid by others. The way I was brought up certainly aggravated my depression, fueled by thoughts that I had failed if I did not prove to be the best in all fields, thinking that my parents' love depended on my school marks. Emotional ambiguity reinforced the depression as well in my odd belief that I needed to hate persons that I was inclined to love, such as my grandmother. And the almost universal rejection I felt from my peers as I grew up confirmed the depression as well. And my depression became my most valuable instrument to minister to dying patients! Depression removes from me any fear of death and makes me eager, rather than scared, to minister to the dying!

My unusual capacity for survival paid off as well during my early years as a medical doctor and even continues to do so today. Though I am not particularly proud to have survived my school years by sometimes plagiarizing homework and by toadying up to teachers, it is a fact that I survived. In professional terms, I am credited as the father (or at this point the grandfather) of geriatric oncology, a subject of study I developed that promises to become critical with the aging of the population and the increased prevalence of cancer in the elderly. My books on geriatric oncology have been translated into several languages and are considered the basis of future investigations in the field. I developed this subject thanks to my ability to survive in seemingly desperate situations.

In the 1980s I found myself in all-but-impossible working conditions at a VA hospital in Florida. Internal political fights risked provoking powers that would accelerate the downfall of any mid-level physician like me. Coping with constant psychological pressures in a rat-race type environment precluded focusing on scholarly activities. I knew I had to get out as soon as possible. But how? I had let my school-days clinical research efforts lapse, so I knew I would be considered too old and too unknown to even consider applying for competitive research grants. My forte had always been teaching, but at the VA hospital there were no students or residents to teach. Furthermore the Internet era was upon us, and I was well aware that my teaching skills were dated.

That is when my survival skills took over: I had to publish something quickly, so I turned to a field still largely untouched by cancer researchers. In 1989 I published my first article on geriatric oncology based on a review of the literature; the same year I presented my results at a national meeting on the treatment of older individuals at the VA hospital where I worked. All I sought was to gain employment in an academically oriented VA hospital where I could use my teaching skills and satisfy my scholarly leanings. From that point on, things snowballed well beyond my expectations. I was asked to publish books and organize national and international conferences. Foreign nations—France, Italy, Belgium, Australia, Singapore—asked my help to organize geriatric oncology programs. The National Cancer Institute in Washington, D.C., earmarked $35 million for research in this new field of study. Twenty years later geriatric oncology is a growing field throughout the world with a society of international investigators.

In the end, one of my least appealing characteristics, my ability to survive through compromise, was pivotal in the generation of a research field of growing interest in the international medical community. And this anecdote from my life also illustrates what I call redemption—turning what seems like a negative into a positive development that benefits many.

I took each step prayerfully. Looking back, I can see God's direct intervention in many places. In 1994, for instance, I was joined by a young Swiss physician, Dr. Martine Extermann, who came to work in my division as an unpaid volunteer for one year. She eventually became the most prominent and well known faculty member on my team. She has been able to generate groundbreaking research and compete successfully for large-scale grants that make important research possible. Her presence was central to the fulfillment of my vision.

I must also credit my upbringing with my ability to provide in writing a passionate but realistic analysis of my life's experience. I am happy to say that my inner insecurities have been transformed to become an essential Christian virtue: humility. Only in humility can a person be completely honest about his or her past.

A few years ago I heard a priest giving a sermon on humility in a church of the Parisian banlieu, as the low-income outskirts of the city are known. Humility, he said, is the ability to recognize our own talents, to get a clear vision of what we are good at, to recognize our own unique role, our sacredness. The idea that humility consists of putting ourselves down is an unfortunate misunderstanding that borders on hypocrisy and prevents us from contributing to society.

Picasso is credited with saying, "When I was a child, my mother said to me, 'If you become a soldier, you'll be a general. If you become a monk you'll end up as the pope.' Instead I became a painter and wound up as Picasso." This statement of supreme pride could be paraphrased into one of supreme humility: "My mother wanted me to become the most successful person in the world, and I did best her wishes: I became what God had planned for me."

I believe that the supreme act of humility is to be able to recognize that we have outgrown other people's expectations and have found our unique role in this world. Whether we are recognized artists, world leaders, humble laborers or homeless street beggars, each one of us is a unique pebble in the mosaic envisioned by God.

The fourth path to redemption through suffering was described by the psychoanalyst Carl Jung in the archetype of the "wounded healer." This vision is found in ancient mythology as well as in the Christian narrative. Suffering gives a unique credibility to the healer, as he or she possesses a personal stake in healing. Unlike the doctor-scientist who pretends to offer objective recommendations to the patient without knowing the price of those recommendations, the wounded healer has experience of suffering and knows what a patient is going through. He or she can muster empathy for the struggle of the patient as well as compassion, while the Oslerian physician (influenced by William Osler), enamored of his or her aequanimitas, at most may muster some sympathy and condescension.

The first mythologic example of the wounded healer was represented by the centaur Chiron. After being wounded by Hercules' poisonous arrows, and recognizing that his wounds would never heal, Chiron gained inspiration from his own disease to heal other peoples. According to myth, he raised the baby Asclepius, who had been cut from his mother's womb and delivered to Chiron by Apollo. Asclepius, the Greek God of medicine, also was a wounded healer. After funding the Epidaurus sanctuary for healing his own wound, he offered his experience in the service of others. (The snake-entwined staff, a symbol of medicine even today, belonged to Asclepius.)

And of course Christ is the quintessential example of the wounded healer. New International Version: "By his wounds we are healed," stated the apostle. A beautiful example of the effectiveness of the wounded healer in the emotional and spiritual field was provided in the 1977 novel and 1983 made-for-TV movie series *The Thorn Birds*. The heroine is Meghann, or Meggie, a wealthy woman from the Australian outback who has a daughter from her abusive husband and a son from adulterous relations with an ambitious priest who eventually will become a prominent Roman cardinal. Everybody except Meggie and her mother thinks that the son is from Meggie's legal husband. As the priest was always her true love, Meggie resents her daughter, while she worships her son, and she is devastated when he decides to enter the priesthood, following the footsteps of his natural father. Shortly after his ordination, which his mother refused to attend, the son dies in a diving accident in Greece. In face of this tragedy Meggie's resentment of her daughter increases to the point that she refuses to acknowledge her during the funeral. Meggie is rescued from her living hell of resentment and anger by her own mother, an aged but still impressive Jean Simmons. As a young woman she also had had an adulterous relationship, and she had conceived a son that she privileged over Meggie in her affections. When she asks Meggie not to repeat her mistakes, the message is heard and heeded because Meggie was aware of her mother's affair and consequently can trust her mother's compassion and concerns. She knows her mother talks from an experience she lived in her own flesh, not out of cold obsequy to some general rules of moral behaviour. By her mother's wounds Meggie was healed.

Sometimes I recite to myself some of the scenes that hurt so badly during my adolescence, using the wisdom accumulated in the last thirty-six years of faith. I ask my father: "Do you realize how much your outbursts hurt mother and consequently hurt me? Do you realize that we are all intimidated by you? We would like to love you. As a little child I slept in your room in our makeshift postwar apartment. I cherished the songs you used to sing at my bedside to soothe me into sleep. I was terrified by the idea I might lose you. Do you remember how much I cried when you went to the coffee shop in Bologna when the train took a long stop, because I was scared that you missed the train and you abandoned us? Why do you now feel the need to curse us every night and kick us around as if we were in your way?

How can you go to the church where you got married and curse your marriage at the same time?" I can imagine my father reacting with violence to my questions, shouting insults at me and blaming mother for my attitude, and walking out of the house slamming the door. I also imagine him coming back silent two hours later and, the following morning, greeting the whole family with a new smile that announces a new day in his behavior. He was a thoughtful person who would have done anything not to lose his family. He just behaved as he had seen his father behaving before him and could not conceive that his outbursts might be interpreted as anything but a bad mood on a bad day, that the words he uttered or shouted at that time might be taken literally by anybody. Unfortunately this conversation never happened, and my reaction to him, when I grew old enough not to fear him anymore, was only confrontational, excluding any form of the understanding for which he had repeatedly begged.

I imagine myself telling mother: "Mamma, do you really not like us? I am sorry but the message you send us is devastating. Sister and I feel sad and disappointed for not having met your expectations, but please don't blame us for that. We don't want to be a battlefield where daddy and you and grandmother wage their battles. You seem to resent that our life has been much easier than yours, but if you saw into our hearts you would recognize that it has not been easy at all. In different ways we both are left adrift on a river without knowing what it is ahead of us. In my heart of hearts I know that this is not what you want. I know you feel lonely and unappreciated in a town you don't know, in a family that seems to disdain you. But you should realize that your loneliness is our loneliness, your pain is our pain. Even if we seem to enjoy the bribes of father and grandmother, the cookies and candies, the comic books, we will be lonely as long as you don't show us that we have gained your affection. And please quit trying to gauge our values from the marks we get at school. Your grandmother did that with the best of intentions and created three generations of people insecure and lost. You have an opportunity to redeem her and your own parents by renouncing her rigidity. Try to see what we are good at and support the growth of our talents with the warmth of your love."

I don't know whether these are pure dreams or instead are also a form of redemption. There is a Kingdom of God encompassing the living and the dead. In the Kingdom of God, where time is not an issue, these conversations may be real, a connection to eternity through mystery. In any case these conversations make me aware that the remedy of the truth was always available even in the darkest moment of my growth. My family suffered from a lack of faith the same way a diabetic patient suffers from a lack of insulin!

Still there is a missing piece to the history of redemption: the motive for seeking redemption. Where does one get the emotional strength to effect redemption, to die for it? The answer, of course, is love, love in the form of *agape*. There are four words for love in ancient Greek. They are *eros*, the sexual passion; *filia*, the affection of friends; *eusebeia*, the affection of children and parents; and finally *agape*, unconditional love, love that may be fueled by an act of reason, love that keeps alive all the other forms of love, which otherwise might wither at the first difficulty. The acceptance of agape was particularly difficult for my generation, which learned to handle its feelings by suppressing them.

The history of a young woman in my medical school illustrates. The daughter of an editor of the Osservatore Romano, the official news publication of the Catholic Church, she joined the Catholic University School of Medicine full of enthusiasm. Committed to seeing in each patient "the suffering Christ," as was the school's proclaimed goal, she was diligent in her religious practices, including daily mass and annual retreats. Soap and water, her only beauty accessory, and long wide skirts had given her an almost angelic appearance of innocence. Her only vice: From time to time she sneaked some cigarettes. In those days I had some thoughts about her as a serious romantic interest, though I never did dare to approach her.

Three years later she had become a different person. She cut her long hair, started wearing makeup and provocative dresses, and I know by hearsay that she elected to go to bed with various schoolmates. (I still cannot call it lust because I believe that sex, to her, was more a form of self punishment or at least of self-investigation than of self indulgence.) Eventually she moved to the state school, a place more in line with her newly found agnostic or atheistic faith, as clearly she still respected the eighth commandment and abhorred lies. The last I knew of her, she became a psychiatrist. I don't know how her life progressed. In one of the few contacts we had between classes, she revealed her mental drama in a simple statement: "Christianity tells you to love everybody, and you make a futile effort to achieve this goal, until you realize that you have become a phony, a hypocrite who pretends to be somebody you are not, because you will never be able to love everybody. That imperative proves Christianity false." Nowadays I would paraphrase her statement: "Christianity tells you to love everybody because Christianity upholds the riches of your own dignity; you can love everybody once you believe yourself and love yourself. If you don't love yourself, you may at most delude yourself that you are able to love anybody."

CHAPTER 18

# Ministering to the Dying

UNFORTUNATELY I DO NOT see much redemption in many of the families I minister to during the trajectory of the death of a family member. How many times have I called the estranged children of a dying parent to hear a polite "thank you for your concern, Doctor!" which I hear as "mind your goddam businesses, you goddam do-gooder. If you really care to carry a message on my behalf tell the old son of a bitch (or the old bitch) that I wish he (or she) would rot in hell!"

Somehow I would prefer it if they would answer with more candor and unload their anger on me. Maybe an outburst would let them disperse and dissolve the hatred that imprisons their capacity for compassion the way a cage of calcium paralyzes the lung of a patient exposed to asbestos. Once they hear themselves uttering their words of hatred, hatred may dissolve like soap bubbles. Hypocrisy cloaked with politeness keeps the cage locked. It prevents people from looking at themselves in the mirror of hatred, the way Dorian Gray regarded the dissolution of her body that everybody saw as forever young and attractive.

Hell is hatred that devours without ever being satisfied, the opposite of agape, according to the metaphor employed by C.S. Lewis in *The Screwtape Letters*, published in 1942, one of the more unusual books ever written. Wormwood is a young devil instructed by his uncle Screwtape, an older devil, on how to effect human damnation. The rules of the game are very simple: Human souls are your food, not to be consumed out of passion, or of desire, or of hunger, or even of anger. They are the devil's food out of addiction to a cold form of hatred that cannot be placated and that is augmented with each and every meal. Wormwood is warned: If you can't devour human souls, expect to be devoured yourself. That is the way hatred works.

Depression, for me, removed any fear of death. In fact, in a depressed state, death is desirable, and to this day I lack fear of death. This outlook has allowed me to minister to my dying patients, to help them face imminent death, to help them understand that this is something that almost nobody can do on his or her own, and to treasure this moment as they would any other moment of their lives.

Here is what I tell them: If death is the ultimate enemy, we all are doomed, as we all are going to die. The only way to defeat death is to co-opt the experience of dying and integrate it into our lives. The message changes, of course, with the individual characteristics of each patient, his or her cultural and ethnic background, his or her religious faith or absence of it.

My favorite metaphor to illustrate opportunities in the proximity of death is a trip to Rome. "If you had only one day to visit Rome," I tell my dying patients, "you may try to cram in as many monuments as you can and find yourself exhausted and without any lasting memory at the end of the day. Or you may climb a hill, such as the Gianicolo (the Janiculum) or the Parioli, have a global vision of the city and decide which monuments you really wish to see, which ones may really have an impact on your life. Then your visit will be meaningful and your impressions lasting and treasured. Try to think of your death as your Gianicolo or your Parioli. It is an opportunity to gain a global view of your life and decide which life monuments (relationships, successes and even failures) you want to save. Then you can make of your own life a distillate, similar to the perfume of Bulgarian roses—where the essence of thousands of flowers is preserved in a drop long after the roses have withered.

"This is the time to tell people you love how much you love them and what their love has meant to you. This is the time to ask for and concede forgiveness and restore any flow of love interrupted by pride, hostility or misunderstanding. This is the time to revisit with your loved ones the moments of your life that had a major impact on you so that they may treasure them with you. This may also be the time to revisit with your loved ones what you consider your failures, because you may find that you learned your most important lessons from them. The most valuable legacy you may bequeath to your loved ones may concern the ways you transformed your failures into successes; this helps them learn how to face life."

One of my first cancer patients was a young violin player who died of sarcoma that spread to the lung. Despite the fact that he and his widowed mother did not have any religious affiliation, they were able to treasure his oncoming death through such a process under the guidance of a sensitive

Baptist chaplain who never tried to sell them on his own beliefs. The young man realized that he had been endowed with a unique talent for the violin, and in his short life he had left a vital imprint on the world thanks to his unique way of interpreting classical music. Also, his violin allowed him to find a faithful girlfriend who bathed him in her love up to the very end. Equally important, he learned that his misgivings during his earlier life, when he was rejected as "strange" by his schoolmates, were the price to pay for being sacredly endowed with a unique talent. Before dying he made peace with the painful memories of his childhood and extended heartfelt forgiveness to the people who had derided or belittled him. The proximity of death had become an opportunity to appreciate and enjoy sacredness and love as he had never been able to do before. Even in the absence of any religious beliefs, his nonverbal aspect at the end of life expressed the sentiment of Thérèse de Lisieux, Sister Teresa of the Child Jesus: "No matter what, everything is grace!"

Since most of my dying patients fear becoming a burden to their loved ones, I insist that they see how taking care of a loved one is one of the more meaningful experiences in anyone's life. Further, the patient shows his or her love by accepting being taken care of and by not denying their families this opportunity. The family learns a greater appreciation of their own value in providing such care to a loved one—care that only they can provide.

Sometimes I share with them my regret for not having been able to minister to my father at the end of his life. I don't share with them, however, that once in an explosion of rage I told my sister, who was regretting not having instituted renal dialysis for him, "If he did not hurry to get out of the way, I would have killed him myself!" However, my regret in not having been able to provide, during my father's last year, the affection that might have eased his passing will haunt me to the end of my days and will provide a powerful motivation to encourage my patients' caregivers to provide the best care they can. Doing so is not just for the patient's but also for their own benefit. It provides a way to discover, affirm and establish their own sacredness.

My own experience of being in the middle of family feuds in Italy turned out to be a particularly valuable asset to address other people's family dysfunctions in America, especially those of the patients who occupy 90 percent of my time. One time I found myself holding the hand of an 80-year-old woman with ovarian cancer while her daughter, who was single and unhappy, accused her of having manipulated the family using the excuse of her disease. The daughter blamed the mother for her own loneliness and aloneness. While holding her speechless mother's hand, I told the daughter that I was sure her mother had realized the negative impact she had had on her daughter's life. "I can assure you that she feels very sorry about it and craves your forgiveness," I said. After abandoning her mother for a few days, the daughter came back and assisted her mother lovingly for the next eighteen months until her death.

Though it is difficult to reconcile family members who have nursed their hostility for years, the same way a bee secretes honey, I never give up, and I hope that people may be reconciled if not in this life then in another life. One of the more disconcerting experiences in this respect occurred when I was a medical resident in Jackson, Mississippi. I was taking care of a middle-aged man with acute kidney failure. I tried my best to help reconcile him with his estranged children. Only a son living in Birmingham, Alabama, took his call. But the answer was: "Next time there is a flood in Jackson, try to ride the wave. If you happen to float to Birmingham give me a call, and I will be happy to take care of you." The hospital chaplain eventually adopted the man, which allowed him to become eligible for dialysis. Soon he died of a heart attack, having made peace with God and having tried to make peace with his family. Medical caregivers see thousands of stories like this play out each day across the country; most of us hope that when the dying patient reaches out, the family will gracefully accept.

Having survived an inner cold war in my own family gave me unusual endurance for ambiguous situations that other colleagues, imbued with the American spirit of directness, find intolerable. Plus other doctors compartmentalize. They believe that the job of Western medicine is to minister to the body, not the mind, and certainly not to the patients' webs of emotional and familial relationships. Not surprisingly many of my colleagues send me the difficult patients, those literally labeled "hateful patients" in medical literature. In a few cases I have chosen to drop them as patients, sometimes because they became so disruptive that the staff threatened to quit, and sometimes for their own good, as I judged that they would receive better care closer to home. And yet I relished tackling the hard cases. Often I managed to provide a haven for individuals who would otherwise have had no medical care and helped improve otherwise dismal outcomes. In addition, I hope I manage to soothe some of the hatred these poor souls have for themselves (and consequently for the world) by letting them know that I love them, and I love them because I recognize myself in them. I have been a worse pest than they are, and they give me the opportunity to pay off some of my own debts by ministering to them! More important, thanks to them, what I considered my major shortcomings (or poisonous assets) are now valuable currency. I can use the tolerance I had learned to develop for myself as a means to soothe their pain.

As much as I do like to think of myself as a leader, I am anything but. My assertiveness was irremediably broken when my parents, maybe with the best of intentions, managed to destroy any spurts of self-assurance. I have a difficult time making painful decisions, and sometimes people suffer from my indecisiveness. Many years ago a smart, skilled nurse scolded me for allowing a colleague to work under my direction despite some evidence of his incompetence. At first I did nothing. Eventually I tried to work with this colleague, who had an unusual capacity for human empathy, and limited his job to the management of chronic diseases. With such patients he could provide compassionate care, which was his forte, while having time to check with me regarding critical medical decisions. I was sensitive to the fact that this colleague was a single father of two (and one of his children had Down's syndrome); also, he was taking care of elderly parents and desperately needed to work.

Of course I turned to my trusted friend, my wife, Claudia. When I asked whether she felt I was a wimp, as everybody seemed to judge me, she refused to call me names. Instead she told me a story:

"A man was in charge of bringing the water from the valley to a Chinese mountain village. He used two jars, one of which had a hole in the bottom, so that he could only bring up a single full jar to the village and had to make twice as many trips to the valley. When asked why he did not find a substitute for the leaking container, he answered that the water dripping through the hole fed flowers that made his trip more joyful. He plucked the flowers to take bouquets to his wife, and those flowers and grasses and mushrooms also fed birds and wild animals. That water was not lost but used for a purpose as vital as supplying the village."

As only a loving spouse can do, Claudia reflected back to me my deepest feelings. By being a jar almost empty of assertiveness, I allowed a young deserving man to feed his family and share with suffering people his capacity for love. In many situations no solution is completely right or completely wrong. I felt newly secure in the fact that I could use the assets I had to do my job, and those assets would pay off. The outcome might have been different under a more assertive director, but my approach also resulted in blessings and good. Again, this is an example of redemption. I perceived my lack of assertivness as a poisonous liability that bestowed on me despisement and derision. And yet this liability became a most valuable asset in protecting the livelihood of a deserving young man and his needy family.

## CHAPTER 19

# Suicide
## *A Convenient End in a Christless Society*

MOST OF MY MOTHER'S cousins lived in Piacenza, a city in northern Italy, and from there came one of the worst tragedies of my family, unveiling the real face of a world my mother had looked to as a lost Eden.

"Let the pastor know that Pietruccio's corpse is going to be there in half an hour."

"What are you saying? Who is this? I don't understand.. . ." My aunt had just dozed off on a quiet Saturday afternoon after a modest noon meal when the phone woke her up. The caller was Cici, an unofficial leader of the family among the cousins, a brilliant lawyer who liked to display a British nonchalance in the face of tragedy. Pietruccio, the youngest son of his youngest brother, had shot himself when on sentinel duty in the barracks of Ascoli Piceno, where he was serving in the military.

A handsome young man, Pietruccio was a successful athlete. His achievements included baseball and basketball, which he played at the national championship level. In addition he proved to be an excellent rock climber, following in the footsteps of his own father. Also like his father, he had been eyed longingly by many a young woman.

Despite his mundane successes, and his ability to confront physical danger without fear, he panicked when confronted by scholastic tests. Twice during high school, he had to repeat university admission tests, and in three years he had not managed to pass more than two exams toward a degree in chemical engineering. His fiancée was putting pressure on him to finish college so they could get married. The pressure had mounted a year earlier; he had already attempted to take his own life with a drug overdose. Returning home earlier than planned from a trip, his parents found and rescued him.

Shocked by the suicide attempt, they realized they needed help and asked the opinion of a renowned physician who had taken care of the family for at least three generations. "Let him interrupt the curriculum for a while and go into the military. Young men live together, get lots of exercise, have a healthy lifestyle. He will be able to set aside his emotions and will come back to you renewed and happy!" was the professional sentence. Apparently it did not occur to the trusted family counselor that in the military you have practically unlimited access to firearms. And firearms are a common way that males commit suicide, not to mention their image as instruments of glory in the protection of the homeland. And that is how Pietruccio chose to end his life.

Forty years later I see in Pietruccio's death the end of my innocence. Pietruccio's life appeared haunted by an avalanche of lies. And, to gain my mother's affection, I had embraced those lies that had suffocated the desire to live in an otherwise promising and jolly young man.

For one thing, the trusted doctor disregarded not just the scientific data, but even the common sense advice that a potential suicide should be kept far from firearms. He also elected to ignore mounting evidence that military service is a unique cauldron of depression and desperation, nurturing suicidal ideation in young men shanghaied from the protective cocoons of their families and subjected to brutal training whose ultimate goal is to kill and be killed at the command of people you don't know and may not trust. The good doctor preferred against all evidence to see in the military a joyful camping vacation where young men learn how to live together and share with each other joy, amusement and enthusiasm. Instead of searching the medical literature on the effects of military life on disturbed young people, he preferred to believe the lie of a romanticized military written a century earlier by Edmondo De Amicis in his book *Military Life* (*La Vita Militare*.) De Amicis is almost universally reviled in Italy for the lies that pervaded his books, which caused generations of young Italians to shed tears over implausible anecdotes of heroism.

Had the trusted family doctor of Piacenza heeded clinical and social experience instead of De Amicis' lies, maybe he would have been able to find some help for Pietruccio; he definitely would not have advised the family that he should join the military! But to be fair, the doctor was doing nothing other than to reinforce and enable a chain of lies that predated his visit. We in the family learned of Pietruccio's previous suicide attempt only after his death. When he and his parents could not attend my sister's wedding because he was recovering from a drug overdose, we were told he had a severe intestinal infection. Even faced with his previous suicide attempt, both his parents and his fiancée did not stop pressuring him to graduate quickly. It did not occur to them that maybe their strategy was wrong or maybe Pietruccio should have pursued a different career. His attempted suicide was considered a form of momentary weakness, like a runner who needs some rest because of shin splints. They did not question the blueprint of his life. And under no circumstances was a suicide attempt going to be allowed to reflect on the emotional stability of an individual with that family name.

For me it was a form of déjà vu! After my parents resisted for many years my request to see a mental-health professional, eventually they agreed to it, but only after I threatened to leave medical school. They selected a professor of neurology in Modena, about 150 miles from my hometown, and they requested that I keep the visit secret. How much the good professor was attuned to my problem is reflected in his main recommendation: After I revealed my conflicts with my parents, my discomfort with my body, my problems in establishing an emotionally satisfying relationship with a woman, he recommended that I quit masturbating!

I could not help seeing in Pietruccio's suicide a form of payback for my own callousness. One year earlier, when I was a medical officer, practicing as a physician in the Italian army, I had been approached by a young man who showed me a collection of Valium pills. During the brief visit he hinted that he might use them to end a life he felt was becoming unbearable. This conversation had occurred with both of us standing in the middle of a crowded room. My previous patient was cussing at me, as I had refused to OK his request for a leave so that he could rest. The soldier after him had just unzipped his pants to allow me to examine his genitalia. In the name of efficiency, privacy had never been a consideration in military medicine, at least not in those days in the Italian army!

Convinced that people who really will commit suicide will never talk about it, I dismissed his prattling. I considered him one of the many freeloaders seeking an excuse to avoid exercise. A few days later, as I was enjoying the equivalent of a thanksgiving dinner with my parents and my newlywed wife, I received a phone call. The young man had thrown himself from a window of the barrack's third floor and was dead on arrival.

My parents and my sister could not finish eating; they started asking questions about the tragedy. Clearly they were distressed by the news. I finished my meal, feigning cynicism and complacency: "Life is transient, and it does not really matter how one finishes it. This young man was not fit for this world. That is the way evolution works." This is more or less what I said, doing my best to sound condescending. I made a point of sipping a dessert wine and savoring the *piada dei morti*, a version of a fruitcake in my hometown.

Though suicide had haunted a large part of my youth, at that time of my life I felt immune to it. With my graduation from medical school, with my marriage, I felt I had reached my emotional balance. I had gained status in society. I could claim for the first time to be normal. From this vantage point I could watch other people's emotional dramas the way a sailor looks at a boat trapped in a tempest from the shore (the metaphor is from the Latin poet Lucretius in "*De Rerum Natura*") and enjoys as a spectator the ordeal of other sailors fighting for their lives.

Pietruccio's death reminded me that I was not immune to suicide at all, that my normality was just a sandcastle. I became fully aware of this lesson only a long time later, however. For the moment I tried to disregard this signal and to keep reveling in my delusion of normality. So much so that two years later I was the involuntary cause of another suicide.

I was in charge of the outpatient clinics at the University of Mississippi. Prison officials brought me a prisoner from the penitentiary one hundred and twenty miles away. He arrived handcuffed after a two-hour journey on the wooden bench in the back of a police truck.

On the way to the clinics, the officers had allowed him a detour to visit his ailing mother. Because of the delay, I refused to see him, though I had no other patients at that time. It was just an inconvenience as I was trying to wrap up my working day. The following day I bragged to a colleague over lunch: "I kicked him back all the way to the prison, where he belongs, a son of a bitch of a murderer." He was serving time for having killed his wife. A few days later we learned he had hanged himself in prison. Suffering from a poorly controlled, very brittle diabetes, he was subject to rapid and unexpected changes of mood. Apparently he had murdered his wife during one of these "metabolic" episodes. When they were not bullying and beating him, the other prisoners ostracized him, because they could not stand nor understand his volatility. Eventually he got to the point that he could not stand himself any more.

More suicides occurred along my route as milestones underlining the lies I was not ready to abandon, as I did not feel enough confidence to abandon myself to the living truth. Of these I must mention one that touched me more deeply because it threatened my dearest memories. It uprooted the very landmarks that I counted upon as references for the development of my own history.

After starring in a high school football game and leading his team to victory, Jim came home, opened the letter that welcomed him as a freshman to Vanderbilt University, kissed his mother, locked himself in his room and shot himself. He was 18, less than a year older than my son. His parents had been the first friends to greet my son's birth, and when my son was born, Jim announced to his grandparents and his uncles: "I have a new brother called Marco!" A few months later we visited his house, and Jim came at us shooting a toy pistol: "Listen to this, you stupid baby!" he told Marco. Marco was sitting on the floor and was marveling with wide eyes at the noisy horseplay. Putting down the gun, Jim hugged Marco as if to protect his younger brother and whispered: "I love you." On other occasions we took the two toddlers horseback riding as well as riding a boat on a pond filled with bass and snakes. Befitting a Southern gentleman, Jim's father, a physician, displayed in the living room, in a glass case, a collection of firearms, from those used during the Civil War to the most modern type of automatic rifles.

Jim and his parents left town so that his father could start a practice two hundred miles north, and we saw each other only occasionally at medical conventions. On each occasion I was told that Jim was becoming a star both in terms of sports and scholastic accomplishments. He had also become one of the most talked-about ladies' men in his small town.

About three years prior to his death his parents divorced, and his father married a divorced nurse with five children of her own. All of the sudden the narrative involved seven children. Somehow I never felt comfortable with the conversation. I remember that riding a bus to a medical function, I tried to change topics; I just could not fathom him as the father of other children beside Jim and his sister.

"Another child mad at his mother for having alienated his father," was the comment of a psychiatrist, a friend to whom we described our distress over Jim's suicide. Technically she might have been correct, but I found her comments somehow callous, like those of a physician explaining to the mourning wife of a cancer victim that the cause of her husband's death was a disregulation of the k-ras oncogene. Analytic psychiatry, like molecular biology, may identify the mechanism through which a life was lost, but it can't embrace the tragedy of death. It can explain how but not why people die nor why other people are left to mourn. I find this minimalist explanation is itself an additional form of lie, one of the many ways through which we miss the forest of life to focus on a small and insignificant bush.

I could not help seeing the suicide of Jim as the end of a rosary of lies, like that of Pietruccio's. Young people were raised to follow their immediate inclination with a faith in the limitless possibility of the future. Epitomized by the gas-guzzling engines that powered gigantic cars, the future promised bigger vehicles, more palatial houses, faster and more comfortable airplanes, and the cure of all diseases. The moon landing reinforced the promise of a limitless destiny. Not even the sky was the limit anymore. To worry about the exhaustion of world resources, about sickness, about the plight of the less fortunate was considered a form of social boycott supported by emotional pathology, worse than defeatism. Still now the political right counts on the nostalgia for this lie to gain electoral momentum. ("Drill, baby, drill!")

Jim's father became a prominent physician and allowed his wife to revel in her maternity; they both enjoyed the mansion on the river. Each of them drove a late-model BMW and shared a Volvo SUV for family outings. They spent the weekends in their purebred horse farm, and during the summer they visited Europe in five-star hotels. To identify, leave alone to mention, any personal concern or any disagreement would have been considered worse than inappropriate, tantamount to a rebellion against the grace of God, the search for the prohibited tree in the Garden of Eden.

"This is paradise," mentioned one of the three friends, protagonists in the movie *Good Neighbors*. In that paradise he ended up masturbating each night to relieve his tension as his wife slept placidly and oblivious beside him. The same woman entertained a year-long affair with the intellectual of the three friends, a college professor who had made it his life goal to remove any trace of prudery from his students. I want you to be comfortable to pronounce the word F-U-C-K at the end of my course, was his self-introduction to his class. He himself felt so comfortable with that expression that could not convince his wife to copulate with him. This is the paradise of lies where Pietruccio, and Jim, and the soldier trusted to my care, and the diabetic prisoner, lost their lives, like flies suffocated by a spider web.

I never learned what motivated Jim's father to abandon his wife of twenty years to marry a different woman, but I am sure that the very lie that supported twenty years of marriage made him prey to a new lie that led to one more marriage. It is irrelevant at this point what lay behind his choice: whether his new wife provided him with excitement that the old one had forgotten how to provide, or that he felt guilty for taking advantage of the favors of a single mother of five during a one-night stand at a medical convention, or that he found the new young children fun while the older children were causes of concern and headaches. Or maybe it was a combination of all these factors. No matter what, he decided to change the players when he did not like the script anymore. Anything but face the lie that had informed all of his life! I could go on, but the history of the suicides that made milestones during my life would become monotonous. At the end there is always a man or woman who could not tolerate the web of lies in which he or she was imprisoned but did not know how to cut.

Perhaps the paradigm of all modern suicides is that of a 23-year-old Danish existentialist, Carlo Michelstaedter, a young Italian-speaking Jew from Gorizia who left the Austro-Hungarian territory to study in Florence.

He shot himself in 1910 after mailing his Ph.D. dissertation in philosophy. Unlike his better known friend Kierkegaard, who had recognized religious faith as a form of personal relation, as the lifesaver that allowed one to survive adrift in a sea of lies, Michelstaedter did not see any way out but to hasten his drowning in the same sea. He identified in the world without God nothing else but a noose of lies closing slowly around your neck. The only way to avoid lifelong suffocation was to anticipate your death, he apparently believed.

I wish to mention the epidemic of suicide among young people who feel bullied by their peers, especially if they are or are perceived as gay. These are poignant examples of the evil of the power in a Christless society that can marginalize and destroy other individuals perceived as being abnormal, out of the mainstream. The rules of normality in a society without religious inspiration are established by the powerful and for the powerful. Instead of being inspired by the desire to spread agape, many are inspired by the desire to overpower other individuals, to hang their heads like hunting trophies on a living room wall. Time magazine decided to celebrate the killing of the first wolf in Idaho by publishing a picture of the hunter in camouflage holding the dead animal by its hind feet. Every time I hear of a bullying-related suicide, I think of the bully in camouflage holding his victim by the feet in a photograph that immortalizes his glory.

A neuroscientist may object that modern molecular biology has revealed an imbalance of some essential neurotransmitters of the brain at the basis of most suicides. I would dispute cause and effect! The environmental lie in which the potential suicides are embedded is the environmental cause of the unbalance of neurotransmitters. Once more, science divorced from the person would confuse the mechanism with the cause.

CHAPTER 20

# Assisted Suicide

*'Don't worry, Doc, this is between you and me'*

TODAY'S CONTROVERSY OVER ASSISTED suicide stems from the lie that Western medicine can offer an objective "good." Some authoritative physicians including Timothy Quill of Rochester, N.Y., and Marcia Angell, M.D., former editor of the *New England Journal of Medicine*, arguably the world's most prestigious medical journal, support the legalization of these practices. Since some form of euthanasia is widely practiced in the dark, goes their argument, it would be more equitable both for patients and providers that it be practiced in the sunshine according to established rules.

In the case of Dr. Angell, the support for physician-assisted suicide has a highly emotional overtone; I have the highest respect and empathy for her experience. Her father, when he learned he had incurable prostate cancer, shot himself. The family had to carry forever the double wound of having been excluded from a life-determining decision and of witnessing the gory scene of his passing. Had a physician been entitled to help him commit suicide he might have shared his decision with his family without fear of being restricted, and his peaceful death, surrounded by people he loved, would have provided the family with a more tolerable, and maybe even a treasurable memory.

The argument in favor of euthanasia and assisted suicide could not be more logical, but its premise is a lie. The lie is that medicine, as practiced in the West, is an absolute good irrespective of the persons it is purported to serve. It assumes that one can establish according to some objective criteria when a life can and cannot be saved and when the patient's wish to end life is a fully free decision. The free decision itself is nonsense from a theoretical standpoint. A decision is free when the person who decides has real knowledge of all possible choices. I am free to select one television set instead of another or one food instead of another because I do know which one I am going to enjoy more on the basis of previous experiences. Nobody then can choose death as a free choice, as nobody knows what it is like to be dead until he or she dies. But this is just a nuance.

The real flaw of the argument is the pretense of defining and circumscribing a living experience that as such can only be lived. This pretense is tantamount to trying to take the person out of the person, to make a subjective experience objective and measurable. As Miguel de Unamuno pointed out in his 1931 work *The Agony of Christianity*, the fundament of any relationship, whether of persons with each other or with God, is that human beings never arrive at the place of comprehending each other or God. If such comprehension were possible, they would cease to be separate entities, and the relationship would end! The fundament of a relationship is the inability to live each other's experiences.

I never practiced euthanasia or actively helped in a patient suicide. But I might have enabled both in situations in which doing otherwise would have contrasted with my sense of compassion as well as with my integrity, duty bound to preserve and protect patients' confidentiality.

"Doctor, if I make a mistake and give Esther a double dose of her pain medication, will I hasten her death? Don't worry, Doc, this is between you and me. I used to be a cop, and I can assure you that this discussion never happened." Esther, a 49-year-old woman with an aggressive form of breast cancer that had spread to the liver, and whom I had treated for nine months, died that very night. What should I have done? Out of fear that her husband might overdose her, withhold pain medications, thereby sentencing her to spend the last few days of her life in excruciating pain? Report her husband to the authorities and sentence her to spend her last hours with a hired caregiver who could not have cared less about her, while her husband languished in prison waiting to be judged for attempted murder, and make her two teen-agers instant orphans? Warn her that her husband might try to kill her and destroy with my warning in a few seconds a relationship that had remained trustworthy for twenty-five years and that had been her main source of comfort as she lay dying? I don't know, and I really don't care whether her husband wanted to hasten her death to relieve her suffering or his own burden or maybe for both reasons. Unlike logic, living experiences support contradictions: When you live a circle is a square and the square a circle most times. What I know is that compassion for the patient prevented me from intervening. I also know that legalization of euthanasia would not have helped to address the problems of any of the players in these dramas that go on each day in America.

"When I am unable to take care of myself I will shoot my wife first and then myself. We both have agreed to it," confided Mr. George to the nurse administering chemotherapy to him. She dutifully reported the conversation to me.

"Mr. George, I have to ask you to see a psychologist, because you expressed your intention to take your and your wife's life." I was trying to sound matter of fact, but I could not maintain my cool. I had known Mr. George for years, and I considered him an old friend. More than once we had sat together at a bar and, over a couple of beers and a burger, looked at pictures of him sailing from Florida to remote Caribbean islands or of his hunting trophies in Wyoming from days of hiking and camping in the wild. I could not be firm with him.

"What if I refuse?" he retorted, defiant.

"Then you will leave me no choice but to Baker Act you."

In Florida, the Baker Act provides for a three-day lockup under certain circumstances. "I have the authority to retain you in the hospital for three days under observation against your will if I deem that you are a danger to others or to yourself."

"But I never imagined. . . ."

"Please, Mr. George, don't make it more difficult. I don't like it any more than you do, believe me. But this is the law. Do me a favor, see the psychologist and thereafter you can leave. I really don't wish to argue and much less to fight with you. You know I love you. . . ."

Begrudgingly he submitted to the mental-health evaluation. I don't know what he told the shrink, but he was released without restrictions or precautions. I am sure he made up lies. What I do know is that I never saw him again. He never returned the calls I was leaving on his voicemail at least once a week. Six months later we learned that both he and his wife had died. I declined to investigate the causes of their deaths.

A fiercely independent northwesterner proud of his self sufficiency who took care of his severely disabled wife, Mr. George had learned that his colon cancer had relapsed and spread into his liver. Neither he nor his wife wished to impose the burden of their care on any of their three children living in different parts of the country.

What could I have done differently?

Try to contact his children and betray the patient's confidentiality and the trust of an old friend? Even if I decided to take this path, had I the right to bestow the burden of the care of older parents on the children, against the will of the parents themselves? The only useful thing I could have done would have been to sit down with Mr. George and his wife and to explore alternatives to suicide. A very intrusive law endorsed by the religious right prevented me from taking the only compassionate, sensible course of action, congruent with the sentiment of an old friendship and genuine concern for the patient's welfare. According to this law I would have been legally responsible for the patient's suicide if I had known the patient's intention to commit suicide and I had not been able to prevent it, even if I had to resort to physical restriction. This law is so repulsive to a physician's integrity that nowadays the majority of psychiatrists initiate a patient interview by stating: "Remember that if you tell me that you have the intention to kill somebody, including yourself, I have to report you to the police." Ironically, this law aimed to protect life prevents troubled patients who may indeed take somebody's life from getting the help they need. This law is based on the same lie on which the legalization of euthanasia and physician-assisted suicide is based. It is the pretense that in a human drama, one can identify with certainty the best course of action to be pursued without hesitation, irrespective of the human cost. This law is an attempt to protect life by eliminating life itself.

The histories of Esther and Mr. George highlight another unintended consequence of modern medicine. It has been able to prolong human life at the cost of human independence. More and more individuals affected by chronic and disabling diseases, from arthritis to dementia to trauma to the limbs or the central nervous system to emotional disorders such as post-traumatic stress, are now alive and depending on a caregiver for their bare survival. I hope that the majority of home caregivers may feel rewarded by this task and see it as an opportunity to exercise compassion and become better, more sensitive human beings, with a deeper appreciation of the meaning of life. I also hope that those who worship the Christian God see in caregiving an opportunity to take care of the suffering Christ, and in so doing to validate their own faith through their work. Christianity holds that every suffering person represents the suffering Christ on this earth. (Whatsoever you do to the least of my brothers, that you do unto me!)

In the meantime it is well known that caregivers for patients with chronic diseases (and in particular those with Alzheimer's) suffer depression, marital problems, increased incidence of diseases and decreased survival. In the United States, the home caregiver saves the health system at least $300 billion a year (by conservative estimate), and nobody tells him or her so much as a thank you.

In fact, people who agree to become a home caregiver submit themselves to a number of legal jeopardies. For many years a woman with severe dementia was my patient. She had breast cancer and chronic leukemia, and her only caregiver was a loving husband. He was forced to leave her alone for eight hours in the afternoon so he could work to balance a budget overstretched by her care needs. He had asked nothing from his children, nothing from the government. More important he was still able to see in this demented woman the loving spouse that had illumined with joy and meaning the best years of his life. His fidelity was enlightened by a vision of transfiguration. Once he had seen his wife in all her glory, all her potential, the same way the apostles had seen Christ on the mountain, and that vision was more real than all the current difficulties or accidents. I could not think of a more devout and motivated caregiver. Yet, a young health-care worker who happened to talk to him reported him for spousal abuse! The reason was twofold.

First the lady smelled of urine at her doctor's appointment, which could not be helped, as she was incontinent. A catheter would have prevented the loss of urine but would have increased her discomfort and risk of infection. Unfortunately, the young health-care worker, brainwashed by the official lie that one should be clean all the time, even when he or she suffers from urinary incontinence, could not accept this simple fact. That smell of urine was offensive to her, and for this reason she preferred the lady to be inconvenienced by a catheter, even though the device would have disrupted the lady's quality of life and ultimately, probably, caused her death by infection. In her young militant mind uncleanness was unacceptable in any form at any time.

The second reason was that the lady was left alone for eight hours, as her husband was going to work and she was at risk of hurting herself. While I don't deny that ideally a demented person should not be left home alone, the only alternative would have been to admit her to a nursing home, where she would have died in few weeks, scared in an extraneous environment to which she predictably would have been totally unable to adapt. She would have been desperate in her solitude made even more unbearable by her inability to understand its reason. Her safety would have cost her the presence of her husband in whose affections was she still able to revel. As this affection was her only lifeline, her supposed safety in the nursing home would have shortened her life by years (as in the case of my wife's Uncle Titti) and would have deprived her of any sense of life.

Eventually the husband was cleared of any wrongdoing, but this came only after a lengthy investigation that compelled him to lose one week of income and forced a brief and traumatic separation from his spouse. Abuse reports trigger a law that prescribes the immediate custody of the alleged victim. The incident turned our once trust-filled and enjoyable relationship into something contentious and confrontational. Eventually he transferred her care to another practitioner so he would no longer face the condescension of the young militant social worker.

In a similar case, the authorities contacted me about a case of supposed neglect. A social worker called me about a patient dying of small cell lung cancer. His wife could not have been a more loving caregiver, feeding her husband for more than two hours at each meal, because he could swallow only small bites. She showered him in the hospital when the nurses were too busy. The only thing she refused was a feeding tube for him, as he had made it clear that he never wanted to be kept alive that way. His estranged children, who hoped to inherit from him, had reported this loving woman in the hopes of profiting more from his imminent death by excluding her from sharing the loot!

And we all had an opportunity to see how Michael Schiavo was called a murderer by the governor of Florida and the President of the United States (George W. Bush) when he decided to execute his wife's will after providing excellent care for eighteen years.

Thus modern medicine poses a number of expensive and unfunded mandates on the patients' families while government and society promote values that are the opposite of caregiving. The same politicians who feigned compassion for Michael Schiavo's wife, Terri, are those who opposed simple provisions to help the caregiver, such as the Family Leave Act. The same society that condemned Michael Schiavo is the society that recognizes the highest human potential in economic achievements. In this view human beings are as disposable, like parts of an engine. It goes without saying that this view puts home caregivers at a disadvantage. Their very mission cripples them when it comes to economic success. This inconsistency by itself should suffice to reveal as a lie the claim that there is an objective absolute good that can be defined without consideration of the person.

Whether Esther's husband aimed to relieve himself of the caregiving burden or to end his spouse's suffering, or execute an unwritten pact he had with his wife, it is clear that modern medicine had failed the couple. Likewise, one may think that modern medicine, which had allowed the survival of Mr. George and his crippled wife, was the ultimate cause of their planned suicide. Like millions of other people, including myself, they had no use for medicine able to indefinitely prolong their survival at the price of their independence. Medical advances occurred despite their unwillingness to employ them, and those advances worked against them. Such advances are supported by taxpayer-financed research and are paid for by Medicare and Medicaid as well as most private insurers. The millions of people such as myself and the Georges who disagree with them still are forced to pay for them!

The pre-Christian world was well aware that being human means to manage contradictions that logic cannot resolve. An intimate fight between opposite sentiments that cannot be reconciled represents the human tragedy. The ancient Greeks crystallized these conflicts in the immortal myths of Orestes, Antigone and Hector. The ancient Hebrews highlighted the mystery of human suffering in the poems of Job.

The myth of Orestes expresses the conflict between two sacred duties. For the physician it may be the conflict between betraying a patient's confidentiality and allowing a patient to take his own or somebody else's life. For the caregiver it may involve the distribution of time and care to ailing parents, growing children and a needy spouse.

Orestes was the son of the Greek king Agamemnon. While Agamemnon was leading the war against Troy, his wife, Clytemnestra, took a lover, Aegisthus. On Agamemnon's return she had him knifed as he was relaxing in a bath in the security of his own home after ten years of battles and perils. Clytemnestra's motive was neither lust not womanly capriciousness. The murder of Agamemnon was inspired by hatred nurtured for ten years. Agamemnon—to placate the goddess Diana and obtain favorable sailing winds for his army—had sacrificed Iphigenia, his own daughter. Mother and daughter were deceived into believing that the event was not a sacrifice but rather a wedding ceremony to join Iphigenia to the most coveted of the Greek heroes, Achilles. Instead of the bridegroom the young girl and her horrified mother met the priest ready to cut Iphigenia's throat. As a mother, Clytemnestra could never forgive her husband for killing her daughter, as the biblical Sarah would never have forgiven Abraham had he completed Isaac's sacrifice.

It was Orestes' sacred duty, as the oldest male son, to avenge his father's death. But this action implied the most unspeakable of crimes, the murder of one's own mother. No matter what he decided to do, independent from his own will, Orestes was doomed. The only choice offered him was between two sacrilegious courses of actions. Aeschylus, the playwright, masterfully engrafted a drama in the drama. As part of the loot after capturing Troy, Agamemnon took Cassandra as slave and concubine. She, of course, was the unfortunate daughter of King Priam, whom the god Apollo had endowed both with the gift of predicting the future and the condemnation of not being believed. This was the god's revenge because the young woman had spurned his love. Though Cassandra had warned Agamemnon against taking the bath, he dismissed her advice with nonchalance. Cassandra was killed at the same time as Agamemnon.

Cassandra's drama is also universal. A deep insight of a situation generates disbelief, belittling and rejection when the truth is inconvenient. And it is certainly inconvenient for the practitioners of medicine or for that matter of any profession to admit that there are situations over which we have limited or no control. Hence the pretense that we can regulate mercy killing with well defined rules, the same way the fictional mafia commission decided to regulate the commerce of cocaine and heroin in the Godfather books and movies.

The myth of Antigone highlights another common conflict in medicine, the one between the written law and one's personal consciousness. It was my legal duty to report Mr. George to the authorities. It was my moral duty to try to discuss the situation with Mr. George and his wife, even if that conversation would have made me legally liable in his death.

Antigone was the daughter of Oedipus, the king of the Greek town of Thebes, who without being aware of it had killed his own father and married his own mother. As punishment for this involuntary impiety, he blinded himself and went into exile in the town of Colonus. Unable to fend for himself, he relied exclusively on his young daughter Antigone as his eyes, his hands and his guide. Antigone chose to preserve her virginity as a sacrifice to her father. She affirmed filial piety as her supreme value.

After his death, Antigone returned to Thebes and submitted herself to the law of the new tyrant Creon, who was allied to one of the maid's two brothers, Eteocles. The other brother, Polynices, instead had decided to fight Creon, whom he saw as usurper of his father's throne. When Polynices was killed, Creon ordered that his corpse be left rotting and devoured by animals as the ultimate punishment (the ancient Greek believed that a soul would never find peace until the body was properly buried).

After soul searching, Antigone decided it was her duty to defy the tyrant and bury her brother even if that action would bring on her death. (Incidentally, the word "autonomy," holding that personal determination is more compelling than civil law, was used for the first time by Sophocles in telling the tragedy of Antigone. Autonomy is also one of the pillars of medical ethic. The patient, not the doctor or the medical system, is the final arbiter of any medical decision. Autonomy is the statement that medical decisions should be consistent with a patient's values. Under the specious argument of free choice, market-driven health-care industry repeatedly tries to deprive the patient of this autonomy.) Unlike another major mythic figure, Orestes, Antigone knew what her most sacred duty was, but she could not accept it without an intimate struggle, as disregard of civil law was a form of impiety that involved rightful governmental punishment. Like many physicians who, out of compassion, help a patient die, Antigone did not ask that the law be changed; she accepted her punishment. Her story demonstrated that human law, while necessary, cannot encompass all human situations and should never become the supreme gauge of human behavior, should never substitute for personal values. I see Dr. Timothy Quill and the supporters of legalized euthanasia as aiming to imprison the human consciousness in a web of law, to substitute personal law with a government law. In the attempt to deny the human drama, they deny human autonomy, the human capacity and duty of self-determination, which is the endowment that makes humans human.

The myth of Hector highlights the value of continuing to fight for what one believes is right, even when the battle appears lost. Hector, son of King Priam, was the most valiant Trojan warrior. In his conversation with his wife, Andromache, in the sixth chapter of Homer's *Iliad*, he admits that the war will be lost and he will be killed in battle, and the citizens of Troy who are not killed will be drawn into slavery, and Andromache will be among them. Still he keeps fighting to delay that fatal day. Any physician, and I hope that this includes the majority of us, who has fought to keep a seriously ill patient alive cannot help feeling an allegiance to Hector. These situations occur every day in emergency rooms and intensive care units and in overseas medical missions. In his book *When Diesel is Gone* my friend Alberto Reggiori, a surgeon from Milan who spent ten years in Uganda, narrates how he was compelled to operate in the dark when there was not enough diesel left to furnish electricity to the operating room. Should have there been a law that stopped him from operating in the dark, because without light he might have floundered? Should the same law have decreed the deaths of all people who needed urgent intervention or those whose operations had already started? The drama of Hector represents the drama of healers— physicians, nurses, psychologists and social workers around the world — who are dealing with limited resources and in doing so may indeed harm some patients. But the law aimed to prevent this harm would also prevent the good that these practitioners accomplish.

According to current regulation, a surgeon may be dismissed from the hospital staff if his or her peri-surgical mortality is too high. Perisurgical mortality is defined as mortality within thirty days from the intervention. This well intended regulation, which is aimed to protect patients from incompetent practitioners, may hurt patients in at least two ways. First it may discourage surgeons from performing high-risk operations that may be life-saving. Second, it may motivate surgeons to tether patients to breathing machines until the thirty days have passed—patients who naturally would have died a long time ago.

The human and economic cost of this practice is easy to estimate. Thanks to these regulations, Uncle Titti could easily get a $50,000 pacemaker that he didn't need, as this well paid intervention was all but without risk. In the meantime he was denied a potentially life-saving operation. After his bowel became perforated, he represented a very high surgical risk. The doctors portrayed their decision as a rejection of risky surgery in favor of the small chance that, with fluids and antibiotics, he would slowly mend. What the doctors really decided was that if Uncle Titti died on his own, nobody would blame them. However, if he died during or after surgery, his death would tarnish their surgical mortality record.

Likewise a physician who endured Katrina with her patients at New Orleans charity hospital and spent a sleepless week at their bedsides was threatened with a criminal trial because she might have hastened the death of some patients. Had she abandoned her patients and sought a safe haven from Katrina, as many other physicians had done, nobody would have blamed her. A medical practice contrary to her values would have left her medical reputation untarnished and prevented her criminal persecution! Again the drama of Hector is not limited to medicine. Think of spouses around the world who fight a daily battle to save their marriages and the health of their children; think of illegal immigrants who flood rich countries at the risk of their lives and of the charities that support this population, sometimes even in opposition to law.

The myth that best illustrates the issues of modern medicine, including its contradictions, is the biblical myth of Job. As it involves questions about human suffering, it may be the most comprehensive of all. The poem that graces the Bible was inspired by an ancient Middle Eastern legend that the anonymous author found appropriate to develop into an inquiry of God. Job was a wealthy and deeply religious man who lost his wealth, his children and his health through a series of accidents for which he bore no responsibility. According to the story it was the devil, then an angel of God, with the task of tempting human beings, that barraged him with grief, to demonstrate to God that Job's love for him was not sincere but was expedient, a ploy to preserve his own perks. Affected by a skin disease comparable to leprosy, this man who was once a civic leader was compelled to dwell outside the city, living on a mound of rubbish, looking for food in the garbage and scratching his skin with a fragment of a pot to get some relief. The same people who previously obsequiously bowed their heads and bent knees in his presence now ignored or sneered at him. But the worst torment of all was the conversation he was forced to carry on with three well meaning friends who insisted that his personal ruin was caused by some grievous sin and that he would be healed by God once he acknowledged his sin. Steadfastly

Job refused to heed their advice and called on God as testimony that there was no guile in him nor was there an understandable cause for his suffering. Eventually God appeared and condemned the three friends for speaking on His behalf and interpreting His will; at the same time He praised and compensated Job for his sincerity as well as his unwavering faith. The message of that Mesopotamian god that was adopted by the Hebrews as their own God could have not been clearer: Nobody is entitled to interpret God's will based on particular events; nobody is entitled to believe in an absolute truth that is good for everybody and allows one to judge in an objective fashion what is good and what is bad. Rather, the discovery of common good is an ongoing process that each generation receives from another and is based on the sharing of personal values. The mechanism through which personal values can be shared is called compassion.

The temptation to blame people for their own suffering is still pervasive more than three millennia after Job! In medicine it is reflected in two situations. The first is when a patient acquires a disease whose cause might have been avoided, such as smoking or sexual promiscuity. The second is where some evidence exists that prophylactic interventions may offer a life-saving benefit, including early treatment of hypertension or screening individuals for cancer even if they show no symptoms. In both circumstances blaming the victim reveals the fear of facing the mystery of human suffering by finding an explanation that may exempt oneself from the same destiny.

A self-righteous lack of compassion is just a mask we wear to conceal our living insecurity to ourselves. Every time we close our hearts to the pain of a fellow human we deny ourselves an opportunity to grow. Compassion is the sentiment that allows us to participate in other people's lives; it is the bridge of mutual communication. It is the expression of unconditional love that is also the only universal human language. Without compassion human interactions are only exploitive, with the goal of nurturing one's own lie instead of embracing the living truth through an expansion of our human experience.

This attitude also involves intellectual and scientific near-sightedness. You may remember how Ronald Reagan and his cronies in the religious right tried to prevent and curtail funds for AIDS research claiming that taxpayers should not be required to support the sinful behavior of homosexuals and drug addicts. (Rev. Jerry Falwell, founder of the Moral Majority, called AIDS a scourge that God employed to punish homosexuality and to purify the world from sin.) They conveniently closed their eyes to the fact that an increasing number of AIDS victims were recipients of blood and blood products, as well as innocent spouses and children. Were it not for a vocal homosexual advocacy movement leading to research and treatment, we would never have developed active drugs against the HIV virus, entire nations in Africa and South America would have succumbed to the epidemic, prominent scientists, artists and thinkers would have disappeared from this world before leaving their life-saving contribution to humanity — all courtesy of a new brand of Job's friends pretending again to speak in God's name.

Equally disturbing, however, is the claim that if you follow current prophylactic guidelines you can avoid deadly diseases such as breast cancer, stroke or heart attacks. More than once, I witnessed professional women between ages 30 and 40 who developed aggressive breast cancers after pregnancy. They had done everything right, they had followed all the screening guidelines and dietary recommendations, they had not gained too much weight during their pregnancies, they submitted to regular medical check-ups and still developed a lethal form of breast cancer. In addition to the pain of dying, of leaving their families and their newborns, guilt held them in thrall because they believed they had done something wrong, that their cancers and their untimely deaths were their fault. That is because advocacy groups have been so successful in claiming, with the best intentions, that death from breast cancer can and should be avoided.

Of course I am in favor of preventive medicine and in particular of cancer screening, knowing that screenings have prevented deaths from cervical, breast, colorectal and lung cancer. However valuable, these interventions are not panaceas. To believe that all diseases can be eradicated as long as we faithfully follow all current health-care recommendations is a lie that causes additional disconcertment and guilt in patients who already must deal with the finiteness of their lives and with personal losses. And this lie stems directly from the mother of all lies (which is also the most common modern human aspiration) that with behavior guided by our reason we can prevent any form of sufferings and disease, we can control the outcome of every human situations. This lie ignores two inconvenient truths. The first is that science is far from explaining and eliminating the causes of all diseases, and may never be able to do so. In fact the increased population longevity has been associated with epidemics of chronic and degenerative diseases , such as Alzheimer 's and other forms of dementia that were all but unknown in the past. At the meantime science is likely to contradict itself overtime. What physicians and scientists used to recite as scientific dogma has been proven as untruth as the fear that masturbation may cause one's hands to become hairy! Just few days ago we learned that moderate obesity is not a risk factor for either death or disease, after piling a mounting guilt on our eating habits over thirty years. Thanks to bad science we disdained poor people who arranged McDonald's birthday party for their little ones, we condemned ourselves to penitence every time we ate at the restaurant by counting how many days of life we were giving up because of the calories we chose to ingest, and we ostracized overweight people the same way we confined smokers to the modern equivalent of a leprosary. Before discovering that blood transfusions may be lethal to critically ill patients we used to pour blood on them freely (and quite often infection tainted commercial blood) explaining that we were improving the oxygenation of their tissues. And recently even the value of screening women for breast cancer with mammography has undergone a wave of criticism. I cannot think of any scientific dogma that has not been overturned during the 45 years since I graduated from medical school!

The second inconvenient truth is that rationality has very little to do with human behavior. I write these lines less than a month after the Newtown Conn slaughter of innocent children by a deranged youth, and very few people seem to agree on the only rational provision, supported by sound epidemiologic evidence, to outlaw the sale of assault weapon. Instead, through the mouth of its executive vice president, Wayne LaPierre, the National Rifle Association proposes to transform our elementary schools into correctional facilities. Likewise, I have not been able to have a single newspaper accepting my letter denouncing recreational sex as a cause of cancer as common as tobacco smoking. It is proven beyond doubt that the $HPV_1$ virus, transmitted through sexual intercourse, is the cause of cervical cancer (the most common cause of cancer death around the world), of anal cancer in male homosexuals, and of the majority of cancers of the head and neck area, at least in the USA.

The myth of Job encompasses all areas of life, as suffering is germane to the human condition. To blame the poor for poverty, divorcees for the disruption of their families, parents for the behavior of their children—all are attitudes inspired by the same motivation as the friends of Job. That is the conviction that we have absolute control of our destiny, that all forms of suffering could be avoided if everyone followed the rules. This pervasive lie prevents us from facing the only real truth about human suffering, that we cannot explain it.

A corollary of this truth is that compassion allows us to express our allegiance to other human beings, that our suffering bridges our private islands, allows us to share our common humanity and relieve our suffering by embracing the suffering of another. The Italian poet Giacomo Leopardi, who was not religious, had reached this conclusion in one of his last poems, "La Ginestra" ("The Broom"), also known as ("The Flower of the Desert") in which he derides the optimism of his contemporaries. The humble plant, ginestra, lives in desolate places without surrendering to harsh conditions, and in doing so it resembles the ideal man, who rejects any illusions about himself and does not ask heaven or nature for help that will never, in any event, come. Inspired by the enlightenment as well as by the industrial revolution, the men of the early 19th century were convinced that the application of rational principles to the conduct of life would stamp out suffering.

Christianity offered a solution to, albeit not an explanation for, human suffering. Christian belief holds that God Himself decided to partake of human suffering by becoming human in the person of the Christ. The human suffering of God allowed suffering humans to partake of the life of God through their very suffering. Suffering became a divine experience, the ultimate form of love. Equally important, the suffering of God allowed humanity to overcome its intimate contradictions through mutual forgiveness. The death of Christ was inspired by hatred for the truth that threatened the Jewish and Roman establishment of the time, in their power and even more in their dearly held convictions. For the Jews this consisted in considering themselves an elected people enjoying a privileged relationship with God. For the Romans and the classical world this consisted in considering themselves the ultimate arbiter of the world's destiny. Roman rule, like any other rule, was founded on power. In his poem the "Aeneid," Virgil crystallized the Roman mission in three verses. Aeneas, founder of the Roman Empire, meets his father, Anchises, during a visit to the netherworld. Anchises proclaims:

"Tu regere imperio populos Romane memento
Hae tibi erunt artes pacisque imponere mores
Parcere subiectis and debellare superbos"

That means, "Your Roman goal is to rule all people with power! These will be your special skills. You will have to impose peace by forgiving your subject and destroy those who resist you." Clearly a god who dies on a cross was a loser in this perspective. He could not be God!

God's death in Christ killed the very hatred that inspired his killing and that represented human hatred for the truth, for freedom to love and forgive each other. In Christian times, the person who hates has the opportunity to allow his or her hatred to be dead with the God that that very hatred had killed. In Christian times, Orestes would not have needed to avenge his father. Hatred for his mother and her lover would have died with Christ. Like a lightning rod, Christ attracted all the hatred of the world. By killing Christ, that hatred killed itself. The cross represented the final confrontation between hatred and love. Love prevailed because God (that is, universal truth) simply cannot be killed. In Christian times, the contradictions of Antigone would have dissipated as the law of love, leading her to bury her brother, would have prevailed and freed her from the guilt of defying governmental law. In Christian times, the fight of Hector would have been integrated in the universal fight for the survival of one's own humanity even at the price of one's own life.

But the modern world, the world emerged from the American and French revolutions, refused the Christian answer. Inspired by the philosophy of enlightenment, the world engaged in the search for a cause of and a final solution to human suffering, that is a search inspired by the mother of all lies. This attempt to kill human suffering has been nothing less than the attempt to kill the person. In valorizing suffering as an instrument of redemption, Chrisitanity recognized suffering as a special endowment of humanity. Suffering is the experience of being alive, as the experience of being alive hinges on feeling. And there cannot be feeling that does not lead to suffering. In the Movie "Ordinary People" the psychiatrist played by Judd Hirsch tells his young patient (Timothy Hutton): "Once you are able to experience pain, you will be free to experience all other emotions."

The hope that rules and regulations may dissipate the human drama is understandable because avoidance of discomfort is only too human. The idea that rules and regulations have resolved the human drama is delusional and expresses the same basic lie that we can recognize an objective truth , independent from the human mystery. Michael R Tobin, a student of Bernanos' theology called this process "disincarnation." That means the refusal to recognize truth as a living experience, the refusal to acknowledge that God, the ultimate truth, in the person of Christ, wore a human flesh, and in that way allowed every human being to experience the truth in his or her real flesh.

CHAPTER 21

# Faith

*An Antidote to Depression*

DEPRESSION WAS THE NEMESIS of my youth and early adulthood. It was the internal worm that led me to the threshold of suicide, to the threshold of divorce, to the inability to recognize and appreciate the gifts of love that others had given me, to recognize and revel in my own talents. And yet depression became, in a strange and wonderful way, a valuable asset in the practice of medicine because it enabled me to be compassionate with the dying.

One may ask whether the priests, Don Oreste and Father Serra, would have been as influential if my depression had been diagnosed and treated at the time. In other words, did they just provide supportive therapy for a mood disorder for which there is now specific medical treatment? These days, my mental state would have been diagnosed as depression (a diagnosis I, in fact, received much later) or even panic attacks and OCD (obsessive compulsive disorder). Now I know that depression had beset me since childhood and that the criticisms I had leveled at my parents might have been more a consequence of my emotional illness than of their personal shortcomings. Antidepressants and talk therapy have allowed me to survive and to thrive in my profession and my family life. At the same time I also believe that neither drugs nor talk therapy alone would have allowed me to receive the love that I craved.

My disease, my upbringing or both had made me, by my late teen years, an unpleasant human being, only too capable of destructive behavior. Though she had meant it in a different way, my first long-term girlfriend had hit the nail on the head in calling me a worm. Like a worm, I had spent my life undermining what other people had built for their own enjoyment. I am sorry to say I did experience schadenfreude, did thrive in others' failures. A banal episode may highlight my attitude of those days.

In summer 1961 I had joined a rock-climbing school, one of the many enterprises where I tried to generate self-respect by pushing myself completely out of my comfort zone. My own self dislike induced me to feel that only by becoming something I was not could I be adjudged respected, lovable and valuable. One day a rope-friction burn prevented me from participating in further exercises. An hour later, as I was nursing my wounds, another young man had the same accident. My exultation exploded uncontained: "Let's have a beer together. Let's rejoice that both of us have suffered the same fate." This insensitive comment occurred after people had been wondering what in the heck I was doing there. I had a fear of heights, and along with my clumsy technique I could not have been more out of place. In fact I had been a burden because to rescue me more than once, everyone else's lessons had to be delayed or aborted. Together with driving school, rock climbing was the only school I ever failed. "You definitely have been the worst of all my pupils!" the instructor said scornfully as he denied me my certificate. So when I rejoiced in the fact that somebody else had experienced an accident and injury, nobody said a word, but everybody looked at me with unmistakable pity and contempt. Like the subjects of the Southwest Airlines commercial, I would have done anything to get away! Nobody talked to me after that incident. The last day of the course as I was walking toward the railway station I caught up with a young woman, also a member of the course, and tagged along with her. She acknowledged my friendly greeting with a furtive look. Though we walked side by side for two hours, she did not exchange a word with me. I enjoyed so little credibility in those days that few people paid attention to me or what I had to say. I was perceived as a nuisance—a gnat or a mosquito. When given a choice the majority of my peers would avoid me.

I have found it crucial to unearth these painful memories to highlight the discovery of the three pillars of my Christian faith: redemption, sacrifice and love in the form of agape.

Of course my emotional conflicts did not lend themselves to a peaceful exit from the family home. My allegiance to my mother impelled me to disown a grandmother I still loved and a father who was at this point doing his best to gain my affections. Because of her status as "victim" in a scenario of bullying, abandoning my mother would have represented the supreme form of injustice in my eyes.

My feelings from this time make me think of Aeschylus' *Oresteia*, a trilogy of Greek tragedies. Orestes, the unhappy son, must choose between two acts of impiety: to leave his father's death unavenged or to kill his adulterous, murderous mother.

On this disagreeable human being whom nobody cared to befriend Don Oreste and Father Serra bestowed the love of God; that is, the love in the form of agape—unconditional love that springs from the unconditional faith that each and every person is sacred, has a unique mission and a unique worth. They knew that the grace and the love of God should not be rationed but given freely and completely where it is needed. They knew what some in the medical profession struggle with today—that you are not entitled to deny life-saving care to an older patient so that you can deploy the money you save to relieve famine in developing countries. No medications but only unconditional love could have eased my existential pain.

My initial idea, to escape from the situation to America, had not been a solution at all. "Why have you sought refuge in America?" my father wrote me in one of his last letters with late insight before dementia veiled his mind. I know now it was a way to ask for forgiveness, and I wished I had been able to answer by then. But at that point in my spiritual development I was not ready to forgive.

My marriage had provided an opportunity to abuse my father-in-law, in whom I saw the incarnation of the almightiness of the Italian man. For example, I felt that we should visit his estranged spouse in Germany prior to our marriage. Though this action was appropriate both as a form of respect to my future mother-in-law and a statement of our independence, I cannot deny that one of my goals was to punish my father-in-law, getting in a jab at my own father at the same time. Likewise I demanded that all relatives (except my parents, my sister, and my wife's father) be excluded from the wedding. The public reason was a form of respect for my wife's mother, who refused to attend because she was scared to come to Italy, as according to the Italian law she could have been jailed for having abandoned her family. But I cannot deny that I rejoiced in excluding my wife's grandmother and punishing by proxy my own grandmother.

In solidarity I adopted some of my mother's prejudices, including a suspicion of southern Italians, who had a tendency to be freeloaders in her view. This view is still common in Northern Italy and it has been enshrined in a powerful political party, the Lega Lombarda, in the last thirty years. Lega in Italian means alliance. The original Lega Lombarda represented an alliance of the major towns of the Lombardia region to defeat the emperor Federico Barbarossa more than a thousand years ago. The goal of the present "Lega" is to divide Italy into Northern and a Southern regions independent from each other to free the productive north from the burden of supporting the unproductive south.

During my tenure as medical officer the year before we moved to the States, out of my prejudice and dislike I administered a serious penalty to a soldier from the south who told me to fuck myself because I refused him a note for a day off from work. He had asked for a day of rest because of back pain, but I told him he was a lazy bastard and better go back to work at once. As a result of my punishment he was transferred even farther from his family in one of the northernmost and coldest military garrisons of Italy. In retrospect, I can see that he was only trying his best to survive the unseemly conditions of the Italian army, where the sons of privilege could avoid all burdensome duties and those without a protector saint are repeatedly asked to perform the work of everybody else (and in wartime they were asked to die for everybody else). I did not like him: I provoked him with my injurious remark and I was only too happy and proud to unleash on him the strength of my prejudices.

Coming to Mississippi I immediately adopted the local prejudice against black people simply because in my fantasy they were similar to southern Italians. I annoyed all of our European acquaintances in the States by offering descriptions of Europe as a decadent country inhabited by lazy and unworthy people liable to soon become subjects of the Soviet empire. I still don't know how my wife tolerated me during those years; I have a hard time tolerating even the memory of myself. Certainly, if Claudia had left me, I don't think I would have been able to sort out, much less escape, this prison of anger, an anger that had gained a life of its own!

After years of exploring my personal history in light of the Christian revelation that occurred later I realized that my family situation was not as hopeless as Orestes' quandary. Our family might have been *Le Noed de Viperes*, or knot of snakes, described by Francois Mauriac in a well known romance novel of the same title, but faith in God would surely have loosened the knot. My family was sick from a lack of faith in God, the same way a diabetic patient develops a coma in the absence of insulin. We all had suffered from a deficiency of faith.

Faith would have stated and illumed the sacredness of each member of the family. As I mentioned earlier, sacredness derives from "sacrum," which means "hallowed" or "reserved for a special function" that only that person can perform. The awareness that every human being is sacred in the design of God is the basis of the human rights enshrined in the U.S. Constitution and defended by the American Civil Liberties Union (ACLU). Short of sacredness, humans are as disposable as lobsters in a tank.

The awareness of being sacred would have allowed my mother to face and confront the abuse to which she was subjected. Out of fear, neither she nor anybody else could face the eight-hundred pound gorilla in the room. For my mother it was the fear of dissolving the family, accepting the fact that for once she had not been able to live up to her duty, to create disillusionment and disappointment in her parents, who could not even conceive of a broken marriage. For my father it was the fear of losing his little dominion, the pedestal from which he felt it necessary to address the world; he would have had to face the fact that his exceptional school successes did not grant him a free ride, that he still had to work during his lifetime to earn the affection and respect of his wife and children. Without the front of a stable family, his life would have crumbled; he would have found himself alone and without resources, like as the main character in Pier Paolo Pasolini's movie *Teorema*. In this movie the life of a successful businessman from Milan is destabilized by the visit of a mysterious "foreign guest." At the end of the film this gentleman finds himself without family, without resources and without convictions.

For me and my sister it was the fear of losing the support of our family, of finding ourselves left alone to fend for ourselves in a hostile world for which we were totally unprepared. It was also the fear of losing a semblance of love that from the outside looked similar to that experienced by the majority of our friends and schoolmates, that allowed us to look with disdain on the gypsy children roaming our community looking for the opportunity of small thefts when charity fell short.

The common source of this fear, and I believe of any fear that supports a self-propagating network of lies, was the absence of the sense of one's sacredness, of one's mission. Without the certainty of having been endowed by God with a unique function that only we can accomplish, we are left to defend our own uncertainty in the self-defeating process called "co-dependency." People choose the means of combat with which they are most comfortable. A spoiled brat like my father will try to bully everybody into obeying his caprices, as he had learned to do since boyhood; a woman like my mother, who had been conditioned to disregard her own feelings, would try to find a rational solution to every situation. A proletariat like my grandmother, accustomed to being deprived of a voice in the decisional world, would proclaim her rights and try to obtain whatever beneficence she could from a world that had skirted her and the likes of her. Though the bullies appear to have the upper hand, in reality everybody is a loser. The desperate solitude in which my father spent his last years (ignored by the people who did not fear him anymore but still were unable to love him) is a tragic demonstration of the ultimate failure of bullying.

Faith in God would have provided the strength to fight the good battle, in addition to providing the strength to face one's problem. The awareness of her own sacredness would have broken the cycle of dependence that subjected my mother to my father's abuse. It would have allowed her to stand up not just for her own self, something she felt incapable of doing on account of her upbringing, but for the law of God, which does not allow any of his or her creatures to be disdained. "God does not create garbage," was the motto of a "marriage encounter" session that Claudia and I attended more than thirty years ago. The fight for our own dignity can be successful only when dignity is engrafted in one's sacredness; that is, on the defense of the role God has established for each one of us. Then the fight becomes a "sacrifice," from *sacrum facere*, to render sacred, reserved, unique. The pain of the fight is the pain of giving birth, to deliver a creature of God. Armed with faith my mother would not have feared her parents' disownment or the town's rejection or her domestic life's disarray, because she would have been fighting for the assertion of God's will. The pain that she would have generated in her own parents, in my father, in my grandmother, in her friends, would have been the pain of the surgery that restores health by draining a life-threatening abscess, rather than the pain of the abscess that spreads and poisons the whole body. A fecund pain that restores health. Not the pain of silent hostility that looks for all occasions to undermine the enemy, that sees the enemy in another person instead of seeing it as a fellow prisoner of the forces of evil that poison our living environment.

Faith in God, the awareness of sacredness, would have also allowed my mother to be more tolerant of everybody else's shortcomings. Faith would have allowed her to recognize that my and my sister's inclinations were the prints of God that made us sacred, reserved to the use and purpose He and She had established for us. My passion for literature, poetry and philosophy should have been nurtured as flowers in God's garden, rather than disregarded in a vain attempt to grow other flowers (math and science) that could never establish solid roots.

Faith in God would have also armed me to stand up for myself, for my mother's dignity, for peace in our family. Faith would have shown me that everybody in my family was a patient in need of a physician, that I did not need to take any hostile action toward my father or my grandmother, that I could fight them without suppressing my love for them, because my fight aimed to cure them of their diseases. Faith would have prevented me from becoming a "reverse Orestes" charged with the killing of his father in order to avenge his mother.

I have been able to find a purpose to my life, a reason to keep living, through the testimony of people who proved credible to me. They became credible by providing the love I had craved, and because of that love they had faith in me and my future. Their love and their faith enabled my faith in myself. When I think of an act of faith that turned my life around I cannot help but remembering an episode that occurred in the early '80s when I was a new faculty member at the University of Mississippi Medical Center. A young medical student, a small young woman with a seeming Napoleon complex, told me: "Dr. Balducci, I really have a hard time believing that I can learn anything from you or any other teacher! My time would be better spent by reading the book and probing my knowledge of the patient without any intermediary. I really have a hard time believing that there is a situation in this world over which I have no full control!" And she said it with a straight face!

Some people like to believe that they may choose their faith (or the denial of any faith, which is in itself a form of faith) as one chooses a present from a Saks Fifth Avenue catalogue. They believe that they possess all the means and time to make "an informed choice." While I don't argue with this approach, my experience has been different. In my struggles, I felt like a man on the edge of drowning in a tempestuous sea who was offered a reliable lifesaver after many futile attempts to float. In my experience life is an ongoing emergency with too little time for picking and choosing our destinies, especially when one realizes that each minute of our lives could be our last.

One may ask what I came to believe with my act of embracing faith. Even if I adhered to Don Oreste's and Father Serra's faith as a lifesaver, I can't say that I knew much of their faith beside the fact that I knew it was good for me. Nor can I say that I would have blindly embraced the whole gamut of their beliefs. For example, my recollection is that both priests thought that the death penalty may be justified in extreme circumstances, a position I cannot possibly share.

So what did I really come to believe?

The core of my beliefs includes the possibility of redeeming the world through sacrifice supported by love. Redemption and sacrifice are made possible by the historical intervention of God in our lives. By engrafting their sacrifices on God's own sacrifice, humans become God's partners in an ongoing work of redemption.

At the beginning of my faith journey, my only firm belief was that Jesus loved me and that his love made me worthy of living and would free me from the predicaments in which I found myself. I did not know how to save my marriage to Claudia, I did not know how to make peace with my father, I did not know how to raise my newborn child once Claudia and I had started a family, and I did not yet know how to bring empathy to the job of ministering to my patients' suffering. All I firmly believed was that I could pray and that my prayer would be well received because Jesus loved me—and that this love would provide, as the Bible says, "a very present help in trouble." Once I had prayed, the ball was in Jesus's court. That is all I understood as I began my journey. I did not yet understand that prayer was the venue through which Jesus would show me how to address these issues, how to share his love.

CHAPTER 22

# Making Peace with Claudia

DURING OUR WEDDING CEREMONY Father Serra referred to the "*amor que devora*," noting that marriage means to consume each other in love. Only years later did I discover the full meaning of his words, when I discovered agape, the source of the full sacrifice of oneself.

In my relationship with Claudia I started appreciating the meaning of sacrifice. I had to get out of the comfort of my niche, as well as my routines, and engage in a number of confrontations, such as the confrontation that occurred with her father over our visit, shortly before our marriage, with her mother. I did give her part of myself. Still I expected a number of perks from my marriage, which included sex at will, appreciation of my achievements, and mostly creation of a family life where we could preempt each other's desires. I was looking for harmony, for the peace I had not found in my original family, where I learned that conflict was only and always a source of division and separateness. I could not conceive of conflict as something positive, as a surgical intervention of sorts that eliminates tumors and infections in the body of one's marriage, conflict like fire that burns unnecessary fences and allows a more perfect union.

Paradoxically, the silhouette of agape began to emerge when my ideal marriage was on the edge of collapse. When Claudia let me know that she did not like what she had discovered of me, I experienced déjà vu. I had gone through this in all my previous relationships, especially the longest one. She had discovered a self-centered man, preoccupied only with satisfying his immediate impulses without regard to anyone else's feelings, hidden behind a façade of professional competence, social commitment and open mindedness (the same crimes I had imputed to my father, ironically enough). She saw through me: Rather than coming to America for the noble goal of learning a more effective way to practice medicine and serve my fellow men, I had come for a confused knot of poorly defined reasons. These included the motivation to escape from myself, establish myself on my own, gain my mother's praise, etc. She felt used as an instrument to pursue my hidden goals, which were not her goals, especially once they had been divested of their cover and appeared for what they were—the confused efforts of an adolescent to punish and satisfy his mother at the same time.

To help me in this selfish and impossible endeavor, she had left family and friends, and she found herself lonelier than ever in a foreign country. If this circumstance were not enough, I also spoiled our short vacations by imposing on her, forcing her to spend time with my rowdy family. Eight people were cramped in a three-bedroom apartment with a single bathroom, with no privacy and no breathing room. And she had come to abhor our sexual relationship, as much as she had been keen to engage in it at the beginning of our marriage, as she was searching for a confirmation that I loved her. Whether I was trying to draw from her some solitary pleasure or to prove my manhood—whatever was in my heart, she felt used and abused. She felt that I was trying to couple with her simply because she was there, that I could have had the same relations with any other woman, that there was nothing special, nothing sacred, in our union.

My first reaction was one of desperation. I had failed one more time, I told myself. I had accumulated one more rejection; I had lost my last chance. My life was a route to dissolution where every single milestone was a rejection. I became obsessed with the verses of one of Giacomo Leopardi's best known poems, "L'ultimo canto di Saffo," or "Saffo's Last Song." "*Virtu' non luce in disadorno ammanto.*" "Human virtues are not allowed to shine when they are packed in a body that is repulsive," states the unhappy poetess as a testament just before throwing herself from a rock into the sea. Was I, too, condemned to live without love because any woman would find my demeanor if not my body repulsive?

The worst temptation was to go back and live a perpetual lie, as I had done with my parents, as I had done in all previous relationships, as I had learned to do in my profession. I had hoped that my marriage would allow me to be myself. Yet the truth that Claudia had unmasked about me, that I was no more than a confused adolescent whose goal in life was to humor and punish his mother at the same time, turned out to be too painful to bear. After a number of relationships, a marriage, a son, an M.D. degree, mastery of three medical specialties and publication of more than a hundred scientific papers, I was not different from the image of myself I disliked most. At 15 I walked home one night with my high school teacher from a representation of a *cinema 'd' essai* ( I still remember it was the golden age of Charlie Chaplin). He ignored me for a while as I was trying to start a conversation. Eventually he turned toward me, looked me in the eyes and told me: "If you were not your parents' son I would have dismissed you from my class a long time ago. You never overgrew your adolescence, and everybody in your class despises you for that," and he walked away, lightened of a burden he had carried for almost two years! I was still there alone, in that dark corner of my old home town, abandoned and disdained by everybody. I even started wondering whether the truth existed at all. Maybe lies were the only way of life, as I had taught my medical student. I knew how to live with lies: I knew how to charm professors and patients into believing that I was a great doctor; I knew how to entertain a social conversation exalting the same family values I was planning to desert; I knew how to obtain a transient relationship with another person anxious for some relief from her own loneliness, anxious for soothing lies; I even would have been able to live side by side with Claudia, two perfect strangers who celebrated the main holidays together. One thing I had learned in my adolescence was to live with ambiguity and tensions. I knew how to negotiate a minefield; I could sit comfortably on a time bomb. What I could not stand was the emptiness of facing truth.

Fortunately our working commitments compelled us to live together for some time despite mutual hostility and failure to comprehend each other. These practical constrictions provided the time to settle our emotions down and to discover our own freedom to love each other, to discover agape as the original and final form of love. A common American tenet is that any type of bondage is intrinsically evil as it prevents one from pursuing his or her aspirations. I learned that the contrary may be true. There is bondage that keeps us from hurting ourselves in times of crises. This type of restraint protects rather than impedes our freedom. Homer described these freeing restraints in *The Odyssey*. On his trip back home from the Trojan War, Ulysses happened to sail close to the mermaids' island. These charming creatures were known for the irresistible sweetness of their songs, which lured sailors to come too close to their island and shipwreck. To be able to enjoy the siren songs without risking the ship and his and his crew's lives, Ulysses deafened his men by putting wax in their ears and asked to be tied to the mast. He also ordered that they tighten the ropes that restrained him any time he gestured to be freed. Like Ulysses' bonds, the bonds that prevented Claudia and me from leaving each other when problems looked insurmountable kept our marriage from wrecking.

As anger and the desperation settled down, I was able to realize three unique aspects of my relationship with Claudia.

First and foremost our relationship has been cemented by some startling, mutual experiences during which we saw in each other the view that Peter, James and John had of Jesus on Mount Tabor. On more than one occasion we had "transfigured" in front of each other; we had seen each other for what we were meant to be. The first of these experiences occurred on the snowfields of Abruzzo's mountains, one year before we formalized our declarations of love.

At that time Claudia, out of love, had compelled me to overcome my hesitations and ski down a challenging slope I had considered way too hard. In that simple situation two important sentiments emerged: love, in the form of *filia*, personal care, and trust. I had recognized her capacity to love, and I felt as capable of love as she was, as if her love were contagious ("*amor che a nullo amato amar perdona,*" says Dante of Francesca da Rimini, a character in the *Divine Comedy*, which means love that compels a loved one to reciprocate that love), and I felt for the first time I could trust somebody else fully. I had discovered two inseparable feelings: love and trust.

Many other experiences like this followed, including our trip to Germany to visit her mother despite her father's opposition and wrath. In that situation we discovered the force of the couple, the independent life of a couple. Being a couple was much more than mixing two wills. It was a will to be together that enabled us to reach goals that separately we would have been unable to meet, because as a couple we had gained a new sets of rights and priorities that transcended each other's individual rights and priorities. I had no reason to visit her mother alone, and she had no reason to visit her mother at that particular time. Together we had to do it, first because her mother represented one of our assets, second because we had to state our independence as a couple. There were some things that as a couple we had to do, and no external influence could prevent us from doing without destroying the couple. Being a couple meant creating a new self that overcame the doubts and the hesitations of each previous self. Being a couple meant to be free to be each other.

There were other occasions, for instance the discovery of each other's intimacy, especially my rediscovery (or first discovery) of true, love-based sex, as my wife encouraged me to be myself, to relax, not to try to perform in the bedroom like an actor or a sports star. For once I did not have to be the first in my class; even better, I discovered that I could always have been the first in my class of one by being myself.

I also vividly remember our brief sojourn in rural Italy where I worked as a primary care physician to raise money to go to the States. There we fully appreciated the joy of being with each other. I will never forget the tears Claudia shed, which I saw from train windows as she left for a few days for Rome to take her medical license exam. Any separation felt like cutting out a part of ourselves.

And how could I possibly forget Claudia's visits to Florence where I spent three months in military school? I started pining for her early Sunday morning. While the other guests of my comrades (there were twelve of us in each room) snored, grumbled, cussed and farted, I wandered away in thoughts that were visions, oblivious of the cacophony expressing the anger of eleven young men, imprisoned in mandatory military service. I felt as if transported to heaven as happened to Paul or Mohammed during prayers. My vision anticipated the time I would get the first hint of her long fair hair, her deep blue eyes with a unique little squint, through the barred window of the barracks waiting hall. On those Sundays together we visited our favored Italian town that came alive to greet and welcome and support our love. The old street, the magnificent palaces, the majestic churches, the frescos of Giotto and Masaccio, the statues of Michelangelo, the ancient shops of the jewelers on Ponte Vecchio became old and trusted friends singing over and over the same soothing song: "We are so glad you have found each other; your love transcends time as much as the masterpiece we represent; welcome to the world of love!" As with Cinderella, the pumpkin had become a rich coach, the mice purebred horses. I did treasure those few hours of freedom the way one tastes a precious old wine whose flavor persists among a person's living experiences years after the last drop has evaporated from the surface of taste buds! That precious taste, that spice of life on which I had learned to count as one of my resources, was bound to Claudia's presence. It would have been lost forever if our marriage had dissolved.

The truth is that together we had laid the foundation of a relationship, and the foundation was still there, solid and imposing, even if we did not like the building that had grown up over it. That foundation was a shared treasure worth the effort to tear down the old edifice and fabricate a new one. That foundation was also a warning. Would we have ever been able to ignore those moments so deeply imprinted in us and to start from scratch? Would it have been possible to see another transfiguration with a different person, or would we have just pursued each other in different bodies?

Second, we had a child. We had conceived him at a time of mutual comfort, though not as a precise choice. Neither of us had had this experience before; neither of us had known what it meant to be a parent; neither of us wanted to relinquish the responsibility of raising that child. That was also a *traite d'union* that we did not want to renounce. In choosing to stay together, did we succumb to guilt? Of course we did, and I am happy we did. We felt guilty about the potential damage to our child if we were to dissolve our marriage. This guilt preserved for us the joy of raising that child together, of watching the product of our love growing and expanding his ability to love, of one day allowing his children to sleep between us in our king-sized bed. Contrary to common psychological wisdom I discovered then that guilt may be as liberating as the restraints that kept Ulysses tied to the mast of his ship when sailing close to the sirens.

I don't think there is a more ridiculous statement than "the children are all right," and I praise the movie of this title that unmasked the fallacy of the simplistic and untrue statement, "If the parents are not happy, the children cannot be happy." Everybody would agree that each one of us should strive to be happy, but happiness is a volatile concept. In choosing to raise our child together, we traded the relief of a moment of oblivion in the arms of a different partner for the excitement of seeing a new life taking form, of helping this new life to identify his role and mission in this world. I believe we traded a delusion of happiness for an experience of happiness taking form slowly and through our fair share of pain and anguish.

The third consideration is that by this time I had found some type of faith. I had learned to trust Christ. I knew that our wedding had been blessed by Christ and as such deserved to be maintained even in the moment of darkness when we could not identify the sense of living together. Though I could not understand them, I knew that Christ had plans for us. To renounce those plans would have meant renouncing my faith.

At last I had discovered that love cannot be renounced like used clothing. I had learned that if we had renounced our love, we would have generated wounds that could not heal (both in ourselves and in others). I came to realize that our love had a meaning that transcended us. In short, I had discovered the nature of agape, of unconditional love.

The young colleague in medical school, the angel who cut her wings as she thought she had discovered that love cannot be imposed and abandoned herself to a rosary of joyless affairs to prove the point was wrong! And I was wrong in echoing her message. We can and must impose upon ourselves to love another person. This happens once we carry within ourselves a whole vision of that person. The special moments I had lived with Claudia on the ski slopes and during our German trips, during our residence in rural Italy and on so many other occasions, were more than photographs in a memory book. They were the proof that I could love and be loved, that I could trust somebody and be trusted. They were the hinge on which my whole life turned. More important, they were the clues to how to look at any other person, to identify the uniqueness, the sacredness of each person, to learn that each and every person represents a unique spark in the firmament in which I myself was supposed to shine. To ignore that person's spark was to disregard my own neighborhood, to treat my permanent residence as an anonymous rented room; that is, to ignore myself. To belittle or to hate that spark was tantamount to belittling or hating the place I was assigned to live, to belittle and to hate myself.

I will never know another person as deeply as I have learned to know Claudia, but my relation to Claudia inspires my way of looking at any new person I meet. I know that each person can be transfigured as Jesus on Mount Tabor, as Claudia and I had been in those special moments that remain the fundaments of our union and of our marriage. Because of this transfiguration in which each person appears as what God has meant for that person to be, each person may be an object of agape.

Finally, twenty-five years later, I had finally understood what Don Oreste and Father Serra had seen in me. When one has been touched by another life the way Claudia had touched me, one has a choice. The first is to live the rest of his or her life in the pursuance of those moments, the way a mountain climber tries to ascend ever-higher and more challenging mountaintops in pursuit of an always purer vision of the sky, no matter how much effort it costs. The second is to give up the search for a more limpid sky either because it costs too much effort or because we are temporarily blinded by the sunlight.

## CHAPTER 23

# An Exploration of Agape

"I DID NOT LIKE the way you looked the day of your first communion," one of my devout aunts told me. "You did not seem particularly happy to receive Jesus." And she could not have been more right, though she did not understand that the apparent coldness of a 9-year-old boy concealed a life-and-death drama. I had been told that my first communion would represent a special day, a form of intercourse with God that I should love more than my parents, my friends, my whole life. I was gravely distressed because I had not been able to muster any feelings toward that wafer, which I had done my best not to touch with my teeth, beyond feelings of suspicion, uneasiness and deception. And I was more interested in attracting the interest of the little girl in a white dress who knelt in front of me than in finding comfort in the food of the soul I had just been fed. I also envied those friends of mine whose first communion would be celebrated with an open house for friends instead of the modest meal my mother had organized for the closest family members.

In 1966 I rationalized my definitive rupture with the Christian faith because I thought that I was unable to love. My crystal clear rationale was a repetition of what my colleague who had deserted her faith had told me a couple of years earlier. Christian faith was based on the loving adhesion to the person of Christ. As I was not able to love, I could not love Christ and consequently I could not possibly have faith. The only way I could return to my faith would have been by learning how to love.

Unfortunately this type of reasoning was very popular at those times. Despite my general lack of credibility with my peers, I helped entice at least three women to abandon the religious life on the grounds that we could not have faith because faith was based on love and we were unable to love.

My rational process was correct and deceitful as is any rational process divorced from life experience. The premise, that we were unable to love, could not have been more wrong and was founded on self despisement or self hatred, on the feeling that we were disposable, cheap, that we had nothing to give. The origins of this sentiment were to be found in a culture that has enshrined reason as the source of all certainty and has rejected any form of immediate certainty, including the certainty of the self. Many people may find it paradoxical, but the father of modern thought, Descartes, had spent a lifetime trying to demonstrate that he did exist. In other words, this culture has discarded human mystery, the self evidence of one's living experience. In proof of its inanity, a self-centered culture had become self-centered by disregarding the self!

The logical trap in which I and other members of my generation had been caught was inescapable because it was so inescapably logical to the point of becoming absurd. We could not be ourselves because we were unable to love, but we could not love because we could not be ourselves. I still remember the desperate tears of one of those young women who had left the cloister, full of sorrow because she had concluded that her faith was an imaginary construction in the absence of love. "Let me go," she pleaded as I was holding her in my arms trying to convince her to spend the night with me: "I cannot love anybody!" As I saw the light of her car waning in the dark as she left me, I prayed that she would not take her life. I prayed though I claimed not to believe in God.

What I and others of my generation did not realize at that time was that our feeling of discomfort with ourselves, our attempt to define who we were, was indeed a form of love, was the statement of our selves trying to break out of the logical prison where we had confined them. It was not love Hollywood style, where a couple lives satisfied forever after encountering a perfect match, nor was it the love that inspired some saints to destroy themselves for the love of God, according to some current forms of lives-of-the-saints stories. What the devil, in its infinite capacity for deception, had done was to deprive us of any reference of love in our family, in our society, even in our churches.

The associate pastor of our church kept proclaiming that our faith was a "rational faith," that it was faith in the revelation of reason. Reason, not divine revelation, told us that God existed, that God was infinitely good, and that our souls were immortal. Sadly many Christians whom I love and respect consider Thomas Aquinas's five proofs of God's existence as objective support of their faith. It is very dangerous to commit our faith to an act of reason that may be contradicted, as any act of reason can. What cannot be contradicted, I discovered later, is the revelation of the self as endowed with the dignity that comes from a unique call and that claims individual immortality. Our culture had robbed of all dignity the sacrifice, the action of making himself or herself "sacred," or reserved for a special function, which is the essence of agape.

In fact, in my family derision was a common reaction to news of somebody's sacrifice. My father and to some extent even my mother made fun of the effort that my aunts (my mother's sisters) made to reach their schools in the mountains or to conduct a simple life deprived of most of modern amenities. A close friend of mine and I would make fun of anybody who would propose any form of sacrifice as an expression of love. Examples may include a person who renounced an academic career to spend more time with his or her family, or a man and a woman who had decided not to violate each other's intimacy prior to marriage. We considered that person a wimp, somebody unable to fend for him or herself.

A modern writer says if Jesus had lived during our time, the Sadducees would not have crucified him. They would have invited him to dinner and made fun of him. I saw this happen on more than one occasion. At parties I heard prominent scientists, writers and politicians proclaim, between drinks, "Jesus Christ was a lunatic, a schizophrenic, a mad man," to everybody's amusement. In a novel many critics consider one of the greatest of the 20th century, *The Master and Margarita*, Mikhail Bulgakov describes Christ as a peasant, a wandering teacher able to seduce only simple-minded people. In *The Gospel According to Jesus Christ,* the Nobel Prize-winning Portuguese author Jose Saramago sees in Jesus a religious boy who is lured to crucifixion by a capricious and extravagant deity that ultimately makes fun of him.

I remember my bitterness when a young woman, a very religious student nurse, gave me a gift I was not ready to receive. She had a particular affection for me and hoped that I could reciprocate her feelings. She confessed that she had given up dinner one day a week to be able to buy me a Christmas present. Why did I react with bitterness? The present was more than just a material gift; it was something of herself that I was not ready to accept and I did not know how to refuse. I could not see the connection of love and sacrifice, and her gift revealed to me the nature of love, which I was not ready to acknowledge. If I had heard of this happening to somebody else, I probably would have made fun of the girl with my friends. I might even have gone one step further, indulging in insensitive male banter by saying, "She is ready for you to ask for her pussy." By making me the recipient of a sacrifice, she had exposed me to a world I did not know; she preempted any sarcastic remark I might have made; she communicated that I had a value I was unable to recognize in myself—that I was worthy of receiving a gift based on who I was, irrespective of how much or how little I had accomplished.

Love as agape, the unconditional love that everybody wishes to receive (the love that sees in the self and in any other human person what God has seen in that person; what Peter, James and John saw in Jesus on Mount Tabor) is then the motivation of redemption that is achieved through the sacrifice of each person; that is, when each person becomes aware of and fully dedicated to his or her mission. In his novel *O Diario de um Mago* (*The Pilgrimage*) Brazilian writer Paulo Coelho provides a powerful description of agape as the force behind the main character's search for his sword along the route that leads from the French border to the sanctuary of Santiago de Compostela. Indeed, the sword represents the redemption of the protagonist and the people around him. Coelho calls agape "o amor que devora" or "the love that eats somebody up."

Avoiding agape, some seek oblivion. But the only way we can reach this degree of oblivion is through addiction to work, to sex, to politics, to power, to drugs. Though oblivion through addiction may sound like a free rational choice, it is a devastating one; it is the choice that brings us back to the drawing board of psychology and makes us ask: Whose problem is this? As if every problem we met were not our problem; as if every life we touched were not also our life. It is the choice between the freedom to discover the world in our neighborhood, or to make our neighborhood out of the world; that is, to walk throughout the world wearing blinders that allow us to see only what we want to see, the construction of the world with which we feel comfortable, like the former slave who could not become accustomed to his newfound freedom in the Chekhov play *The Cherry Orchard*.

So agape is unconditional love because it is a voluntary love whose determination to love is born out of the determination to save and invest the assets we have accumulated in our lives. Included in agape is the intimate joy of being responsible for other people, to discover our own sacredness as we help the people around us to discover theirs. Agape is the joyful soul of our redemption endeavor.

Two questions arise concerning agape: Is religious faith necessary to the practice of agape? Can you love the people you don't like?

I don't have an answer to the first question. I can say only that for me faith was instrumental to the discovery of agape, and I cannot see how somebody can discover agape without discovering God at the same time. How can you profess unconditional love without believing in unconditional love? How can you believe in human sacredness without believing in a God that assigns each person a unique role? How can you overcome hatred for the people who hurt you without believing that these individuals were assigned a special role in your life? Having said that, I must admit that I have known people who lived agape without having a precise vision of God. These include Claudia, who has practiced agape more assertively than I ever did, though she maintains more doubts than I do about God's existence and will. In his Nobel Prize-winning novel *The Plague,* Albert Camus describes the character of Dr. Bernard Rieux, a physician who wishes to practice love toward the whole community but is unable to believe in any god.

The answer to the second question is much simpler. In my life there have been plenty of people I don't like, including the arrogant woman who preached to me and my colleagues about our bureaucratic duties in the conduct of clinical research. (And any individuals who make a living by impeding other people's work, including three nerds with prideful smiles who showed up on the front page of Time magazine few years ago. They were proud to have stopped the life-saving research going on at Duke University, at the cost of hundreds of millions of dollars, because of a deadline violation — the investigator reports had not reached the funding agency in due time. As ministers of a bureaucratic god they were proud to make human sacrifices to their regulatory deity.) Add to these virtually anybody reminding me of somebody who hurt me or incarnating an idea that I despise.

Though I cannot and I should not erase my feelings about these individuals, I may still comprehend them in agape. First because I must humbly recognize that none of us has a monopoly on truth and that they are here to defend important values such as patients' autonomy that otherwise may be disregarded. It is through ongoing confrontation that we may reach an equilibrium through which we can respect individual freedom without compromising the conduct of life-saving research. The second and more general reason is the one articulated by M. Scott Peck in his book *The Different Drum: Community Making and Peace.* Peck points out that people we don't like represent an important reference point for the building of a society more congruent with our beliefs and aspirations. One of my high school mates said, "My fortune has been that my father had died when I was very young. This allowed me the freedom to be myself!" Though I feigned a disconcerted and scandalized reaction to this statement, as I had deemed it inappropriate, in my heart of hearts I could not have agreed more. How many times had I fantasized about the disappearance of this burdensome presence that expected to be the magnet of all attention and kept the whole family enslaved to his will and walking on eggshells so as not to disturb his peace! Almost sixty years later I came to the conclusion that my father had been an important presence in my life, despite—or maybe thanks to—his real or perceived shortcomings. He had represented a reference around which I have been able to build my own paternal presence, as an old building represents a reference for the construction of the new. And for this reason I can and should love (agape) everybody I meet including the persons whose presence I perceive as disturbing.

CHAPTER 24

# Rationalism Has No Use for Christ

LET'S FORGET FOR A minute all the moral concerns related to abortion and human cloning and focus on the issue of eugenics. What are the stated goals of eugenics? In addition to eliminating all forms of inherited and congenital diseases, by eliminating their bearers, eugenics promises designer human beings labeled the fittest, the smartest, the most attractive. I have heard many times the proposal to clone the best lovers. I never once heard the promise to clone the most loving human beings, those who are ready to sacrifice themselves for the love of others. I wonder how many potential parents willing to trust their progeny to human cloning would choose to clone Jesus Christ, if he were clonable; I bet that Jesus would remain an embryo without takers, as in the eye of the eugenicists he was just a loser.

The choices of eugenics provide definitive proof of the master lie underlying our scientific and technologic progress (if there were any additional need to unmask it). The dream of eugenics is to design powerful human beings, not to design loving human beings capable of gathering our suffering humanity under a tent of compassion where everybody is welcome because everyone is validated by mutual love. That mutual love allows seeing every human as the unique indispensable stone of a mosaic that we all recognize as an act of love, even if nobody can embrace its full scope.

Let's face it, eugenics may finally accomplish what rationalism, science and technology have dreamed of accomplishing: a world centered on an objective good, progress, a world indifferent to human sentiments, where human beings are robbed of their humanity, a world without love. As Georges Bernanos said in his 1946 masterpiece, *La France contre les Robots* (*France Against the Robots*), "A world won by technology is a world lost by freedom!"

At this point it may be helpful to illustrate the meaning of love, probably the most abused word in our time. One has to wonder whether society speaks so much of love nowadays because society has lost its meaning, as so many people do not know how to find nor how to recognize it. When I heard a good friend, a world-prominent oncologist, saying about her teenage daughter: "One has to question whether it was worth it to have a child," I could not help wondering whether the world may soon come to an end due to a scarcity of love even before it will come to an end due to scarcity of water and other natural resources. Because love and only love is what inspires us to give and to support life. The fault of the 13 year old? She was rebellious and talked back to her parents, like the majority of teen-agers do, especially those who seek their parents' attention, because both parents are involved in time-consuming professional endeavors that support an always risky academic career. In particular she had bought a revealing dress for a New Year's party without the approval of her mother.

"Don't you see that she is trying to elicit a reaction from you?" I wanted to shout at my friend. "Any reaction, even anger, even disappointment, is better than the emotional desert where she believes she lives because you and Fred seem to ignore her. I don't argue about your love for your child. I am sure that both you and your husband would sacrifice your life for her. But try to see things from her viewpoint. How would you interpret the fact that you are in California and Fred is in Holland and at least once a week you both are gone at a time when she feels she needs guidance enveloped by affection? I am not telling you to give up your work, I am telling you to listen to your child and to make feel her loved all the time even if you have to be gone!"

Unlike the other ancient Greek definitions of love, agape is a love of choice, and the choice is supported by one's realization that only agape can generate and support life.

What eugenics tries to accomplish in the name of rationalism is a world without agape. There always will be plenty of eros as an unending source of power. Power for the so-called sex workers, men and women, who are able to excite sexual passions in others while remaining indifferent to sex themselves. Power for a special type of lingerie epitomized by Victoria's Secret. Power for all types of entertainment where sex is always a best seller.

But divorced from agape, the only reasonable outcome of eros is abortion, destruction or prevention of life. Life is an unbearable encumbrance to eros.

There will always be some form of friendship, if only because human beings need to feel gregarious from time to time. Recent research shows that all mammals and maybe even birds need to be gregarious, not just humankind. There will always be some form of *eusebeia*, as it is well known that most mammals including horses and elephants recognize their own offspring after years of separation. But agape is the real enemy of rationalism, the love that allows somebody to die for a loved one, the love that induces a person to die to make room to another person, the love that induces a person to die for the salvation of others.

Rationalism does not see the need of sacrifice to generate and support life, as reason is sufficient to this goal and so does not see the need of agape.

Some people may take exception to my claim that the refusal to clone Jesus Christ is characteristic of our times. Already in the Middle Ages some *clerici vagantes* or "wandering clerics" (university students in the vein of challenging the current political power) had written satirical poems and chants critical of the church and religious beliefs. I remember a poem according to which Pope Boniface VIII during a triumphal church ceremony encounters Jesus carrying the cross on his way to calvary. Pope Gaetani (the secular name of Boniface), was well known for his avarice, his thirst for political power and honors, for his lust, and for his skepticism in matters of religious faith. When he encounters Christ on his road he sees this as an opportunity to acquire more public recognition by helping Christ to carry (notice to carry, not to avoid) his cross. Disgusted by the duplicity and the hypocrisy of the new High Priest, Christ kicks the pope in the butt and knocks him to the ground, forcing him to lose his golden papal hat and soil his precious ceremonial clothes. Infuriated by this offense to his high office, Boniface himself decrees the crucifixion of the Christ.

Most of us are familiar with Dostoevsky's description of Ivan Karamazov's play in which the great inquisitor decides to condemn Christ to the pyre at the time of his second coming.

In these examples, however, Christ is still the supreme role model employed to shame his servants on earth for their hypocrisy and their near-sightedness. Rationalism instead has no use for Christ. According to eugenics Christ is just an undesirable child, whose message, agape, is anathema to the goddess reason.

I highlighted the mother of all lies: the rationalist dream of an objective reality with no relationship to human feeling, capable of ruling human behavior as an electronic center rules a world army of robots. The dream of disincarnation as Tobin described it. The ultimate arbiter of this world is power in its different and often contradictory forms. Whether wielded by a political tyrant, by the majority of people, by an economic oligarchy, or by a cadre of well-meaning but elite and misguided medical professionals, the common goal of this power is to destroy agape and with it to destroy mystery. Without mystery life is a withering flower without roots.

## CHAPTER 25

# Pro-Abortion Arrogance and Liberal Contempt for Religion

"It is high time for these people to end their love affair with the fetus," stated Joycelyn Elders, M.D., the surgeon general under President Bill Clinton, in reference to the pro-life folks that she designated, disdainfully, "the anti-abortion gang." Perhaps the bluntness of Dr. Elders may be partly excused on account of her personal history. As an African-American person growing up in the South in the '50s she could have been offended by the hypocrisy of people feigning deep compassion for the unborn or for cells grown *in vitro* when the same people had tried to prevent the access of black kids to public schools and public hospitals and had attempted to bar people of color from the voting booth. Not to mention that some of these same people had shown neither restraint nor hesitation when it came to hurting and sometimes killing black children. And even if they had professed racial tolerance, they had been reluctant to distance themselves from Bull Connor's attack dogs, from George Wallace's unwavering support of segregation and even from the assassins of the three civil right workers in Mississippi.

Nonetheless, as Surgeon General Elders was speaking on behalf of the President of the United States, she told Grace's parents, who had treasured the embattled birth of Grace as a gift from God, and millions of individuals like them, that the United States was not their home anymore. With a few careless words she had disowned millions of people because of their religious faith!

The people she exiled and made homeless were the very individuals who had built this country as a welcoming center for the oppressed and the rejected from across the world. They had done so with their hard work; they had done so with their honesty that inspired mutual trust and a common sense of justice and decency. Mostly they had done so with their religious faith, which has been the source of both their vision and their virtues.

Let me make something clear: I consider abortion an issue of science, not of faith, because modern biological science provides clear and incontestable evidence that human life begins at conception. But in the vision of Dr. Elders (that is, in the vision of President and Mrs. Clinton and of the intelligentsia that propelled them to power), opponents of abortion are a bunch of Neanderthals irremediably affected by religious prejudices who cannot be converted to embrace rational truths and deserve only to be stamped out. Never mind that Nat Hentoff, a secular civil liberties leader, had denounced abortion as a violation of the basic right to life. Never mind that Pier Paolo Pasolini—a prophetic Italian poet, novelist and movie director—had also decried abortion as the destruction of human life. After his expulsion from the communist party, because he had declared his homosexuality (in postwar Italy the communist party had adopted a "don't ask, don't tell" policy when it came to homosexuality, in obsequy to the Italian ideal of masculinity), Pasolini rejoined a leftist organization whose goal was and is to promote the civil liberties enshrined in the Italian constitution. He parted ways with them, as he found support of abortion incongruent with a commitment to uphold civil liberties.

The article in which Pasolini declared his condemnation of abortion is particularly moving. Because of his differentness he was persecuted throughout his life. (He was eventually killed in a horrendous way by a male prostitute, in 1974, when the young man beat him unconscious and ran over him with his own car.) The only consistent affection, the only trustworthy presence in his turbulent life had been his mother. In the dead of night she escaped with him from his northern Italian town to Rome, after he was maliciously accused of having abused a male pupil, and she shared months of seclusion, poverty and fears in the Roman *borgatas* where people survived on petty theft, prostitution and charity, before he was cleared of the accusation. In the article Pasolini pays tribute to his mother when he says that he remembers the peace he enjoyed "in utero"—the only peaceful, careless time of his tormented life!

Apparently the intelligentsia shows little tolerance of intelligent discussion when this challenges their prejudices. Social scientists who have never left the ivory tower of academics prescribe the working habits of millions of people in the field who break their backs every day. Medical ethicists who have never visited a hospital ward decide when life-saving treatment should be administered or withheld from patients on the verge of dying based on the position of commas in the informed consent document. All become despondent if it looks as if the poor ignorant populace does not appreciate the treasure of wisdom they freely bestow. Let me correct myself: the shedding of their wisdom is not free at all! They expect to be paid to make trouble in people's daily lives for their own good, of course.

Here is an example of the sort of intellectual arrogance that misses the point: As a physician-scientist, I was once summoned to a two-hour talk. When it was all over, it made me think of the way Jewish people were gathered from the Roman ghetto and compelled to listen to the supposed injuries of hate-filled venomous preachers during the holy week in papal Rome. The speaker—a young woman with a master's degree—proclaimed to an audience more educated than she that medical research is a privilege and each scientist must be held responsible for how the paperwork of the research (not, mind you, its results) is managed. This woman in her ignorance may not have known that such a standard would have jailed the discoverers of insulin and penicillin and the multidrug treatment of AIDS—and all because of paperwork not properly filled out to someone's liking.

A well respected oncologist at Albany Medical College, Dr. Alexander Spiers, was banned from doing clinical research for five years. His fault? Without proper consent documentation he had cured several patients suffering from hairy cell leukemia with Pentostatin, a drug that he had developed.

While doctors such as Spiers are persecuted, physicians in America daily commit atrocities in the name of conventional Western medicine. Every day in the United States, for example, out of fear of prostate cancer, men with elevated PSA levels are castrated with expensive drugs. This practice occurs at a cost of approximately $50,000 a year and without any evidence of life-prolonging benefit. What's more, evidence of damage abounds, and not just in loss of libido. Men who undergo chemical castration with LHRH analogs (common drugs used in hormone therapy) also experience increased risks of bone fractures, heart attacks, anemia and diabetes. But castration is considered standard treatment; it kills patients, but does not put them at risk, in the view of the intelligentsia.

Paradoxically, Dr. Elders' outburst achieved the opposite of what she had intended. Her bluntness contrasted with the smooth tongue of her boss yet expressed his deeply held views, revealed to the world, that religious-neutral politics is a delusion. Dr. Elders' statement was inspired by the very emotion that is the essence of the intelligentsia: contempt, and in particular, contempt of religious beliefs. Contempt is the motivation underlying battles to prevent mention of religion in public schools or to prevent the display of religious symbols in public places. The clear message is people are free to practice their beliefs in their private lives, the same way they are free to experiment with their sexual preferences or to practice other shameful habits, such as smoking. The public square belongs to those who have been enlightened and despise religion as the vestige of obscurantism.

The members of the intelligentsia are the modern heirs of the French Jacobins who guillotined millions of Christian believers during the French *la Grande Terreur*. Under the leadership of Robespierre, the Jacobins killed people to protect their freedom from superstition and to enlighten them, bringing them to the devotion of the Goddess Reason. A little more than a hundred years later Stalin ordered the killing of approximately 13 million individuals who did not want to recognize the authority of the Supreme Soviet as the seal of all freedoms. In the carefully crafted language of rightward politicians nowadays, both Robespierre and Stalin were practicing "tough love."

Perhaps the cartoonist Al Capp crystallized this situation better than anybody else. His honest cop Fearless Fosdick succeeded in having all canned beans outlawed because one of the cans had been poisoned. He shot and killed thousands of people who were trying to satisfy their craving for beans in order to prevent the death of one of them from eating from the poisoned can!

I agree wholeheartedly with whoever objects to my observation that religious persecution has been and continues to be the hallmark of religions, including Christianity, because this is my point. One cannot escape religion in the public square: Once we have eliminated all signs of more traditional religions, we are left with an atheistic or agnostic religion that decrees the death of all traditional deities. Like every religion, this religion represents the convergence of multiple emotions. For many it may stem from deception and disillusion. In addition to the individuals who have been physically abused by the clergy, many more have felt emotionally abused as a result of mishandled or misunderstood religious teaching.

Many physicians of my generation belong to the group of individuals proud to believe only in measurable entities. One of my first medical experiences sticks in my mind. As a young physician I spent six months in rural Italy as a primary care provider. I once made a house call on a pregnant woman who lived on a farm. She was suffering from deep vein thrombosis. I found her in the marital bed, with a sick child sleeping in a crib close to her. At the head of the bed there was a reproduction of the so-called Virgin of the Rosary in which a crowned Virgin Mary holds her child, looking with condescension on Saint Rita, kneeling at her side with rosary in hand.

This reproduction is very popular in rural Italy. My grandmother, who disavowed any particular devotion, had a similar reproduction hanging on the wall above her headboard.

I noticed that she already had six children. "Did anybody ever mention to you that another pregnancy may kill you or leave you disabled?" I asked her with the tone of an impatient teacher addressing a recalcitrant pupil. "You know, there are many ways to make love to your husband without getting pregnant." At that time of my life I felt it was my duty to promote public health by dispersing the superstitions that still infected the remote countryside of Italy. Somehow I felt as much of a missionary as my aunt walking ten miles each way each weekend to teach mountain children how to read and write in the post war havoc. Like Dr. Elders speaking about abortion I knew what was right and wrong, and I resented having to waste my valuable time taking care of ailments that might easily have been prevented by mental and reproductive hygiene. If this woman had been less scared of a mythological hell and more scared of a very real risk of pulmonary embolism she would have used birth control, and her problems would have been over. It was as simple as that. I must add a personal note that reveals how ridiculous my arrogance was. Up to that point in life, sex had been for me much more a source of frustration and hard work rather than pleasure. And yet, from the height of my M.D. degree I pretended to teach this country woman how to enjoy her sexual life.

Her answer was as disarming as it was soulful. "We are poor people. All we have is the hope for a little place in paradise; we don't want to lose it on account of our sins!" The contrast between me and that farm woman could not have been more startling. She had values; that is, she knew what was really worthy to her. She had convictions to live and to die for. And in her case her convictions concerned life itself; that is, the most vital of all convictions. Irrespective of whether birth control is justifiable or not by moral theology, she felt that her ability to carry and to give life was a unique privilege with which she was endowed and that made her sacred; that is, reserved to the function God has assigned to her. She believed in something so real that she could witness it grow within her body and take a body on her own, not just an idea, like democracy, or a romantic construct such as homeland. On the other side I had relegated all of my values to the delusion of an objective science, of a rational truth. Like the main character of Unamuno's *Amor y Pedagogia* I believed that the secret of human happiness resided in a rational word, in a word without feelings; that is, in a lifeless world.

As I listened to this woman I had hard time not expressing my derision. Certainly my smile that wanted to be polite conveyed my condescension. Years later I learned that my contempt was just a form of defense aimed to conceal my poverty in term of values. Faced with that farm woman I would have looked like a beggar knocking at the back door of a mansion, fearful to enter because my poor rags would shame me when compared with the precious garments of the house master. And that is the way I see Joycelyn Elders, President and Mrs. Clinton, Planned Parenthood, NOW and all the advocates of abortion rights when confronted with the riches of a mother who decided to carry to term a child with Down's syndrome.

The same year, after moving to Canada, I had a similar experience. "Goddam religious fanatics," shouted a psychiatrist who stormed from the room of an American Indian woman, chewing the butt of a cigar with his nicotine-blackened teeth. With his thin hair raised at both sides of his scalp like two small hornets, he provided a good impersonation of a comic-book devil. A lowly intern, I walked into the room trying to find out what was going on. The woman was distressed because after six children her husband had heeded the recommendation of a local family planning organization and had had a vasectomy. As I tried to convince her that she should try to look at her husband's decision as a misplaced form of love and care for her, she shook her head: "It is just wrong, Doctor! We have six children already and all of them are healthy. Why could we not have more? It is wrong to interfere with God's plans." Once more I was faced with that particular form of riches that are called values, which for myself I had deposited in a trust fund dominated by reason.

Whether this assortment of people are nostalgic about faith or envious of people of faith (as Georges Bernanos said of Dr. Delbende, a country physician who eventually commits suicide in *The Diary of a Country Priest*: "He never forgave himself for having lost his faith") or simply hold a totally irrational faith in rationality that leads them to despise people of faith as uncultured, two things are clear: First, they are not indifferent to religion, and, second, they preach and proclaim an alternative form of religion.

Let's face the fact: Religion involves the deepest human emotions and so does any form of god denial. Why don't we agree on that, get over the artificial separation of church and state and try to work with our emotions in a constructive way?

Let's look at the issue of evolution and creationism (or, in one of its forms, "intelligent design"). At present two armies of different zealots are facing each other in a war of exhaustion without end in sight. Evolution is a reasonable albeit unproven scientific hypothesis; creationism is an article of faith that cannot be demonstrated nor disproven with scientific methods. At present one field pretends that evolution is an established truth and the other field that creationism and intelligent design have scientific legitimacy. This confusion would be avoided if the teaching of religion had been allowed in public schools. If both subjects were allowed, a science course could teach the theory of evolution while the religious course could explore the relationship between scientific findings and religious beliefs. Religion is the horse on the dinner table, the eight-hundred-pound gorilla in the room of U.S. politics. In my view, the solution is to acknowledge the problem rather than skirt it, as leftist intelligentsia by and large tried to do with disastrous consequences for their political agenda. Never underestimate the liberal capacity for self defeat!

The word "politics" (from the Greek *politika*, modeled on Aristotle's *Affairs of the City*) defines the life of the community. Rather than being jeopardized, this life is enriched by individual experiences, as U.S. history demonstrates. To resist change and to suspect people who are different from us is a human reaction. Yet the incorporation of different cultural groups within mainstream America has widened the cultural opportunities of any person growing up in this country, in addition to making the American people the most tolerant in the world and enriching the country with the world's most diverse workforce. All this has occurred despite the occasional persecutions of all ethnic minorities (from the Japanese, to the Italian, to the Irish and mostly to the African American and the Native American). This cultural osmosis keeps promoting understanding and solidarity. But this process can only proceed when every human experience is at the table, and attitudes toward religion (either of acceptance or rejection) are the ones that more than any others shape our public communication.

To its credit, the religious right recognized at least thirty years ago that the exclusion of a religious interchange from the public forum was a form of injustice that excluded the majority of the U.S. population from participation in national community life, not to mention being a recipe for political disaster. It was this inclusiveness that made Ronald Reagan so popular. It made him look real, a representative of everyday people. This, despite that in his private life Reagan was much less devout than his presidential adversary, Jimmy Carter, a deacon of his Baptist church! Likewise George H.W. Bush lost the election in part because his commitment to religious values appeared artificial, an afterthought. By the way, this discussion of religion in politics shows once more that critical decisions, such as national elections, are directed by personal emotions rather than rational determination!

I do applaud Texas Gov. Rick Perry for calling a Day of Prayer and Fasting on Aug. 6, 2011, for the country, and though I could not travel to Texas that day, I joined in his intention in my personal prayers. It was thoughtful and timely to ask for prayers during a difficult time. I disagree with Gov. Perry and with the majority of the religious right because I find their agenda by and large antithetic to the Christian principles they profess. When I look at their agenda I am reminded of the owner of Isaiah's vineyards: "He looked for justice, but behold, bloodshed; for righteousness, but behold, an outcry!" [English Standard Version]. I found it particularly disturbing that Gov. Perry claimed that he did not lose a minute of sleep over the execution orders he signed, more in number than any other governor's in the history of the country. Irrespective of one's feelings concerning capital punishment, I cannot possibly fathom how a Christian can send other people to death without feeling the sorrow of ending a human life.

Christianity upholds love in the form of agape; that is, unconditional love, love inspired by the fact that each person is a brother or sister, a son or a daughter of the living God. No Christian, even if he holds high political office, is entitled to refuse another human being this condition of God's childship that is a direct consequence of Christ's advent and sacrifice. No Christian is entitled to throw on another human being a look less perceptive than the look that Christ cast toward each human being with whom he came in contact: a transfigurational look capable of seeing in each person that which God has seen when He and She created him or her. In addition, is Gov. Perry so impervious to compassion that he is not able to overcome the horror inspired by a crime and see a human person as the culprit—a human person who has been a child (and shared every child's aspiration to love) before engaging in a path of crime, a person who elicited tenderness and hope in his parents, his friends, his companions? The night before he was put to death, the mother of Ted Bundy, the serial killer of women and girls, called him and told him: "You still are and always will be my beloved son." Is it possible that Gov. Perry is not hurt by the hurt of a mother who is going to lose her child? Or in his view does a person's crime forfeit his or her right to love and be loved?

Unfortunately, liberal forces disdained the possibility of engaging with Gov. Perry in a discussion of Christian principles. Had they entered into such a debate, they could have easily demonstrated that Perry's agenda—from his sexual prejudices to support of the death penalty to the denial of decent health care and livelihoods to the majority of Americans—contradicted his own claim to uphold Christian values. But the liberal intelligentsia prefers to lose the election rather than even engage in a religious discussion, as if this discussion were demeaning and might contaminate the purity of their anti-religious beliefs!

CHAPTER 26

# This Is What I Call Faith

THOUGH FAITH MAY BE a source of joy, the awareness of one's sacredness is mainly a source of comfort, the ability to accept events that one cannot understand, including disease and death. A soldier engaged in deadly battle is more inclined to fight when he knows that he has been trusted with safeguarding his friends' lives, whatever his allegiance to the fight's ultimate goals. The worst suffering of Job was his inability to understand the sense of his suffering as more than the personal losses, more than disgusting scabies that excluded him from the human consortium, more than the reproach of his friends. Once he became aware of the presence of God in his life, all the other causes of his suffering became tolerable.

Once again I feel the need to claim *"Credo ut intelligam,"* as St. Augustine said: Only through faith can I make sense of my life; that is, I discover my sacredness as the final human aspiration. Or at least my final aspiration is to feel and know that I am unique, indispensable, endowed with individual talents. Even more, as Luigi Giussani said in his book *Can You Live Like That?* having faith is to distinguish among several dots fluttering on the horizon the one boat that represents the vessel with a load of fish that will ensure our food supply for the day. Faith is vision, is learning how to jump at opportunities to redeem; that is, to rescue from neglect and self-destruction that world we happen to negotiate.

Faith is the essence of a joke that has inspired my life. A Jesuit priest, whose golf game was delayed by three blind people trying to play in front of him, asked the course director, "Why don't they play at night?" Even a handicap, even a disease becomes an opportunity for a person of faith. In my own life I realized that the very depression that had set me apart from my peers and led me to the threshold of suicide represented a unique opportunity when ministering to terminally ill patients. Unlike most of my colleagues I was not afraid of dying, and consequently I felt comfortable when it came time to communicate with individuals close to death. Only a few days ago a friend who had been jobless for six months, after reaching the top of her medical career, confided in me, "When I was fired I felt that my whole world was crumbling. I almost could not face my former colleagues. Yet I came to realize that this interruption of my activity could not have come at a more appropriate time. I had the opportunity to take care of both my mother and my mother-in-law, who died three months apart. Had I been busy traveling around the world and meeting world dignitaries, I would have all but missed this treasured experience at home." This is what I call faith.

For many Christian and Muslim believers the hope in eternal and unshakable happiness is the main source of solace and the main motivation for a life free of sin. I do believe in an afterlife; I do believe in a Kingdom of God that encompasses the living and the dead. In this kingdom the resources of good will are joined together and may be used by children, spouses and friends to redeem the debts left unpaid by their loved ones. I feel motivated, as I will explain later, to contribute to this bank of good will as the supreme manifestation of love. But more than the hope for an eternal reward, my faith represents a reassuring interpretation of my everyday life, the ability to see an opportunity in any occurrence, even those that are adverse on the surface; the ability to see a brother or sister, rather than an enemy, in every new person I learn to know; the ability to acknowledge a meaning in my own and other people's suffering.

But let's not underplay the joy of faith. Though I have demonstrated repeatedly throughout my life that I am, too often, refractory to joy, I have been privileged to be able to borrow other people's joy. Experiencing Grace's mother's outlook, watching the growth of my son and my grandchildren—I thrill at reveling in the joy of people I trust and I love.

Not so in my early days of doubt and despair. My situation was crystallized in the words of a major character (literally, "the Unnamed") in Alessandro Manzoni's *The Betrothed* (*I Promessi Sposi*), a novel considered the most widely read and influential in the Italian language. The Unnamed had arranged the kidnapping of Lucia, a devout farm girl betrothed to Renzo, a silk worker in Northern Italy in the 1600s. The Unnamed had planned to make a gift of her to Don Rodrigo, one of the many bullish landlords of the area, who had bet with his cousin that he could take the girl's virginity before her fiancé had the opportunity to marry her. She pleads, in the name of God, to be let go, but the Unnamed lashes back at her:

"'God! God! Always God!' said the Unnamed. 'Those who are too weak to defend themselves always make use of the name of God, as if they knew something concerning him! What! Do you mean by this word to make me --' and he left the sentence unfinished."

Why did the Unnamed not finish the sentence? Why could he not say the word "afraid"? Because, in reality, he was petrified. Likewise, I had felt that my desire for God had been a form of weakness, a compensation for my lack of backbone and assertiveness.

During puberty I avoided washing my genital areas for weeks because a priest in the confessional had told me that any touching in that area was a mortal sin. A mortal sin brings with it the consequence of eternal damnation. Later I blamed the Catholic Church for the emotional abuse that my mother had received from my father, at least in my view. Had divorce been available in Italy, my mother could have broken out of her emotional prison, in which I was confined as well by my allegiance to her. Thanks to the pope's meddling in political affairs with his stern opposition to divorce, she had no recourse. She and I were destined to remain imprisoned together for our lifetimes, tormented by the common rancor against my father. I saw the pope as nothing more than another heartless politician intent on scoring political points by grandstanding against divorce, inattentive and indifferent to the suffering of millions of people that divorce would have alleviated.

Eventually I escalated to blaming the Catholic Church for my insecurity, my lack of confidence in myself, my inability to be in contact with my feelings: "It looks as if that boy never existed; he is all phony, he wants to show up but he does not even know how and when to show up," complained my prom date to my friends. For its telling me what I was supposed to feel and not feel, I held the Catholic Church responsible for having suppressed my ability to recognize and express my own feelings. If I wanted to have any social life, I had to feign the feelings that people around me expressed, I had to copy their expressions of joy, amusement, sadness and anger. And of course I was about as convincing as Al Gore in expressing outrage in the pivotal presidential campaign debate with George W. Bush.

At that time I had not come to appreciate that religion was the only lifeline that prevented me from drowning in those difficult years, that I owed much to a couple of Catholic priests who generously listened to me, allowing my conflicts to find a forum and an outlet that prevented me from blowing up. In fact my search for God was the only sincere spontaneous feeling I had experienced, and it should have been the cornerstone on which to build my emotional life. In order to find my true self, I had to deny the only certainty that existed in me, my desire for God. Once more it looked like the devil, however one imagines the devil to be, enjoyed extracting from his own victims their own death sentences!

Other individuals, maybe the majority, felt deceived by God. They had the impression that God failed them, like the main character in the Ingmar Bergman movie *Through A Glass Darkly* who waits for the second coming of God and encounters God in a gigantic spider descending from heaven and ready to swallow her (the helicopter that will eventually take her to a mental hospital in the city, away from her vacation retreat on an isolated island).

"The world has already suffered too much in a futile search for God," a close friend in medical school concluded as an announcement that he was going to abandon all religious practices — this, after several hundred hours of psychoanalysis. At another time he had stated, speaking of his family: "I never met four people whose life had been more absurd. God will have to account for it." In vain he had tried to make sense of the tragedy of his life: his blind mother, his philandering father, and his sister who lived at home trying to negotiate some type of relationship between her parents. We had bonded since my first days in Rome. Different from most of the other senior students who tried to force me to submit to painful hazing, he had invited me to his room, shared expensive Turkish cigarettes with me and tried to sooth my disconcertedness and confusion as a freshman. We spent long hours in his room, after evening meals, listening to Beethoven and Bach and trying to make sense of our life experiences, between one puff and the next.

He was particularly attentive to the trumpet calling to retreat in the barracks across campus: He perceived it as an authorization to relax, to let himself go, as the declaration that his day of pain was over. In addition to a disconnected family, he had left a young woman behind in his small Southern hometown with whom he had been petting for years, day after day. As soon as her mother left for her evening shift as a home nurse, he was admitted to the house and shed his clothes. They spent hours in bed. While she tried to capture his attention by catering to his pleasure, he was trying only to quench his inner turmoil in a rosary of orgasms that had left him more and more devoid of feeling. Emotional emptiness was the only form of relief he had experienced. He was the incarnation of Burt Lancaster's line in the Luchino Visconti film *The Leopard*. Impersonating a Sicilian landlord during the tumultuous years of the reunion of Italy, the actor states to a visitor from the northern city of Turin: "Our sexuality is just desire for oblivion."

Together we engaged in a cooperative search for God. We attended daily mass, we held weekly conversations with our spiritual assistant at an appointed time to unravel our litany of doubts, and we spent long night hours reviewing our lives. I still remember how excited he was when he began psychoanalysis. He felt assured that after a few sessions he would find answer to his unspoken questions. Instead, after hundreds of hours, he had decided to throw away the only lifeline he possessed, because he had not been able to find relief for his suffering. For him, too, God was a gigantic spider or maybe a gigantic snake ready to devour him. I was devastated: For months, our conversations and our exchanges had provided an anchor to my faith in a world that otherwise seemed indifferent or hostile. And now, with a simple statement he was withdrawing his support. He jerked the rug from under my feet. Once more I was left alone with my wavering faith that felt more like a burden than a consolation in a world that did not seem to have any use for it. I was left with the perennial question that haunted my adolescence and my youth, whether my belief in God was nothing more than a cover up for my human failure.

Unlike Mother Teresa and other deeply religious individuals who experienced this emotional desert (the "Dark Night of the Soul" of John of the Cross) and yet persisted in waiting for God's answer, as did Job, individuals disappointed by God often succumb to their emotional fatigue as well as to worldly distractions while nurturing resentment toward a god that seems oblivious of their needs and pains. Diego Fabbri provides a thorough description of such individuals in his play *Processo a Gesù (Trial of Jesus)*. Whereas prostitutes and thieves defended Jesus because they felt understood and validated, an assortment of ex-seminarians, ex-altar boys, and ex-members of Catholic associations were among his more fervent accusers. They accused Jesus of deceiving simple-minded and destitute individuals. In their view, faith was responsible for maintaining the vicious cycle of poverty and ignorance: Faith in Jesus impeded the poor, preventing them from learning to fend for themselves. Whether they had embraced the philosophy of Marx, Auguste Comte or Nietzsche, they were united in their belief in this deception, and a common indictment of Jesus stemmed from this deception.

And there are the "children of the century"—those who have been raised to believe that all forms of religious faith are unworthy of intellectual consideration. These are direct descendents of the enlightenment, best impersonated in Juliet in the 1994 movie *Heavenly Creatures*. The main characters include two 15-year-old girls from New Zealand, Pauline and Juliet. Pauline is the daughter of a middle-class family whereas Juliet lives in a mansion as the daughter of a British university dean and a psychologist who believes in free love. Juliet's life style and unconventional behavior charms Pauline, who establishes a homosexual relationship with Juliet. When Pauline's mother tries to interrupt the relationship, Pauline, with Juliet's help, murders her. One of the peculiarities of Juliet (in the 1950s, Christchurch was embedded in a dormant form of Christianity) is that she did not believe in heaven and hell. Her parents had instructed her that the afterlife was fictional. Yet they had not dared to break the terrifying news to her that death was the end of all human experiences. So they invented a form of afterlife for her own benefit. They instructed her that after death, she would dwell free of pain in a special place where she could keep fooling around unimpeded with her girlfriend. In their heart of hearts, the enlightened Juliet's parents did not believe that the personal aspiration to immortality, which their daughter shared with the rest of humanity, could be silenced. They understood that personal dissolution as end of life was incongruent with the deepest human aspirations of immortality. I cannot help finding it humorous that they offered their child the hope of an afterlife of their own making in an attempt to spare her the belief in an afterlife to which millions of Christians had adhered for more than twenty centuries.

In my times of deepest doubt, while searching for God, at the same time I had been scared of God. And that is when I lost my innocence, trying to establish myself outside of God's plans for me; trying to make sense of a world that, without God, had no sense whatsoever. It followed that I engaged in a number of destructive relationships. That is why Betsy's rediscovered innocence after her brain-tumor diagnosis was my rediscovered innocence. Her joy became my joy. Our paths had been quite different, but they converged when we both discovered that we depended on God in order to be ourselves.

In the last chapter of "Purgatory," the second part of the *Divine Comedy*, Dante describes how he achieved a vision of God. Beatrice, his guide, the spirit of the woman he had loved and who had died young, had waited for him at the top of the Mountain of Purgatory. From there she started looking at the sun and was transported in that way to God's empire. By watching Beatrice, Dante was able to acquire himself, through Beatrice, the vision of God. Like Beatrice for Dante, I myself, and many others in the parish, achieved a vision of God through Betsy's vision.

The Catholic Church has been criticized by all Protestant denominations for promoting a cult of saints, which in many people's devotions may receive more attention even than God. While these criticisms are reasonable, they miss an aspect of sainthood that I learned through Betsy. Saints are a physical venue to the vision of God, a venue congruent with our need for concrete manifestations of our relationship with the divine, our need to see God with our eyes, hear Him and Her with our ears, feel God through our skin—because that is the way in which we love.

Religious faith stems from an act of faith. This includes the belief in something that cannot be proven based on the credible testimony of the senses or of another person. Betsy definitely was the occasion of many acts of faith. Her contagious joy revealed much to anybody able and willing to see that she was up to something good, something liable to transform anguish into enjoyment even in the presence of suffering. People who happened to meet her could not help yearning to learn all there was to learn about her source of joy. Her close friends, those who had known and somehow partaken of her history, were comforted by learning that there was a way to break the chain of addiction and soothe the anguish of dependence. Her intellect, her education helped make her credible and her faith credible.

The simplest act of faith was described by C.S. Lewis in the first book of the *Chronicles of Narnia*. Peter and the other children were disturbed by Susan's claim to have discovered an alternative world at the end of the wardrobe in the house old attic. They expressed their concern to the professor who hosted them in his mansion in the English countryside to escape the bombing of London during World War II. After listening to the story the professor concluded—to the disconcertment and frustration of her siblings—that because Susan did not seem a liar or a fool, then the logical solution was to believe what she said. This simple reasoning could be applied to Jesus. He did not appear a liar, he did not appear a fool, he underwent passion and death so as not to disavow his message. The most logical thing, of course, is to believe him.

Even if I had been ready to take this jump in the dark at any time of my life, a number of intellectual problems would have put the brakes on my determination. The historicity of Jesus's passion and crucifixion is incontrovertible. Everything else including the nature of his miracles and the content of his message may be open to critical analysis. Even those who take the Gospels literally cannot help noticing inconsistencies that make the historical accuracy of the whole narrative questionable.

Some inconsistencies: The Sermon on the Mount occurs on a mountain according to Luke and on a plain according to Matthew; the genealogy of Jesus in Luke and Matthew is completely different.

And even if one agrees that these incongruities are to be expected in any eyewitnesses account, how should one interpret some of Jesus's expressions, such as "the poor in spirit," not to mention the theological debate between various Christian denominations on subjects such as transubstantiation, predestination, Peter's primacy and Mary's perpetual virginity and regality? One may certainly adhere to a message of redemption through suffering, but one needs to find in his or her own experience the practical application of these principles.

For this purpose a church, a community of faithful, what the Second Vatican Council called "Peoples of God" where centuries of human experiences have been treasured and bequeathed is invaluable.

CHAPTER 27

# Popes and Wars
## Part I

"THE CITIZEN PARINI HAS no place where the citizen Christ has no place." With these words Giuseppe Parini refused a seat in the parliament of the Repubblica Cisalpina (Cisalpine Republic), the first attempt at democracy in the Italian region of Lombardia, after the Austrian empire had been overthrown by Napoleon's army.

A poet and a priest, Parini decried the excesses of the clergy-enabled aristocracy in his poem "Il giorno" ("The Day"). A day in the life of a young aristocrat (whom Parini had mentored) consisted of a series of leisurely pleasures paid for by the hard work, and sometimes the blood, of the servants over whom the aristocrats exercised life-and-death power. A classical section of the poem describes how a servant was fired because he kicked a small bitch called Cuccia (the foolish virgin Cuccia) after she bit his shin. While the man and his family were freezing and dying of starvation in the streets of Milan, Cuccia's owner was describing the terrible ordeal of her pet to horrified guests who, all the while, were savoring refined food and drink, served by the impassible colleagues of the man who had been punished with loss of livelihood and protection for him and his family. Parini's social sensitivity and concerns garnered him an invitation to be part of the parliament, though he belonged to the hated class of the clergy. The republic had eliminated all images of the crucified from all the government halls.

Parini was a mediocre poet and probably a mediocre priest; one of his poetry collections included a number of love declarations to different women, though truth be told female companionship was not unusual for a priest in the 1700s. After all, priests vow to remain unmarried, not to remain celibate, or so the thinking went. His refusal of a parliamentary seat, however, makes him a prophet and a historical giant.

He had understood, maybe before anybody else, that social justice can be obtained only through love, and a political body divorced from the source of love cannot deliver justice. He had witnessed the massacres committed during the French Revolution ("la Grand Terreur") in the name of justice. He had foreseen the possibility if not the size of the massacres committed by 20th century dictators in the name of justice. He had understood that any form of government, whether representative or tyrannical, would eliminate the possibility of redemption if it became dissociated from religious faith. By definition, a world without the possibility of redemption can only accumulate more debts over debts and evil over evil (in the form of hatred, suspicion, disenchantment). Such a world cannot help becoming so overburdened with moral debts as to declare moral bankruptcy; so overwhelmed by evil as to implode and destroy itself. The massacres of the 20th century as well as the proliferation of weapons of mass destruction (whose threat still hovers over the world, as thousands of nuclear warheads remain unaccounted for after the dissolution of the Soviet Union), testify to the veracity of such prophecy. To this one should add the ongoing unrest in the Muslim world, some of whose leaders look for some type of confrontation with the Great Satan, and the endless warfare throughout the African continent, which displaced millions of people, many of whom are looking for relief from a population-saturated West.

In opposing the rise of secular democracies, the Catholic Church might have done the right thing for the wrong reason, like the prophets of the Old Testament unwittingly predicting the birth of Christ while addressing current events. Though the main interest of the clergy in opposing modern democracies might have been to preserve power and resources, they were right on point when they predicted the dissolution of society and especially the loss of the rights of the poor, who without the support of the church would have turned into modern day slaves.

The figure of Pope Pius the IX is particularly relevant. At the beginning of his pontificate, the longest in history, the young pope tried to sympathize with the nationalistic aspirations of some northern Italians. To show his commitment to the liberal cause he sent troops to help fight the Austrians during the first Italian independence war. He soon became disillusioned when he realized that the majority of the so-called patriots were openly averse to religion, and it would have been impossible to marry religion to a movement with secular roots, its supporters believing religion a hindrance to human progress.

From the new awareness of this incompatibility emerged his famous "Syllabus of Errors," read and denounced by Italian liberals as an example of religious near-sightedness and ignorance. Two hundred years later the same document now is seen to represent an example of clear long-term vision, a lasting landmark, with the claims of its detractors proved wrong and untenable. The pope had prophesied the famines, sweatshops, child labor and class warfare that contaminated Italy and other Western countries (especially France and England) until the beginning of the 20th century, whereas the ruling class enjoyed, oblivious, its privileges.

After the goddess reason, the world that rejected the Christian God discovered a new deity, the god of free market. This new deity anointed a new and more perverse class of aristocrats. The so called "robber barons" had no qualms in destroying, along with human lives, the common patrimony of environment and natural resources. In reserving for themselves large portions of uncultivated land for their own whims, the old aristocrats performed a social service: They preserved environment, wildlife, clean water and air that the whole population eventually would be able to enjoy. Just outside of Rome, in the small town of Tivoli, two water and forest parks, Villa Gregoriana and Villa D'Este, are examples of private-owned land preserved for public enjoyment.

In less than a hundred years, the new aristocrats of the god free market have destroyed thousands of species of plants and animals, exhausted the world fisheries, polluted the major cities, and made water so scarce that in more than half of the world it must be rationed. In a capital city like Delhi it is delivered for only two hours a day. Water deprivation is responsible for deaths from starvation and disease in many parts of the world (look at the African horn).

My home town of Rimini provides a small but vivid example of the robber barons' devastation. In the late 1940s, family breadwinners would fish for sole at sunset, so abundant was this delicacy. Though many of them were jobless and could not afford a decent suit, each night they could provide their families a dinner delicacy freely delivered by an unpolluted sea. Seventy years later one can no longer find any type of fish on the northern Adriatic coast. Industrial discharges as well as discharges from the pig farms common to that area, in addition to overfishing, have depleted my sea of its natural riches. The rare fish that is still harvested many miles from the coast is sent, early in the morning, to Milan, 200 miles north of Rimini, and from there it is distributed by a national distributor to a network that includes Rimini. Most of the time the fish is frozen and its cost prohibitive. And this rape of nature is called progress!

No pope in modern times has been more disparaged than Pius IX by the Italian intelligentsia. In a sign of hatred and contempt, a mob tried to throw his coffin in the Tiber River when he died. And that because his "Syllabus" of 1864 had prophesied how the new government, deprived of religious principles, would thrive on slave labor and rob the poor of common resources.

Social injustice in the modern world has been at the heart of a number of papal encyclicals. From the Greek, "encyclical" means "directed to the world" and is the most authoritative papal declaration short of the proclamation of a new dogma, a controversial papal prerogative that has been used only once in history, when Pius XII proclaimed the Assumption of the Virgin Mary.

In 1891 Pope Leo XIII, in the encyclical "Rerum Novarum," proclaimed that human beings should not be considered merchandise and working conditions should be consistent with each person's God-given dignity. The core of human dignity is the unique role assigned by God to each person in the process of redemption. Disregarding human dignity means to lose opportunities for redemption, to throw away unique sources of currency with which pending moral debts may be paid. In ignoring each other's dignity in their sterile fights, my parents left me and my sister and my wife and my sister's husband and our children to deal with the emotional and moral wounds they opened and were never able to close. Of these, my hostility toward my father has been the hardest for me to overcome, the reality that led me close to moral bankruptcy, close to the collapse of my marriage and at risk of leaving my own personal talents untouched and untapped. Moral bankruptcy, the moral implosion from absence of redemption, may be individual as well as universal.

In 1933 Pope Pius XI emphasized the same principles in "Quadragesimo Anno," issued to commemorate the fortieth anniversary of "Rerum Novarum." At the beginning of his pontificate, Pope Paul VI issued "Populorum Progressio." The pope emphasized that economic injustice today is the main cause of social turmoil and invited those who hold political and economic power to relinquish it so that each human being can obtain recognition of his or her dignity and become partners in the creation of a just society where agape reigns supreme in lieu of profit.

The teaching of these popes was based on sound theology. To the dismay of right-leaning Christians as well as the few remaining communists, it was the theologian Aquinas of the High Middle Ages and not Marx who first stated that capital exploits human labor. What he said was that the laborer should be paid *"ipsa merce"*; that is, with the products of his own work. In other words, the laborer should have a voice in his or her working conditions and should be allowed to negotiate both his or her commitment and compensation! To my knowledge this was the first social interpretation of Christ's statement: "The Sabbath was made for man, not man for the Sabbath" [English Standard Version] which may also be read as "the profit is for mankind, not mankind for the profit."

World War I was definitely a product of the inquietude of Western democracies deprived of the means of redemption (of the ability to make up), and the war demonstrated on a relative large scale the capacity for self-destruction of a world in moral bankruptcy and oversaturated with evil. In addition to reason and free-market deities, a new deity—nationalism—had emerged from the ashes of Christianity after the French Revolution. Nationalism provided a much needed emotional component to the new religion. As people are moved through their emotions, not reason, it was necessary to stir up the emotions of people deprived of confidence in a God that loved them and cared for them. People still needed a reason to live and something to die for.

Of course nationalism should not be confused with patriotism that represents pride in one's heritage and the desire to share one's asset with neighbors for common enrichment. Nationalism is the statement of the superiority of one's heritage over all other heritages and the right to force others to submit and to destroy people on account of one's own superiority. A patriot is a child proud of his house, his parents, and his toys who invites other children to visit him and enjoy his assets. A nationalist is a child bragging that his dad is stronger than any other child's dad, that his dwelling and his toys are more valuable than any other child's, who challenges the other children to a fight to overwhelm and humiliate them. Nationalism is a child (or a twin, or the emotional face) of a free-market system that made power the most desirable achievement of human activity. Conflicts always mean big profits for ruthless entrepreneurs thriving on arms sales, as well as on hoarding material goods to be sold on the black market, which is the extreme form of free market.

Having understood that the conflict represented the implosion of an evil-saturated world, Pope Benedict XV denounced the war as "useless carnage" in 1915 while so-called patriots in Italy were shouting loud requests that their country join the glorious fight. Fifty years after finishing grade school, I still cannot understand how our teachers and our schoolbooks could call that war a major victory when 600,000 Italians (counting just military casualties) and probably more Austrians died so that a piece of land smaller than Connecticut could shift from Austrian to Italian control. The majority of people living there were happy with the Austrian government that had always proved less corrupt than the Italian one and the Italian carpetbaggers who invaded that area without even having shed blood for it. The war was promoted by nationalists who believed in the supreme sanctity of the fatherland and, in the name of nationalism, disregarded the sanctity of human life, especially that of people other than them. The war was fought by and large by the poor, most of them illiterates, most of them not giving a damn about the need to restore the "the natural boundaries of Italy," which was the sanctimonious nationalistic proclamation aiming to justify the carnage. To add insult to injury, Italian Chief of Staff General Luigi Cadorna, who had obtained that command thanks to his family's connections, and despite his incompetence, believed in routinely decimating his troops as a form of encouragement for the soldiers to be brave! The worst of these massacres occurred after the defeat of Caporetto, due to Cadorna's and his staff's incompetence. More than a thousand of these poor devils were slaughtered on such occasions by their own comrades under orders from a commander in chief more interested in killing than in winning.

Six hundred thousand dead! Maybe some anthropologist studying modern history will conclude that nationalism should be considered a form of population control, like ritual infanticide during ancient civilizations, when birth control was not easily available. This consideration would be amusing were it not supported by the universal pain, the starvation of millions, the dissolution of rural families that the folly of the Western democracies did cost. To these one must add the problems of the millions of survivors, many of them disabled from mutilation, many of them without work or resources, all of them encumbered to some extent by PTSD (post-traumatic stress disorder). And yet the majority of these survivors, instead of heeding papal counsel and seeking peace, inflated the fascist movements and prepared for a new war. They were incapable of recognizing that the pope was right and they had been led like sheep to the slaughter by leaders who had freed them from the "tyranny" of religion. Rather than trying to soothe their own pain, they elected to join a movement poised to inflict more useless pain in obedience to the Nationalistic Leviathan.

A family drama caused by this useless carnage, emblematic of a million similar dramas, was described in the book *La Miglior Vita* (*The Better Life*) by Fulvio Tomizza. The author pretends to have been the sacristan of a church in the extreme northeast of Italy, in a rural community deprived of manpower by the war, as the majority of men had been drafted. Coming home from a night walk with the priest, the sacristan glimpsed a corpse floating in the channel. After rescuing it they recognized one of the women whose husbands had left for the war about three years earlier to fight for a land that at most had represented a malignant stepmother to him. Her breasts were engorged; she had committed suicide after discovering she was pregnant. The compassionate priest immediately covered her body so that nobody could discover her condition, ordered the sacristan to state that they found her dead in the street, possibly felled by a stroke, and presided over her religious funeral. While she was drowning, her two small children were sleeping in the same bed, not knowing that they would wake up orphans, and that their very survival was in jeopardy courtesy of a republic that had freed them and their parents from the tyranny of the Christian faith and transformed them into animals headed for the slaughterhouse. Having heard the calls of my child when he was a toddler and now of my grandchildren, I had to stop reading at this point. Too late! I became obsessed by the thought of the joyful call of these children for their mother's hug and kiss when they woke up from their innocent sleep overseen by the picture of the king of Italy and the Italian prime minister instead of the cross of Christ or a picture of the holy family!

The reader is left to decide whether the tragedy stemmed from the fact that this woman had given in to lust, or had been raped in the field where she was forced to spend her days since her husband's departure trying to support a meager harvest just adequate to nourish her children, or had prostituted herself trying to provide for a family whose main breadwinner had been shanghaied and was for more than three years on the front lines ready to be slaughtered for the glory of the fatherland. The reader is also left to decide whether the man who impregnated her had been able to avoid the draft thanks to connections and money and whether he had been deaf to her pleas for help in finding a solution to the problem he had caused. No matter what, she and her family were just an example of the millions of victims sacrificed at the altar of nationalism, which represented (together with reason and free market) the new Leviathan of the modern era, a Leviathan made free to roam the sea as its main nemesis, the Christian God, has been dispossessed and discarded.

Two movies have powerfully described the horrors of World War I. A French movie, *À l'Ouest, rien de nouveau*, is a graphic portrait of universal carnage as well as of inner destruction. American readers know the work: the Erich Maria Remarque novel and the 1930 American movie *All Quiet on the Western Front*. A young German man is lured into wearing the uniform by a high school teacher who is a believer in supposed German superiority. The young man comes home for his last leave, having learned how to kill and having seen his best friends and companions fall around him. He cannot tolerate the delusions of his hometown and decides to return to the front earlier than expected. His old professor asks him to give a talk to his new class, and when he states that war is just carnage where human life is cheap, and honor and patriotism are empty words, he is shouted down as a coward by the enraged pupils. They prefer to believe the professor's delusional dreams of destiny rather than the hands-on experience of a returning soldier. As he enters the pub for a beer, he is surrounded by four elders who discuss the best strategy to win the war and invite him to their table to give his opinion. When he states what should have been obvious, that the war was going to be lost, that the soldiers had no supplies and that the losses were so heavy that they had to employ child soldiers, the old men call him a defeatist and ask him to leave. Then they will be free to pursue their dreams of glory. At home his mother comes by his bed and recommends that he protect himself from the cold weather; for that purpose she had added wool underwear that she had knitted to his backpack. We are dealing with a chain of self-perpetuating lies that preside over the self destruction of the people entrapped by the lies. This chain of self perpetuating lies that seems to preclude forever the path back to the truth is what psychiatrist author M. Scott Peck described as "evil" in the book *People of the Lie*. It is the oversaturation with evil as the unavoidable consequences of the loss of the meaning of redemption.

The only sweet moment of the movie is a conversation between the soldier and his sister when they remember their childhood passion for collecting butterflies. This memory will cause his death at the end. As he stands in the trench he sees a butterfly on a flower outside the trench. He had read the bulletin "*a l'ouest rien de nouveau*" (all quiet on the west front), so he feels safe in reaching for the butterfly and in doing so becomes an easy target for a French sniper concealed among the branches of a tree!

*Paths of Glory* is a 1957 Stanley Kubrick movie starring Kirk Douglas and depicting the use of decimation in the French army during World War I. A general blames his troops' cowardice for a failed operation that would have brought him glory and promotion. He asks his commander to be allowed to decimate his troops. His commander convinces him to lower his request to three lives, and so a kangaroo court martial quickly takes place. Despite the passionate speech of Kirk Douglas as defense lawyer, the three men are found guilty and condemned to die. In their cell the three men try to cope with their last night on earth, while the honorable commissioned officers of the French army enjoy a fine meal. The general responsible for the killing does not seem to have any remorse for inflicting a foolish operation on his troops. He dances elegantly with a lady he probably will bed that night. Good food, good music and good sex are the best preparation for witnessing an early morning execution of three troops without name, history or advocacy. For a career military man to show any emotion in advance of somebody else's death is a sign of cowardice. I let the reader conclude how the elimination of God from public—and at certain times even in private—places has freed French laborers from the tyranny of religion.

## CHAPTER 28

# Popes and Wars
*Part II*

Let's face it: The French Revolution was aimed to promote the bourgeoisie to aristocracy, not to cause the downfall of the aristocracy; to increase the number of masters, not to reduce the number of servants or even improve the working conditions of the populace. Many will be surprised to learn that under the Sun King (Louis XIV, famous for supposedly stating "*L'Etat, c'es moi,*" "I am the state"), the farmers in the French countryside held more rights than during the first republic. (This was courtesy of the Catholic inspiration of the monarchy for which the sovereign was responsible in front of God for the welfare of his subjects.)

A personal anecdote will show how the myth about the nobility of World War I was resistant to dying. In 1949 our family had our first vacation in Brixen, the former capital of *Süd* Tyrol, the Austrian region Italy occupied after World War I and christened with the Italian name Alto Adige. My pious aunt immediately found a church and was impressed by the religiosity of the local people. She announced to me, a 6 year old, that she planned to write an article for the Catholic journal titled "Austrian people are more religious than we are." I promptly informed my mother, who got enraged, and I overheard her shouting at her sister: "How can you possibly do it after the Austrians have been our enemy for a century and after we fought a bloody war to liberate our country?" In her scolding, my mother was fully supported by my father—one of the few times I can remember them in full agreement. My goodness! The war had concluded more than thirty years earlier; my parents were educated and knew history. The scars of fascism and Nazism that spurted out of the ashes of World War I were still with us, albeit revealed only in part. Despite all this, my parents were enraged because my aunt, with her childlike innocence, had just expressed a truth that was visible to everybody unless one was blinded by the faith in the goodness of the secular governments that had just presided over the destruction of millions and millions of lives for the second time.

Though it is difficult to pass judgment on the social and political interventions of Pius XII, arguably the most controversial pope of the past century, with the Vatican archives still closed to the historians, it is clear from his letters that he tried to prevent World War II through diplomatic efforts and warnings to German and Italian leaders. He also tried, in his numerous talks and encyclicals, perhaps unjustly forgotten or dismissed, to find a way to marry Christianity to the modern world.

Though I am much less familiar with the social theology of Protestant churches, I do know for a fact that, if anything, they have been more involved in social issues than the Catholic Church from the beginning. Both Luther and Calvin promoted literacy at the time when the Catholic Church opposed it to prevent the individual reading and interpretation of the scriptures. Though literacy was meant to enable people to read the Bible and obtain their personal interpretations, to be shared with and validated by the ecclesial community, literacy meant access not only to jobs but also to government. In this respect two issues of Calvin's teaching deserve highlighting.

First, he mandated free public education, something that many American Presbyterians happily forget. Second, while he promoted a capitalistic approach to the economy and recommended obtaining the highest possible profit as a sign of God's blessing, he also saw in private profit a means to support the public good. He did not support a communal life as described in the first chapters of Acts, but he would have joined Peter in punishing Ananias and his wife, Sapphira, for having kept for themselves part of their gain. "Then Peter said, 'Ananias, why have you let Satan fill your heart? You lied to the Holy Spirit, and you kept some of the money for yourself.'" [New Living Translation] He would be horrified by the growing income gap among the haves and have-nots of modern America, and he would disavow the appellative Christian to accurately describe the United States.

Neither Calvin nor Luther conceived of a government indifferent to Christian principles. No Christian denomination has ever endorsed a religious-neutral government. This idea spurted from the French revolution, an anti-Christian movement that was aimed to deprive the poorest and the most vulnerable citizens of the protection and the dignity afforded to them by Jesus Christ himself!

The year 1968 might have represented a revolt against the deity of nationalism and free market, but it was a revolt without direction. While in medical school, I remember participating in many of the manifestations of that time. The message hammered into us was: "We will destroy their roads, their houses, their factories, their powerhouses." It was a message of hatred of people who had identified the lie of the previous generations, the lies on which their parents had thrived. There was not a single word about reconstruction. The lies had been revealed, but the way out of lies remained elusive. I remember a discussion I had with one of the leaders of the student movements, who was also a close friend, Gino Tosolini: "We are a fucked-up generation. All we can do is to destroy a world bequeathed to us as a lie." In other words, 1968 was a time to uncover, not to discover. One may say that by being indifferent to the very existence of the truth, 1968 endorsed the ultimate lie.

CHAPTER 29

# Physician of the Soul

ST. AUGUSTINE RECOGNIZED IN *The Confessions* that anyone can inflict wounds, anyone can dismember a body, but only a competent physician can mend it. But where to find this physician of the soul, able to recompose a disassembled personality, restitute a sense of life, direction, enthusiasm to a world suffocated by the boredom of endless sensations, changing and repetitive as the patterns of a kaleidoscope?

The account of my religious experience would not be complete without a description of my own intellectual and emotional difficulties in embracing Christianity. I would like to share how I overcame some of these problems and how learned to live with others. Mostly I wish to state my allegiance to people tormented by the same doubts and incertitude.

Problems are either intellectual or emotional.

*Intellectual issues.* "The existence of evil demonstrates that God cannot be at the same time almighty and good," stated Albert Camus in *The Myth of Sisyphus*. If God created evil, God cannot be good; if evil exists in spite of God, then God is not almighty. Camus professed his atheism based on the rational impossibility of reconciling the idea of an almighty and a good God. At the same time, the same Nobel Prize-winning author created the character of Dr. Bernard Rieux. In the novel *The Plague*, this physician regretted not believing in God, because only the belief in an ever-loving God could justify his aspiration to sacrifice himself to the wholesomeness of the world. Unable to overcome this inner fight between intellect and aspirations, he commits suicide when an epidemic of plagues is on the way to resolution and his help is not needed anymore. A few years later Camus himself died in a car accident seen by some as a suicide.

To reconcile the construct of an almighty God with the presence of evil, German philosopher Gottfried Wilhelm Leibniz developed the concept in *Theodicy* that is as complex as any other thoughts of this German thinker. In simple words, theodicy means that an almighty God will somehow take care of evil in His and Her infinite wisdom. It is an invitation to trust God that leaves the problem of evil all but unresolved. One way to read theodicy is: "without the Iscariot we would have not had Jesus. The almightiness of God is revealsd in the redemption of the evil, that is in overcoming the intellectual impossibility to transform evil into goodness."

Many philosophers, maybe the majority, have tried to provide an intellectual explanation of evil. To me the most ingenious appears that of German philosopher Arthur Schopenhauer. In his book *The World as Will and Idea*, he proposes that the chaos described in Genesis as pre-existing the creation was "the absurd." The absurd implies the possibility of contradicting itself: a good God derived from the self contradiction of the world of evil.

The most classical Christian explanation of evil has been human free will: God has so desired to be freely loved by humans that He endowed them with the terrible ability to deny Him and in that way to destroy themselves. Yet how can a loving God create individuals destined to suffer for eternity? And what happens to God's own eternal happiness when the people He and She loved are destined to rot in hell? The reformed doctrine of predestination did not help clarify the issue. Luther found assuaging the awareness that his salvation depended on God's will rather than on his own merit, and I myself find salvation by grace rather than by merit a comforting thought, the answer to the terrible question of the "*de profundis*" in Psalm 130, "*si iniquitatem observaveris domine, domine qui sustinebis?*" which means, "Lord, if you kept a record of our sins, who, O Lord, could ever survive?" [New Living Translation] But this comfort about one's personal salvation does not quench the fire of compassion elicited by human suffering, which prompted Paul to say [New Living Translation]: "For my people, my Jewish brothers and sisters. I would be willing to be forever cursed—cut off from Christ!—if that would save them." Moses had earlier articulated the sentiment.

St. Augustine struggled with the same problem throughout his works, and his solution was my solution: "*Credo ut intelligam.*" I can understand my nature and the world around me only by believing in God. In other words, I cannot justify the presence of evil in the world, but this difficulty does not impede faith that is based on the possibility of understanding my role in this world. I basically subscribe to St. Augustine's acceptance of God, and I add to it an emotional tone. When you are on the edge of drowning and somebody throws you a life line, you grab hold of it without asking whether it has undergone all the necessary safety certifications. This has been my experience with Christ. When I felt desperate and had lost any hope of loving and of being loved, my faith in Christ showed me the possibility of agape and through agape the way to redemption. The testimony of Christ hinted at the possibility of transforming my worst liabilities into my most valuable assets, once my suffering was engrafted into Christ's own suffering.

Patients with heart failure started enjoying the benefits of a digitalis infusion two centuries before anyone understood the mechanism of action of the medication on heart muscles. Since the Middle Ages, patients with a chest cold or with abscesses have been deriving benefit from home remedies such as warm packs, though the physiology of inflammation was defined only during the last fifty years. So I feel perfectly justified in hanging onto a medicine, a spiritual medicine, that has turned my life around even if I can't explain all of its effects.

The biblical account of creation and salvation does not help, either, at least in its more literal forms. A modern movie director, Luis Buñuel, and a modern Portuguese writer, Jose Saramago, took particular delight (or at least so it appears) in highlighting the contradictions of the biblical account. Without making a pronouncement about God's existence, these artists seem to proclaim the absurdity of believing in the Christian god.

In *Viridiana's* culminating scene, Buñuel makes an orgy out of the Last Supper. Viridiana, a young woman who has been violated during her sleep by a libidinous uncle and hopes to redeem his sin and her loss of virginity by ministering to the poor, is disheartened by an outcome that reveals her redemptive mission as all but impossible. She renounces her commitment, sends the beggars she had collected in her house back to the street and returns to a life of privilege in the Spanish aristocracy. Christ got tired of being crucified, pulls out the nails that fix him to the cross, makes an obscene hand gesture toward the people attending his death and goes to get drunk somewhere with the marauders crucified at his side.

In the 1969 film *La Voie Lactée* (*The Milky Way*) the director provides literal Bible interpretations in a succession of scenes aimed to highlight the incongruity of the sacred book. At the opening of the movie, two mendicants on their way to Santiago of Compostela peddle goods to a conservatively dressed old man who asks them how much money they have. He refuses to give any money to the one who is penniless but offers a rich gift to the one who has a few cents in his pocket, stating: "[He] who has will receive more and [he] who does not have will lose whatever he has." As he walks away, a child suddenly appears at his side, and soon a dove flies away from them, clearly a mockery of the trinity. After a number of similar scenes, the movie ends with the two mendicants forgetting the sanctuary of Compostela and coupling with a street prostitute according to the imperative that God sent Hosea: "Go and marry a prostitute and have two children. Call one of them 'ye are not my people' and the other one 'no more mercy.'"

In his novels *Cain* and *The Gospel According to Jesus Christ,* Saramago depicts God as a capricious master that appears to enjoy the suffering inflicted upon people. In *The Gospel According to Jesus Christ* God and the devil have the same face (only the devil has a beard) as if they were twin brothers. The devil begs God to forgive him, promising he will become the most faithful and loyal of his servants. God won't have any of it, and he continues to rule as a capricious and absolute sovereign over his subjects who from time to time are punished for an offense that has never been defined. His rule seems inspired most often by sadism (see Isaac's or even Jesus's sacrifice) and never by love.

Without subscribing to the blasphemy of these artists, I must admit that a lot of statements in the Bible are far from clear. For example, who were the "sons of the gods" who cavorted with the "sons of men" and gave origin to the giants? One may accept the request that Abraham sacrifice his only son as a statement against human sacrifice. But if that is the case, why did God not stop Jeosaphthah from sacrificing his own daughter in the Book of Judges? Were David and Jonathan lovers with the approval of God when David sings: "Jonathan whose love was sweeter than the love of women" or did God condemn homosexuality with the fall of Sodom and Gomorrah? And why did a loving God love Jacob and hate Esau, love David and hate Saul? Likewise it is problematic to try to explain why our sweet Jesus used physical violence against the temple merchants or used his divine power to wither a fig tree that did not satisfy his hunger. Though I like to read biblical epistemology and archeology, I don't consider myself a scholar. My approach to the Bible is a common-sense one, with my opinions backed by a number of students and scholars. The Old Testament is a collection of writing from different authors from different times who became progressively aware of the nature of the deity, through a number of real experiences that we can interpret only in part. I do believe that Moses somehow established a personal contact with God both in the burning bush incident and on the mountains of the law giving, though we modern individuals have lost the clue to that type of communication, as we have unlearned how to listen to nature.

In any case, my view is this: The books of the Old Testament may be divided into three groups: the Torah, which is essentially a theological, liturgical and disciplinary text, whose theology is borne out in part by ancient legends; the historical books; and the wisdom books (which includes the prophetic ones). The historical books (part of Torah, Joshua, Judges, Samuel, Kings, and Chronicles) are exaltations of the almightiness of God seen with the eyes of writers belonging to ancient cultures. They looked at God as they would have at an absolute monarch of their times. So it is not surprising that in their eyes God turned out to be as capricious as one of those ancient Eastern monarchs from Hammurabi to Nebuchadnezzar.

There is, indeed, a basic difference between the history of the Isaac sacrifice and the history of Jeosaphthah's . The aborted sacrifice of Isaac was an ancient legend with two important theological teachings: that obedience is due God even when we don't understand His and Her will, and that God abhors human sacrifice. The history of Jeosaphthah on the other side, is the account of a simpleton of a human being finding himself in a quandary from which he tried to escape by killing his daughter. God had not asked for nor approved that sacrifice; it was all Jeosaphthah's doing. Yet, even in the historical Bible books, God's compassion generally overwhelms His anger and His wrath. Not once did God reject his repented people when they asked for forgiveness and help. God is ascribed a magnanimity unknown to the absolute monarchs by historical writers. Over centuries of evolution and revelation, these writers grasped the concept that God's justice is founded on love.

The wisdom books represent, in Old Testament scholar Walter Brueggemann's words, a trial of God by man. In these books (think mainly Job and Ecclesiastes, but one may include many pieces of Isaiah, Jeremiah, Ezekiel, Hosea, and other prophets) human beings ask a triumphant God the meaning of life and human suffering. The answer to these questions is not provided in the Old Testament. It is somehow provided in the New Testament. In the figure of Christ God provides a practical, not a theoretical answer. By sending his son to become a human being, God embraces human suffering and makes of this suffering an instrument of redemption. Through his suffering Christ redeems the debts that keep human beings enslaved to the power of evil. Christ gives a meaning to our suffering, does not eliminate it; nor does he explain its origin. By embracing human suffering God proclaims His brotherhood with all human beings and provides, through agape, the means to maintain that brotherhood. Once again, for somebody like me who was often drowning in a sea of resentment and incertitude, this lifesaver is more than sufficient to trust in for the rest of my life.

The person of God the Father who exacts the torture and the death of his own son, not to mention that of each human being that was born, as a satisfaction to His and Her outraged divinity has represented a stumbling block to my faith. I could not help asking even before Buñuel's movies and Saramago's novels whether God was indeed a sadistic tyrant, playing a cat-and-mouse game with humankind. After reading and re-reading the prayers of Christ in the Olive Garden ("Father, if thou be willing, remove this cup from me" [King James Bible]) it dawned on me that God the Father and God the Son represent a dialogue of God with Him and Herself. Like a disappointed parent who asks sometimes whether it is worthwhile to have children, God asks Him and Herself whether it is worth all these troubles to try to share His and Her love with a humanity that appears at best indifferent to it. The comforting answer that God gives to Him and Herself is that God could not be God without sharing the suffering of His and Her children. The acceptance of human suffering is the ultimate declaration that God is Agape, and denying Agape would mean to deny Himself and Herself. Maybe this realization more than any other allowed me to feel my allegiance to God. Not only God needed to redeem our humanity, but also God needed to be redeemed by our humanity, as the old movie of Jean Delannoy's *Dieu A Besoin des Hommes* (*God Needs Men*) implied.

*Emotional issues.* Undoubtedly my hostility toward my father, along with the use of guilt as a means of subjugation by virtually every member of my family, has colored my religious experience. Such sentiments belong to my past, however, and do not represent a current difficulty impeding my faith.

I wish to emphasize as well that my faith never vacillated even when faced with the excesses and the indiscretions of the Catholic Church and of other Christian denominations. As scandalous and as ahorrent as I find them, the lust for power and sex of the prelates of the Middle Ages and the Renaissance and pedophilia and other forms of child abuse that have emerged in the modern church are nothing more than the expression of human frailty in an institution that Christ had wanted to be fully human. For the record, one of the priests who was accused of pedophilia against more than a dozen boys in the Tampa diocese, Father Robert Schaeufele, had a critical role in healing my hostility toward my father.

A few hours before I left the United States to attend to my father during his agonizing illness, I went to Father Schaeufele for confession. As I revealed my hostility toward my father that I did not feel capable of overcoming on my own, he grabbed my hands and ordered the evil spirits of rancor and hatred to leave me. I was healed. Apparently he was a man who had violated a number of human and divine laws and inflicted serious pain on people who trusted his ministry. Yet, by the grace of God, this man of sin still knew how to be a priest. Likewise, the pope who prevented the extermination and torture of American Indians by ordering missionaries to baptize them, making them as protected as any other human beings, was the same Alexander VI (Rodrigo Borgia) known for his luxurious lifestyle as well as his murders, which have been attenuated, rather than dramatized, in the HBO Showtimes series "The Borgias."

Of course I find the crimes of clergy and abuse of church power abhorrent and hateful and decry the pain they inflicted throughout the world. The splitting of the church by the Protestant Reformation has its roots in the visit of a mystic Martin Luther to Rome. There he witnessed the corruption of the Catholic Church and was inspired to start a reformation (that soon was corrupted as well by the support of the princes of Northen Germany who wanted to gain political independence from the Roman empire). But I learned to expect all manifestations of human weakness in an institution that God wanted to be human.

Gratuitous lack of compassion, instead, disturbed and to some extent still disturbs my faith. Unfortunately I was forced to witness many examples of it. In 1949 our family hired a helper, a teen-ager from Predappio, a small country town famous for having given birth to Mussolini. Her name was Edda. In 1951 her father committed suicide by hanging himself. She was left with the task of dealing with the corpse. The local pastor, Father Vittorino, a Franciscan friar who was nostalgic for the fascist rule, denied the family the comfort of a religious funeral, as suicides were treated that way during those times. Edda grabbed two fallen three branches, made a rudimentary cross of them and marched, holding that cross in front of the coffin. Much before the issue of women priests was even discussed, Edda became God's minister for her father. Like Christ's love, her love overruled the Sadducees that ruled the temple and brought her family and her father the unconditional love of Christ. I must admit that I am more offended by the rigidity of Father Vittorino than by the reported incest of Lucrezia and Cesare Borgia, daughter and son of Alexander VI. A few years later, I don't remember whether it was 1952 or 1953, my uncle had to have brain surgery that by that time was still experimental and very dangerous. My uncle had lived a disorderly life—no school, a lot of women, at least one case of a sexually transmitted disease, and a legal condemnation for the theft of German rifles at the end of World War II. My father recommended that he go to confession, because the surgery had a 50–50 chance of taking his life. He obliged. Unfortunately he met a friar who asked him if he belong to any political party. When my uncle admitted that he was a registered socialist, the friar told him he could not possibly absolve him if he did not rescind his association with the party. Perhaps appropriately, my uncle told him to fuck himself and stick his absolution up his ass. The ill- advised friar was enforcing the rule promulgated by Pope Pius XII. This was the same pope who had remained silent as millions of Jews were carried to the slaughter; the same pope who had facilitated the escape of Nazi criminals to South America. Yet he ostracized anyone who belonged to two parties (communist and socialist) that represented the only possible refuge for millions of Italians laborers seeking a decent livelihood for themselves and their families. At that time Italy was a developing country where the masters wielded almost absolute power over the lives of their subjects. In some southern regions, the *ius primae noctis* was still applied de facto (giving the lord of the manor first rights to local brides on their wedding nights). I still remember the warning attached to every confessional in Italy: "It is a mortal sin under pain of excommunication to vote for the Communist Party and for the Socialist Party." Why have I never seen written there: "It is a serious sin not to pay the laborers a living salary; it is a mortal sin to let the emigrants leave without their spouses; it is a mortal sin to split the families that God has united; it is a mortal sin to reserve enormous properties for one's own amusement while millions of people are starving"?

The culminating scene of the 1961 movie *Judgment at Nuremberg* shows Burt Lancaster, a Nazi judge undergoing trial, standing up and asking Maximilian Schell, his defense lawyer, words to the effect: "Are we going to repeat the same infamy of twenty years ago all over again?" Twenty years earlier, as a judge, he had condemned to death a Jewish man who had been like a father to an Aryan girl and had held her on his lap and kissed her as a father kisses his daughter. In cross examining the girl (Judy Garland), now a grown woman, Schell insinuated that the judge had done nothing else but respect the law because, indeed, she had been kissed by the Jewish man in violation of the law.

"Are we going to commit this infamy all over again?" I cannot help asking my church. I refer to the most egregious betrayal of the poor in the church history, described accurately in the 1986 movie "The Mission" starring Robert De Niro. Following the discovery of America, Jesuits had built seven missions in Brazil, Paraguay and Argentina. These missions were independent cities for and by the indigenous peoples, whom the Jesuits had educated in the principles of a flourishing economy, run according to the Christian principles of justice. For me those missions were and still are the example of what Christianity can do when it respects the tradition of local communities and engrafts into them the Christian principles of love and justice. For the first time in history those missions represented a truly Christian society where religion was spread by its inner force rather than with the sword as it had been in the religious wars of the Middle Ages.

These flourishing communities, these living examples of Christian sociology, displeased the kings of Spain and Portugal, who considered the indigenous peoples a source of cheap labor and exploitation, when they were not valuable merchandise in the slave trade. They complained to Pope

Gregory XIII, pope from 1572 to 1585, who ordered the dismemberment of the Jesuit order and the destruction of the missions. Many of the priests elected to die with the indigenous peoples they had served, now under assault by Spanish and Portuguese cannons. They elected to die for their people, like Christ died, but they are considered rebels by the Catholic Church the same way Jesus had been considered a rebel by the temple priests!

I must confess I don't even try to be objective in this description. My affection and gratitude for Father Serra and for the Jesuits who influenced my own family life makes me feel personally offended by the persecution of this order. This order would have made the world a Christian world if the popes had been more concerned about saving human souls than protecting the privilege and exploitive practices of the powerful! More in general, pervasive human suffering that we witness every day represents an emotional difficulty for my faith. The issue of suffering is real and, at times, overwhelming. We are almost desensitized as we learn that millions of people, mostly children, die every day from preventable causes such as starvation and infectious diseases. We are no longer upset to learn that, for the amount of money we spend trying to prolong for a few months (often without success and with a lot of pain) the lives of a few thousand cancer patients, we could fill the developing world with decent dwellings and clean water. Yet we may not be ostriches when faced with the poverty we find in our own back yards.

When I moonlighted in the emergency rooms of the Mississippi Delta, I had to take care of babies whose skin had become like parchment from dehydration. Twenty years after Bobby Kennedy had visited the Mississippi Delta and received an impression so devastating that he and others worked to overturn a well rooted Jim Crow, poverty and ignorance were still rampant. I saw teen-age mothers not wealthy enough nor smart enough or who did not care enough about their children to take care of the diarrhea that might have killed them. I saw children eating dirt in front of their parents and grandparents who did not care to intervene. Indoor plumbing was still a luxury, skin diseases and sexually transmitted diseases were endemic. Still now throughout the country, emergency rooms are filled with gunshot-wound victims on Friday nights resulting from the deadly mixture of alcohol and bullets. We can see with our own eyes our disabled veterans begging for a living on street corners in major cities, and sometimes mixed with them we find some old man who cannot survive on an inadequate pension because the cost of living and medical expenses have become unaffordable. And every day we read or hear on the news horror stories of babies and small children abused and even killed through neglect or violence by their parents. The victims of the Holocaust are still with us, despite the unconscionable attempts of some to deny its size or even its occurrence: Not too long ago a patient showed me the serial number marked on his forearm in Auschwitz. And victims of the Holocaust were mostly the very people God had selected as His chosen, and some of the perpetrators were self-proclaimed Christian believers!

I don't look for these experiences. They come to me. I try to see in each suffering person Christ asking for my help. I try to remember to say, like the blind man of the Gospel, "Domine, ut videam" ("Lord, that I may see" [Darby Bible Translation]). In this case it means, "God, let me see this person again in your kingdom." But I cannot rid myself of a sense of guilt and feeling revolted at the same time.

CHAPTER 30

# A Few Stories of Redemption

I CANNOT LEAVE THE issue of human suffering without describing some small rays of hope that derive from my own experience. As a veteran physician approaching old age, I still can remember patients literally screaming their way to death because doctors and nurses were all but desensitized to the management of pain. Even as late as 1973 a report showed that in the Mount Sinai Hospital of New York, arguably one of the most prestigious institutions in the world, patients with acute myocardial infarction, or heart attack (that is associated with the worst possible pain) received only homeopathic doses of narcotics. It is not farfetched to state that the dying experience in the late 1970s was similar to the one depicted in Atlanta in the movie *Gone with the Wind* after the rebels abandon the city and Yankees batter the hospital and the wounded inside with their artillery. I remember it well.

As a physician in training, the patients' requests for pain relief annoyed me when my colleagues and I were trying to decipher the intricacies of the scientific nature of their conditions. I remained unmoved by the prayers of an 18-year-old and her mother to spare her the fifth very painful—and totally unnecessary—arterial puncture trying to establish whether her blood pH had risen by a few units. I discharged against medical advice, for insubordination, a paralyzed young man with sickle cell disease. His crime? His towering mama, reminding us of a grizzly protecting her cubs, had shoved out of the room a medical student who had tried to do a blood stick to learn what sickle cells looked like. Indeed, sometimes we inflicted pain on the so called "hateful" patients. I remember inserting thirty unnecessary stitches in a hair dresser abandoned by his wife who sought my attention for superficial lacerations of his forearm. On the pretense of a suicide attempt, he had made some very shallow lacerations of his forearm implying that he had meant to cut his vein. The lacerations would have healed on their own with some pressure applied. It was clear that he did not mean to kill himself, just wanted to catch some attention from the staff. But he had disturbed me during a conference, so I wished to inflict pain on him to punish him, instead of trying to listen to him and console him. Also I needed some additional training in stitching.

Almost single-handedly Dr. Kathleen Foley overturned this state of affairs in Western medicine. She could not accept the tolerance that most physicians displayed for other people's suffering. During forty years of indefatigable work, this brilliant neurologist, who is also a person of compassion rooted in a deeply held Christian faith, succeeded in eliminating all the myths and the prejudices related to the management of pain. She demonstrated that the idea that patients build up tolerance of narcotics is a myth, as one can increase indefinitely the doses of these medications and consequently there is no reason to wait until the pain is severe for the administration of these drugs. She demonstrated that in patients with chronic pain, narcotics are best administered around the clock rather than "as needed" to keep the pain under control throughout the day and allow patients with serious and terminal diseases to treasure the last days of their life free of pain. She demonstrated that the fear of killing the patient with excessive doses of narcotics was totally unfounded and that pain, rather than pain medications, was the major cause of death, disability and discomfort. She gave origin to a new branch of medicine, palliative medicine, that has reinserted the much-needed ingredient of compassion in a Western practice of medicine that is becoming, every day, estranged from and deaf to human needs.

Unfortunately, political representatives of the religious right threaten to undo the achievements of Dr. Foley and of palliative medicine. With a self-righteous grandstanding about preventing the occasional death from overdose, they successfully pushed for passage of laws in many states aimed at scaring physicians into not prescribing pain-relieving medications and pharmacists into not storing them.

Remember Fearless Fosdick? The cartoon character tries to prevent one death from a single poisoned bean can by killing thousands of bean eaters every day. Cynical Bible-thumping politicians skirt the difficult yet effective ways to prevent drug abuse. This would include the acknowledgement that the war on drugs has been a major disaster and conclude that the legalization of drugs may be the only way to prevent both drug abuse and the organized-crime connection to it. But admission of failure and mistakes is not an option when the goal is to win elections. Furthermore, quashing of organized crime may also prevent the flow of money into electoral coffers. The easy way to score points in the war on drugs is to let patients die in pain and to harass, and sometimes jail, physicians and nurses who use compassion rather than expedience as the compass of their practices.

The other ray of hope has been the privilege to observe the missionary work of the movement called Communion and Liberation." During a recent visit to Paraguay I met Don Aldo Trento in Asuncion. This remarkable Italian priest left his hometown of Treviso about twenty years ago. During one of his recurrent crises of depression, he had fallen in love with a young widow, and his feelings were keenly reciprocated. The conflict between his newfound affection and his vocation (his commitment to be married to God) aggravated his emotional status. Following the advice of his spiritual director, Father Don Luigi Giussani, the charismatic founder of Communion and Liberation, he transferred to Paraguay to work in a parish.

During the first few years in the new country, he spent most of his time studying the work of the Jesuits in South American missions and wrote a number of scholarly books on the subject. One day, while he was celebrating mass, somebody brought to his doorstep a terminally ill patient who had been discharged from the hospital for lack of funds. This encounter sparked a new awareness of his mission. He was there to help those who could not help themselves, and there were plenty of them in Paraguay.

In a few years, with the help of his friends from Communion and Liberation, he built three houses around his parish: one for the terminally ill, one for abandoned infants, and a third as a school for orphaned or abandoned children. Each house is a church. That is, each house possesses an altar in the middle where he celebrates mass, while his staff (composed mainly of international volunteers) ministers to the suffering. Thanks to Father Trento's mission, Martha and Mary encounter each other in the Paschal sacrifice. In the biblical tradition Martha represents the active life, as she endeavors to prepare an adequate meal for Jesus and his followers. Mary Magdalene, her sister, represents the contemplative life, as she sits at Jesus's feet and listens to his teaching. Eventually Martha complains to Jesus: Why don't you tell my lazy sister to get up off her ass and help me? The tension between the contemplative and the active life is common in Church history. It has been common for missionaries risking health, wealth and life in hostile settings to complain about the peaceful lives of monks in their isolated monastery. These missionaries are not only found in remote countries. Virtually most parishes in Europe had become de-Christianized. In his book *Les Saints vont en lenfer* (*Saints Go To Hell*), Gilbert Cesbron describes the struggles of Catholic priests working as laborers in the assembly line. In the mission of Father Trento, with an altar in each building, contemplative and active life go side by side. Whoever works in his mission to take care of the poor has the opportunity to witness and to be witnessed by the living God, dwelling in the tabernacle.

When I was there, one of the people brought to him was a dying AIDS patient from the local jail, where he was spending time for drug trafficking. Father Trento interrupted the service, well aware that the Sabbath is for man and not man for the Sabbath. He sent the policeman away: In the house of God, there are neither policemen nor jails, he said. After hugging the man, who could not speak due to his extreme fatigue, he asked him: "If you know that Jesus loves you, do lift a finger." After the man did so, the priest administered the sacrament of absolution. "That is what reconciliation is about," he explained to me. "To be aware of the love of God. I myself make a point of going to confession every week to be told by Jesus that I am loved." Before dying, the man's estranged wife and children, whom he had abandoned ten years earlier, lured by a drug lord promising easy money, visited him. Through the mediation of Don Aldo, he died in peace with God and the world. In a few hours of agony, he perhaps taught more things about God's love to his family than he might have done in a lifetime of honest work.

Don Aldo's parish is located in one of the most derelict areas of Asuncion. The street around the parish is sullied with rotting garbage, dead animals, excrement, used syringes and condoms. The contrast with the interior of the houses could not be more impressive. Each room is clean to the point of being luminous thanks to the reflection of sunlight and is enriched with fresh flowers. Soothing church music is played each day and throughout the day. Cleanliness is the most basic form of self respect, beauty the most basic form of self love, and music is a universal language highlighting the brotherhood of all people — and the only one that can overcome the recurrent threat of more and more Babels, according to Father Trento. Entering the building from outside, one cannot escape the impression of having entered heaven.

Now Father Trento is building a new church for his mission and wants the church façade reproduced exactly as the façade of the Jesuit mission that was destroyed by Spanish and Portuguese forces with the acquiescence of the pope four hundred years ago. There was a redeeming work left to accomplish, and he feels privileged to have been called to accomplish it.

What about his depression? He still takes medications to control his mood that at times may be paralyzing. Otherwise he is grateful for a depression that enabled him to find his vocation, a vocation to infect all individuals he meets with the contagious and redeeming love of Christ!

The operation of Father Trento is a heaven for people from around the world, not just from Paraguay. During my visit I met, among others, a disturbed young woman from my hometown, Rimini. She found a profoundness to her life in the service of the poorest of the poor after looking in vain for relief from her depression in the arms of a number of men. They had pursued together the illusion of freedom by sleeping in expensive hotels, visiting expensive resorts and indulging in expensive meals and drug habits.

A young woman from Germany was there for a completely different reason. She had been disturbed by the knowledge of how much children around the world were suffering, and she finally found a way to relieve their and her own suffering through her service. In addition, young members of Communion and Liberation around the world labored to provide a solid infrastructure for Father Trento's work, and in this way they found the meaning of their own lives in a valuable investment of their unique talents.

A surgeon, Alberto Reggiori, father of seven children, spent more than ten years in Uganda with his family. After braving the bullets during the civil war that devastated the country and even at times entered the operating room, he was asked to move to a southern town. He was charged with the task of making the local hospital functional, a task that appeared unfeasible to almost everybody else. His experience is described in his book, *When Diesel is Gone* Diesel, or gas-oil, was the source of all energy. When the local supply was depleted, the only solution was to provide emergency care in the dark.

But his major initial challenge was to make the 500-bed facility operational. Local people were so disenchanted that when he asked for admission to the operating room, the kitchen or the pharmacy, the answer was always the same: "The man with the key is not here." When he left five years later the hospital counted 10000.00 admissions a year, 1,500 major surgical interventions and 2,500 deliveries of babies, in addition to a fully functional operating room, delivery room, emergency room and intensive care units. He credited not infusion of money or of new resources with creating this miracle. Infusion of motivation through faith in themselves enabled people to learn that they could make a difference in their own lives by serving others.

Perhaps Gilda, an illiterate Ugandan woman, represents Reggiori's best success story. When she was pregnant with her third child, her husband asked her to have an abortion. When she refused, her husband abandoned her and the children. The child was born HIV infected; Gilda had been infected by her husband.

Shunned by her own family and by the community, not unusual in that country for carriers of transmittable diseases, she retired to her hut at the edge of the village waiting to die, together with her children. Things turned around when a social worker from Reggiori's center asked if she could offer care for her youngest, HIV-infected child. "What for?" the mother asked with both diffidence and discouragement. The social worker retorted, "Please do remember that your spirit is stronger than the virus that infects you and your child. If you want, you can make a difference in millions of people's lives, not just in yours and that of your family."

The social worker's persistence paid off. With proper treatment, the child is now a college student, and Gilda has been advocating on five continents for AIDS patients in developing countries.

It is difficult not to think of the angel who touched Isaiah's lip with a burning coal and enabled the stuttering prophet to speak on behalf of God when one hears the eloquence and witnesses the inspiration of this illiterate woman. One also may remember the words of Jesus: "I thank you, O Father, Lord of heaven and earth, that you have hidden these things from the wise and understanding, and revealed them to little children." [World English Bible] Gilda had found that Christianity turned her life around and that of her child and had given her a mission. For her survival, her Christian faith was as essential as the air she was breathing. Just as she did not need to know the chemical composition of the air to know that air was essential, so she did not need any complicated demonstration of the existence of God to recognize that the Christian God was vital for her. She had been able to face the mystery of life.

These examples are nothing but drops in the large sea of missionary work conducted both at home and abroad by all Christian churches. This missionary work brings redemption to the evil of the world and of the church itself. Somehow the evil inside the church represents a training ground for the faithful to learn how to bring about redemption.

The same is true with families. Christian families are a training ground for redemption if spouses learn how to talk with each other, if they learn how to make up after a fight, rather than live a form of delusional harmony. I agree with a priest who said that the best gift parents can give to their children is to show their children how to make up. To be able to make up after a disagreement, to clear the air after hurting each other, is the first and most essential form of redemption, is the first manifestation of agape, "the love that devours." Couples pursuing harmony based on denial of problems and feelings pursue a delusion that deprives their children of the practice of redemption.

I believe this was the major shortcoming of my own mother's upbringing in her strict and devout Christian family. She never learned how to use a family fight as a form of redemption for herself and her husband, my father.

Fight was construed as a denial of spousal love, to be avoided under any circumstances.

I keep hammering on redemption because my experience has taught me that redemption is the ultimate goal of life, not just an option. I gained my self-esteem only when I learned that I could be an instrument or redemption, that my own liabilities could become assets for the redemption of my world, beginning with my own family, and that love as agape finds its ultimate expression in the work of redemption.

## CHAPTER 31

# That I Were Not Born

"I WOULD HAVE PREFERRED never to have been born." My father-in-law used to conclude most meals with this statement. His family and his few friends, including Father Serra, had learned to ignore his repeated declarations of existential discomfort. Clearly they were aimed to shock the audience and to affirm that he was still in charge of himself and aware of the burden of living. Nobody was deceived by the pleasantries we had exchanged at the table, his smile, his enjoyment of good food, or even the uncontainable expressions of affection he had for the grandchild he worshipped. Despite all these daily treasures, life for him was still a painful and burdensome duty that he confronted with the same stoicism with which he had confronted the Abyssinian rebels on the battlefields of Ethiopia.

May be it was the *ponentino* (the breeze that predictably refreshes Rome in the early afternoon) flowing through the open window. I surmise that the Holy Spirit was riding the *ponentino* on that tepid spring afternoon. In any case that particular day I felt inspired to respond to him: "Silvio, you are quoting the Bible, today." An expression of surprise and disconcertment crossed that stern face, accustomed to concealing any emotions other than anger, disappointment or reproach. Clearly, the impression that my small talk generated in him was so swift and deep that he had had no time to hide it.

"You are quoting several books of the Bible," I egged on with nonchalance, as if I had not noticed his stupefaction and was continuing a social conversation to kill time between coffee and the siesta. "More than once Job cursed the day he was born and implored God to let him wane in the night of death away from his suffering. 'Cursed be the man who ran to the field and announced with pride to my father that a baby boy was born,' snapped Jeremiah when God burdened him with the power of prophecy, which cost him rejection and torture and put his life at risk more than once. And more than once the psalmist asked God to withdraw from him His look, to leave him alone for a second without being subject to His scrutiny. You see, Silvio, the Old Testament may be read as a process of mankind to God as much as an exaltation of God's action and a revelation of His law. No book makes the point better than the Ecclesiastes, which starts by claiming *'Vanitas vanitatum et omnia vanitas,'* which means everything is vanity. The priestly writer of the book goes on, insisting that human actions do not entice the benevolence of God, and people who disregard the law are not punished while those who follow the law are not prized, a theme echoed in Psalm 49. The author belonged to the priestly cast and did not believe in eternal life, just as you don't seem to believe in it! You are in good company, Silvio. I just wish you could acknowledge that you don't own the copyright of your unhappiness and dissatisfaction. You express the very sentiments that the deepest thinkers of all times have expressed, including the authors of the Bible. Isn't something that a book like the Ecclesiastes, that may be read as blasphemous, was included among the holy books?" I added the last statement purposefully. As a good military man, Silvio was accustomed to blasphemy. On top of that, he was of Tuscan descent, and in Tuscany blasphemy had become a form of oratorical art. I wanted to make a point: our religious book enshrined blasphemy as a legitimate expression of faith and love for God, there in the book of the Ecclesiastes. Disappointment and anger are as legitimate expressions of love as tenderness and closeness.

I only regret that I didn't go one step farther. I wish I had informed him that the main drama of his adult life, his wife's abandonment of him, was enshrined in the book of Hosea. This book reveals that Silvio's disappointment at having been unable to convince his wife to come back to him and to love him is nothing less than God's disappointment in a humanity that does not seem to have a use for Him and Her, despite the daily blessings of life and despite the emptiness of a life without God. I guess that the Spirit of God vanished as the *ponentino* became feebler. Or maybe the spirits contained in the bottle of wine I guzzled during lunch had chased the Spirit of God away, as my eyelids were becoming heavier by the minute.

Silvio lived four more years after that conversation, and I could not help noticing subtle changes in his behavior. He appeared more relaxed and less eager to highlight his skepticism and his disappointment with life. He acted like a person who had found a powerful allegiance and the vindication of a life that up to that point he had seen as a solitary struggle of Promethean proportions. For almost ninety years of life he had felt that nobody could get an insight into his torment. Like the author of the Ecclesiastes, he had felt endowed with a burden that he must carry by himself, that nobody could help with. Like myself in my adolescence, he had felt excluded from the enjoyment that all his neighbors seemed to draw from life. In one of his rare moments of confidence, as we were watching Marco, my son, play soccer in a league with other boys his age, he admitted: "When I was a child I could not afford to play any sport. I could not even own a bike. As I learned to live without these perks, I developed a form of disdain for them. Even later, when I might have been able to afford them, I never could enjoy them. I am so happy that Marco seems to be able to enjoy life." The experience that moved him most was to see the people he loved enjoying life.

Claudia always remembered with tenderness, even during the times she felt hostile toward her father, how he was eager for her to discover Sardinia in the 1950s, when the region had not yet become a shining star of international tourism, and how he urged her to try expensive food such as lobster, which he would have never himself indulged in. As I myself learned to do, he learned to revel in other people's joy. Claudia described the commotion in his eyes as she was looking over her bridal gown and accessories—this, despite the fact he had not approved of our wedding at that time. When Marco was born, Silvio's first statement was: "From now on the goal of our lives will be to make this little person happy!" and for the following twenty-five years he was true to this goal with a tenacity that paid off with interest. At his funeral Marco could not stop crying, and he cried all night, something unusual for Marco, who had not mourned any of his other grandparents: "I will miss his affection forever; I lost a part of myself," he said between sobs.

In the meantime the official persona he adopted could have not been more cynical, though cynicism in him was tempered by a sense of humor that emerged almost in spite of himself. One of his favorite comments was: "My neighbor exists only for my own trouble and discomfort!" With such a claim he closed any conversation related to helping one's fellow man and relieving the misery of the world. One night when we drove to downtown Rome for an ice cream at the renowned gelateria Ciampini in Piazza Navona, he warned us about the risk of being robbed. After we returned safe, and he learned that we had paid ten thousand liras for ice cream, he commented: "You were lucky! You were robbed only by Ciampini!" But perhaps the most amusing of his verbal creations occurred during the war in Ethiopia. As a commanding officer, he characterized one of his subordinate officers in this way: "This man is harmful to everybody except to the enemy!"

After that somnolent post-lunch conversation, Silvio seemed to have realized that he had never been alone in his struggle with the truth; that is, with God. The tragedies of his life might have set him apart from the majority of humankind, but they made him part of a select group of people who had not shied away from facing the truth, from asking God some difficult questions. He had dared to confront God, and he had been burned, the way Moses looked like when he came down from the mountain with the tablets; he had been scarred the way Jacob limped after a nightlong fight with an angel that turned out to be God. That experience could not be shared with anybody else; that experience prevented him from enjoying festive celebrations aimed at bringing oblivion to a world drifting along. In that erstwhile post-lunch conversation he learned that his living experience made him alone but not lonely. Instead of being distressed by his unique pain, he should have been proud: his aloneness, his questions, even his frequent blasphemies had made him part of a select group of individuals that God had chosen to prepare the world for His and Her message. Some of them had authored the most troublesome books of the Bible; others, such as the pharaoh Ashkelon or the priest Melchizedek had been graced by the revelation of this troublesome God even if they had not belonged to the "chosen people." And this tradition of trying God persisted throughout Christian times. How could Nietzsche construct the superman if not because he tried to justify the Christian experience of the suffering servant without being able to believe in the Christian God?

Silvio was baptized as a Roman Catholic, but he never received confirmation or first communion. Those are essential milestones for full participation in the life of the Roman Catholic Church. He came from a family that was indifferent to the Christian message. He himself always considered the church as an instrument of power and longed for the days of Pius XII when communists and other of society's rebels were threatened with fire and brimstone. Despite his agnosticism he always professed a special feeling toward the Virgin Mary. One day he told me in another rare moment of confidence: "There is no way I can agree with the Protestants. They do not venerate the Virgin Mary. For me she is a reference perhaps more meaningful that God himself!" In my view he saw in her the accepting woman that neither his mother nor his wife had been for him. He received the Roman Catholic sacrament, the anointing of the sick, before dying. And most meaningful, the night he died he asked the Polish nurse who assisted him to pray with him. Unfortunately we arrived in Rome only after his passing.

Like Job, Silvio did not find an explanation for his suffering, but he found the allegiance of God. The first reading of his funeral mass, celebrated by Father Serra, was appropriately from the book of Job, the biblical character that he had impersonated throughout his life, though he gained a vague awareness of it only a few years before his death.

Sivio was born at the beginning of the past century in Alexandria, Egypt, into a family of Italian immigrants. His father spent long months in southern Egypt, away from home, to supervise archeological excavations. The first of six siblings born over a fourteen-year time span, he was marked with two interwoven emotions: responsibility and guilt. Guilt was the stick that led him to live up to his responsibilities. Graduated from an accounting school at 16 he started immediately working in a bank, turning his salary over to his mother to help her manage an expensive household. In exchange, he was informally invested as the "man of the house" to whom all authority was delegated during the prolonged absence of his father.

In that capacity he managed to inspire the hostility of his two sisters, whose virginity he felt charged to protect. Forty years after these events I had the opportunity to hear the grievances of the two women from their own mouths. I learned how he used to send them home from the seashore when his friends were joining him to prevent the mingling of the two sexes—dangerous temptations to his sisters' virtue. This was about 1920. One of the siblings was the same Uncle Titti who came to live near us in Tampa. He soon learned how to survive at Silvio's expense. Unlike Silvio, he spent his adolescence on the soccer and basketball fields, when he was not visiting the brothels of Alexandria. Eventually he was sent to a boarding school in Milan, at Silvio's expense, but he never completed the curriculum. As soon as the opportunity presented itself, he enrolled in the Italian marines and continued until his death the life of a perennial vagabond, well aware that Silvio would rescue him, even if begrudgingly, every time he got into financial trouble. Another brother, Gastone, became a successful accountant at a young age, but unlike Silvio he employed his income to build a personal fortune, besides indulging in the pleasures of sex and gourmet. Eventually he joined the navy and was taken to Australia by the English as a prisoner of war. Still in chains, he managed a money-making operation under the nose of his very captors. After the end of the war he became the dealer for Alpha Romeo in Australia and settled permanently there. The last brother, Raoul, became a physician thanks to Silvio's financial support and became the first and best known anesthesiologist in Italy. Besides Silvio, he was the only one that contributed to the support of the elderly parents and of other family members in need. Still, toward the end of his life, Silvio underwrote the cost of an adult-living facility in France for one of the sisters affected by dementia (in the family it was called Parkinson's, as that disease sounded more dignified than Alzheimer's). From age 16 until age 97, when he died,

Silvio took responsibility for his family and at the same time resented this burden.

To assist his parents and his younger siblings during their move from Alexandria to Rome, Silvio abandoned the only type of life he really had been able to enjoy—the army. Despite the mortal dangers lurking behind every bush and any sand dune twenty-four hours a day, seven days a week, Silvio had only fond memories of the time he spent in Ethiopia as a commanding officer of a fort in rebel territory. The need to follow orders and the certainty that his own orders would be followed without anyone's talking back relieved him of the pain of uncertainty and guilt. This is not surprising: Marcel Proust, who translated neurosis into a form of supreme literary art in *A La Recherche du Temps Perdu, (Remembrance of Things Past)*, stated that the military service was the only period of his life during which he felt free of his neurosis and able to enjoy the experience of living in its immediacy. In this most prominent work, also called *In Search of Lost Time*, Proust brewed his history into a potion whose taste he and his readers could savor in small sips. Except for the military service, life for him had been a burden of overwhelming sadness. Through the filter of his memory he could finally get pleasure from a life that in its immediacy proved a crushing burden. The so-called "freedom of choice" is the worst of slavery for sensitive people with an insight into the consequences of each choice. When I drive in an unknown direction I love to find one-way streets that prevent any distress at having to make a choice at each crossroad. Like Inspector Javert in *Les Miserables* Silvio's peace of mind was offered by clear guidelines to follow. To my and Claudia's dismay he always defended his punitive attitude toward his estranged wife because the government and even Church law (that prohibited divorce) were on his side. The law prevented him from examining his emotional shortcomings, and these represented the cross of his entire life. They originated in the knot of guilt and responsibility that he had been unable to unravel on his own and for which he had been resentful toward his mother and his siblings.

His marriage was the tragedy of his adult life. As one of the few Italian officers who could speak English fluently (thanks to his Egyptian birth and upbringing) he was chosen in 1945 to rescue the Italian soldiers who were prisoners in an American detention camp in Germany. By then he was 39 years old, had recently obtained a Ph. D. degree in economics and had an executive position in a government office prior to being recalled to the service. He also had a mistress, I learned from Claudia, who had learned it from her grandmother. Apparently he had a strong emotional tie to this woman. Though he did not plan to have any children, he had seriously considered marrying her. More than once his mother dissuaded him from this intention, insisting that he was still young and had a lot of life ahead of him to explore. Seemingly the Italian matriarch, who never had a kind comment about any daughter-in-law or son-in-law, did not wish to engage in a fight for Silvio's attention and support. I do know from different sources that the guilt of abandoning this mistress was added to the burdens of all his other guilts, to the point of being a source of ongoing tension in his short married life.

In Germany Silvio met a beautiful and charming woman fourteen years his junior. She came from an ancient and aristocratic family. To support her own family, devastated by the war and to save their vineyard in the Mosel region, she was employed as interpreter by the American army. Within three months they were married. From outside it looked like a storybook wedding, but Silvio confessed to his mother that he had wished for a car accident on the way to the church. He felt guilty about his Italian mistress. He felt guilty toward his family in Rome that he had not notified of his intention to wed. He felt guilty about the young woman that he was involving in the incertitude of his own life.

After the wedding he and his military attendant bought a used car and started a trip back to Rome with the new bride. The trip took forty-five days. Even by foot they would have been able to cover the distance between the SAAR region of Germany, which had been occupied by other European powers, and Rome in a shorter time frame. I don't know how he managed to delay the moment of the truth for that long. Just before his marriage was revealed to a hostile family, his bride discovered to be pregnant, and she suffered all the discomfort of an early pregnancy.

It is easy to understand how things went downhill from there. This young woman did not speak a word of Italian (she and Silvio had always communicated in French). She, who had never left her own country and was about to become a mother, instantly became the target of less than benevolent scrutiny by a contentious Italian family. With six people crammed in a two-bedroom apartment on the Tiber riverside, and Silvio's salary as the only income the family could count on, the family was prone to see her as an intruder who had exploited the caprice of a lonely soldier, not to welcome her as the better half of a beloved son and brother.

In a perverse dynamic typical of an Italian family of those times, that unexpected wedding became an occasion for payback for the family, which, up to that time, had been subjected to Silvio's authority and power. The matriarch saw in the unannounced wedding a form of intolerable rebellion against her primacy. It was inconceivable that a son might not seek his mother's blessing before choosing a bride, a privilege that was conceded only after a prolonged vetting and that never was unconditional.

As an extreme example, the wife of my high school principal, a cultivated teacher of Latin and Greek, got sick on all of her three sons' wedding days. Tired of repeatedly rescheduling their weddings, all three married without her presence. To avoid the problem, her only daughter eloped with her lover. The mother refused to see her children again, even for her husband's funeral. When her husband had to go on an outing for business, she timed him to make sure he did not go surreptitiously to visit his grandchildren. Unspoken tribal law held that the compensation for the abuse a wife received from her husband during her lifetime consisted in making the lives of her daughters-in-law miserable. They eventually would gain the same privilege. Bequeathing such abuse from one generation to the next underlay the lie of the happy and close Italian family. Silvio's marriage was an open challenge to that lie; that is, to the tribal law. It could not and should not have been tolerated. Acceptance would have meant to destroy a century-old culture, to undermine—society the way it was known.

Silvio's mother wasted no time in letting her new daughter-in-law know that she was unwanted and must work hard to gain her benevolence, without the promise that this gain would ever come. In the meantime, one of Silvio's sisters started resenting the beautiful young woman. After imposing a virtual chastity belt on his own sisters, now Silvio pretended that his sisters must submit to the wishes of an attractive stranger who could not even speak their language. One of the sister's welcoming acts toward her new sister-in-law consisted of aiming a teapot full of hot water at her head!

After Claudia was born, my mother-in-law went back to her native Germany with the secret design of never returning. She had a number of encounters with Silvio in Germany. These encounters confirmed her determination. As is almost a rule in these situations, she started resenting intimacy that was not supported, in her view, by any communication, let alone communions. I have encountered younger couples saying that they understood each other very well when horizontal but ceased understanding when on their feet. In the case of my mother-in-law, according to what she told Claudia, their sexual encounters were as burdensome and devastating as their discussions. When she decided that any form of understanding at any level had become all but impossible, she filed for and obtained divorce in Germany. (Divorce was unlawful then in Italy, and a woman who had abandoned her family was considered a felon.) In response Silvio filed for and obtained sole custody of Claudia in a German court.

As soon as the judgment assigning Claudia to Silvio was rendered, Claudia and her mother escaped to France under assumed names. With the help of some Alsacian friends, who also resented the German occupation, Silvio succeeded in tracking them down. Claudia still remembers the scene that followed. It became imprinted on her brain. It colored the rest of her life more than any other incident in her childhood.

At her mother's side, as she was coming back from a stroll in the French countryside, they saw Silvio hurrying toward them. He grabbed Claudia by the hand, her mother grabbed her other hand, and both started pulling. Claudia did not know what had happened next. She might have fainted. All she remembered was that they were all at the gendarmerie (the French military force carrying out police matters) where Silvio's right to Claudia was established in a review of the court papers. During their travels back to Italy, Silvio told his estranged wife that she would be welcome to come home and be his wife anytime she wished. She declared that she would never come back. Silvio took Claudia, who by then did not speak a single Italian word, back to Rome. By his own admission, at that point Silvio made it the mission of his life to win back his wife, to reunite the broken family.

Claudia received letters, phone calls and presents for birthday and Christmas from her mother, who had learned Italian to communicate with her daughter. However, for ten years Claudia did not see her mother. It is not clear whether Silvio ever reported her to Italian authorities for abandoning the family. The fact is that Claudia's mother never felt comfortable enough to cross the Italian frontier, fearful of this indictment. Even when her own mother died in the Italian Riviera during a vacation, Claudia's mother waited for the corpse to come back to Germany.

When Claudia was 14, her father discovered a diary in which Claudia recorded her longing to talk to her mother about an infatuation she had developed for a school mate. Silvio arranged for the girl and the woman to meet in Switzeralnd under his control. For a year they repeatedly saw each other, all the time with Silvio asking her to come back. When he realized it would not happen, he called off Claudia's contact with her mother. The contacts were re-established, but always under Silvio's control, a few years later when Claudia's maternal grandmother died. Claudia eventually became independent of Silvio with our visit to Germany shortly before our wedding.

Claudia's mother never remarried. We don't know whether she established any intimate relationships with any men. She spent her time in Munchen visiting with a small group of friends. Her circles were aristocratic and cultural. One of her best friends was the director of the Deutsche *pinakothek* (German art museum). Another one was a Russian baroness who lived in Wien together with other aristocrats who had fled Russia after the revolution. A third one was a famous pianist. Claudia's mother soon realized that she would never achieve her own lifelong goal of becoming a renowned pianist, and she ended up writing novels and essays that were never published.

Silvio did not engage in sexual relationships. He had vowed in front of a priest not to betray his wife, and he felt duty bound to respect that vow, even in the absence of any declared religious beliefs. By the same vow, he felt duty bound not to soil the family life of his daughter with the presence of a mistress.

But of Claudia's parents, it was Silvio and what Silvio represented that was most influential in my own turnaround.

His choice of celibacy as well as his persistence in pursuing a woman who disdained and resented him for having deprived her of her child was looked at almost universally with derision, as if he were a modern day Don Quixote, fighting windmills. He was seen to be living in a fairy tale of lifelong marital devotion that was no more realistic than the endeavors of King Arthur's cavaliers. Nobody except Father Serra was inclined to see the tragedy of his history. When they cannot get along, normal people split and try to engage in a new relationship, went the wisdom of the time, even among devout Catholics who practiced their faith seriously. When political battle over legalization of divorce divided Italy in 1973, a number of Catholic priests and committed Catholics defied the pope and bishops and openly supported divorce. Perhaps the most noticeable among them was Carlo Carretto, the leader of a youth movement known as Catholic Action. After being disappointed with politics, he retired to the desert to a novitiate, The Little Brothers of Jesus. After a night of prayer Carretto wrote an article published in all of the major Italian newspapers expressing his support for divorce together with a stinging rebuttal of the official church position. He denounced the opposition to divorce as another expression of the church's lust for power and disregard for charity.

In addition to derision, many looked at Silvio's attitude with hostility and loathing if not hatred. When I met Claudia, I myself identified in Silvio the enemy to defeat. Not only did I feel endowed with the mission to rescue Claudia on my white horse from the malignant giant who kept her prisoner in the tower of a castle, but I also found in him a target against which to unload the hostility I had nurtured against my own father, whose prepotency and dominance I saw in Silvio carried to their extreme.

One must recognize that as his own worst enemy, Silvio did his best to elicit these sentiments. It is easy to see an act of violence in the way he took Claudia away from her mother, and more in general in the way he founded his claims to his wife on government and religious law without any consideration of hers or Claudia's feelings. He acted as if he were unable to acknowledge that any personal relationship, especially the one where intimacy is involved, needs to be nurtured with an ongoing dialogue including conflicts leading to deeper understanding. He gave the impression of believing that when the law is on your side you can own another person, you can expect his or her affection, as long as you yourself don't break the law. To that one should add his frequent statements that his wife's abandonment had dishonored him as a man and, worse, dishonored his family. In his view only blood could redeem this offense to the unspoken tribal law—"But it was not worth being jailed over her." I heard him say this more than once.

I began to see Silvio as the worst threat to our marriage. Despite Father Serra's assurance that Silvio cared only about our marital well being, I felt he was trying to put a wedge between Claudia and me and to bring Claudia back under his own subjection. Ironically enough, I did not realize that this fear meant I was affected by the same faults I ascribed to Silvio. Like Don Quixote, I felt endowed with the task of freeing an innocent damsel from her prison. Worse than that, I felt that Claudia was a prize to be conquered in an epic battle with her father. I must confess that more than once I wished him dead.

To everybody's credit and thanks to Father Serra's mediation, things got better and better over the years, especially after Marco's birth. The happiness of having a grandchild became for Silvio a more compelling mission than the conquering of his estranged wife. And I could not help but be moved by the affection Silvio poured on Marco. Assured that we had a common mission, I took a much more benign view of his life choices. I started seeing in him a kind of *heautontimoroumenos*, (self-tormenting), as in a protagonist in a play by the ancient Roman playwright Terence (Publius Terentius Afer). In the play, a man in Rome decides to retire to the country and engage in a number of deprivations to punish himself for the death of his wife.

Only after Silvio's death did I become ready to fully appreciate that his life had been a tragedy of biblical proportions that he fought alone, surrounded by derision and loathing, and without the support of the faith at least up until the last few years. Perhaps I am deluding myself, but I firmly believe that the casual conversation we had on that spring afternoon in Rome allowed Silvio to recognize the allegiance of God, to accept that his suffering had a meaning that was not known by him, but was known by God.

Two more considerations are germane to this case. In his 1882 play "An Enemy of the People," the great playwright Henrik Ibsen wrote, "The majority is always wrong," which means, "Power is always wrong; the power of the mob is no different from that of a tyrant, is always an attempt to suffocate the truth through power." In the case of Silvio I associated myself with the mob that ridiculed him. In my heart of hearts I could see only a desire to overpower a woman who had wronged him, had rejected his love and dishonored his tribe in the context of his proclaimed devotion to the sanctity of marriage. That was the way the mob saw it, and I bought into the mob's lies. I joined and led the mob in his moral lynching. I associated with a power that was way more destructive than the power Silvio had claimed over his estranged spouse.

Some of Silvio's claims were and are clearly indefensible. The honor of a person is untouched by the rejection of another person even if this other person is his or her spouse. And tribal honor is a pagan construct that all major religions including Islam have rejected.. Islamic scholars reject the "honor killing" practiced in remote areas of Islamic countries. Despite these shortcomings, Silvio's lonely battles in the defense of his marriage contained a fundamental truth that the mob dismissed: "A new relationship makes the problems of a troubled marriage worse."

When you no longer like the script, it does not make sense to change the players. Silvio's fidelity, whatever its motivation, deserved to be enshrined alongside the fidelity of the prophet Hosea to his estranged and adulterous wife, alongside the fidelity of Father Serra to my personal growth despite my frequent denials and rebellion, alongside the fidelity of God to His and Her people even when those people curse, deride or, worse, ignore God's name and His and Her indefatigable love .

The second acknowledgement has to do with my marriage. I've told how I see my marriage as the landmark that allowed me to find myself; that is, the meaning of my life and of unconditional love. Without Silvio, without his stern upbringing of Claudia, my marriage, the way I know it, would have been all but impossible. Silvio and Claudia and I were assigned the same portion of the Lord's vineyard to work in, and after many attempts we learned together how to produce our unique type of grapes.

A young man that was a good friend of Claudia told her that in marrying me she was marrying her father. Though we both dismissied this assertion as a pleasantry it might have proven true more than I could have possibly conceived

CHAPTER 32

# I Felt as if I Were Breathing the Life of God

I FELT AS IF I were breathing the life of God Him and Herself!. My parents believed I masturbated and urged me to leave the bathroom at night. The reality was quite different. As I did not have my own room, I had to share my sleeping room, which also served as family dining room, with my sister. So the ability to lock myself in the bathroom gave me the feeling of freedom. In the evening I loved to open the window of the bathroom and to breathe the night air coming across the solitary back road — a combination of flowers, sea, stale gas and stardust. I felt as if I were breathing the life of God Him and Herself! Somehow I always felt enamored of God. I just did not learn until much later where and how to encounter Him and Her

As I believe it was for Silvio, the turning point of my life occurred when I realized that God was talking of me to me, when I discovered my personal history within the context of sacred history. It is impossible for me to identify an Antiochian road where God revealed Himself and Herself to me. Rather I recognize an ongoing process that continues up to this day, and may not even stop with my death, a process that favors my relationship with God as I discovered myself in God's will. As I've said, I don't expect to comprehend God lest I lose my relationship with Him and Her, the same way I don't expect to comprehend Claudia or Marco, or my grandchildren, or any of my most treasured relationships.

I must admit that I always had a feeling for God. Even at the time when I rejected God and blasphemed God's holy name, I was longing for God, and I was angry for not knowing how to find Him and Her.

When I was a small child, almost an infant, just after the end of World War II, my parish church had been destroyed by the allied bombs. Rimini was the most bombed of Italian cities, as it represented the eastern border of the so-called Gothic line, where Germans troops had settled the boundaries for their retreat. A couple of my oldest patients have admitted to me, "Doctor, I am sorry to say, but I bombed your hometown!" Religious celebrations were held in the garden of the house my family and I inhabited. A good friend of my father's allowed us to use an empty apartment in his mansion until we could find a stable dwelling.

Though I could barely speak I was charmed by the religious celebrations. My grandmother had stitched together some rags for me that I pretended were clerical garments, and one of my favorite forms of play was to celebrate the mass. For an altar, I used a wooden desk that my uncle had assembled with wood discarded by a local carpenter. Until age 13 that makeshift desk functioned as the night table and writing table where I sat when I felt inspired to compose poems. Somehow it kept functioning as an altar where I accomplished my own sacrifices.

When it was thrown away because my family could finally afford designer furniture, I secretly cried as if at the death of an old friend unable to survive the changes and challenges of the world. During my adolescence I felt ambivalent about religion, yet religious stories still charmed me.

On a rainy day that prevented outdoor activities during Boy Scout camp, I assisted in a slide presentation on the life of St. Francis of Assisi. As Francis elected to be poor and live on the charity of friends, all the dirt of addiction to luxury was washed out, and he became as free as the birds to which he talked, as clean as the sky of his homeland, whose luminosity enlightens the Renaissance paintings of Pietro Perugino. That evening I found the same sky in a carpet of stars, washed by the recent rain, which smiled at our camp in the middle of the forest and seemed to call with an everlasting joy transcending the small miseries of our community life. I longed for the neatness and the freedom of Francis, and I took that longing with me back in town. For days, unknown to everybody, I carried on a conversation with a God whose support was as certain as His and Her face was unknown.

When the associate pastor of our parish mentioned as a joke that I would make a good priest, I took that suggestion seriously, and for more than a year I reveled in that dream, as an oasis from my distress, under the loving regard of God. I believe I was not more than 9 years old.

Why did I not persist in the only thoughts that were bringing peace to my heart? Why did I not abandon myself to the love of God? Why did I disdain and desert my only solace? Sixty years later the details of that early life have lost reality, and the memory of those times plays more like a musical or a movie than as a series of photographs. The material for studying these questions is all but dissolved like the content of a dream in the morning. Yet I do perceive some persistent themes from those times. Rather than trying to be objective (who can be objective about himself or for that matter about anything?) I will try to fish out these fragments (or figments) from the sea where the river of my history has mingled in its waters.

Shortly after my sister was born I imagined for some time (one hour? one day? one year?) that my mother, my little sister and I took off as if the bed where we slept together had become a flying carpet. We reached the sky smiling at each other, and our smiles blended into more smiles from the whole world. By then I had never heard of flying carpets; it was all my creation. That image ceased abruptly, as if it were chopped out of my head the way one removes a brain tumor. I remember that pain, though not the circumstances of the intervention. It felt as if I could no longer use an arm or a leg that had been severed. Somehow I had learned to believe that I was not entitled to peaceful dreams. From then on I started nurturing dreams of conquering or of revenge. I guess that was one of the mechanisms through which I failed to dwell in the comprehension of a loving God, as a child.

The parallel universe—which might have provided the strength to negotiate the universe where I was compelled to live and act—became closed to me, the way the Eden was closed to Adam and Eve after original sin. One may call this experience a contact with reality. I am more inclined to see it as a deprivation of reality, as an immersion in a lie where I risked drowning for the following forty years. As I came to believe that I was not entitled to the peace of God, I also learned I had no right to hope. I could not make any sense out of my existence. I had become as disposable as the dead leaves that the garbage men packaged every morning, in early fall, from the road to the sea.

Early in my life, witnessing the contrasts between my parents, I decided that love was a figment of my imagination. I ceased to believe in love. As an adolescent I stated in a group of friends that love was just a passing season, that all families I knew were disrupted by resentment and hostility, that family life was an ongoing fight that brought people apart as drought undermined and brought apart the horn of Africa.

"It is clear that you never witnessed a couple in love," concluded the most authoritative among my friends, the informal leader of our group, with the assent and approval of all present.

My naïve declaration made me ostracized by my peers and underlined once more that I was different, that my family had made me different. For a 13 year old, to be deprived of faith in his parents as representing the norm is like a marathon racer having his legs amputated. As I had already learned on more than one occasion, I learned again that to be accepted I had to feign emotions and beliefs, that only through a lie I could gain friendship and respect.

The reproach of the pastor who joined our conversation underlined this lesson. "You should be ashamed of yourself, you spoiled brat! You were endowed with two parents who are a fulgid example of Christian love, and instead of praising God for this gift you feign a skepticism that is inappropriate to your age!"

Was the dissension of my parents real, or was it just another figment of my sick imagination? I could not help asking. Certainly the priest knew what he was talking about. "There is something terribly wrong with me," I thought. "In any case from now on let's pretend I live in the most harmonious of families!"

I also started resenting love like a child who resents an expensive gadget denied him despite his strong desire for it. Yet my friend's cruel remark made me aware, in a mysterious way, that love might exist, though such experience seemed denied to me. Resenting love, disdaining love, ridiculing love—by this, I did affirm love, in my own way. The painful revelation that I had been excluded from love also stated the existence of love. Toward that love out of my reach I could have acted like Iscariot and pursued its death or like Peter who told Jesus, "Go away from me, Lord; I am a sinful man!" [New International Version] By recognizing his shortcomings, he gained access to the very love that had seemed precluded to him.

Many years later I would learn to access love in the same way. My denial of love was tantamount to a denial and renunciation of God: You cannot believe in the source of love if you don't believe in love. In First Corinthians, Paul stated positively that to believe in God is to believe in love and to believe in love is to believe in God:

"If I speak in the tongues of men and of angels, but have not love, I am only a resounding gong or a clanging cymbal. If I have the gift of prophecy and can fathom all mysteries and all knowledge, and if I have a faith that can move mountains, but have not love, I am nothing. If I give all I possess to the poor and surrender my body to the flames, but have not love, I gain nothing." [New International Version]

Clearly, by denying myself love, I denied myself God. Perhaps even worse, out of despisement or hatred I started undermining those who possessed love. I needed to convince myself that love was a figment of imagination, and so was God, and these delusions threatened my status. I needed to state a new normality, supported by a network of lies. Emotionally paralyzed, I had to convince myself that all the normal world sat in a motorized wheelchair and people standing on their own should be made paralyzed or killed. Their normality was an intolerable threat to my normality: either me or them!

Adopting an emotional perspective like this, it is easy to comprehend Hitler, or Lenin, or all the dictators who inflict unspeakable pain on other human beings. They were not just aiming at power, but also they needed to create a new normality founded on the absence of love. Only then could their own existence be fully justified. It is also easy to comprehend young people who grab guns and massacre their classmates or teachers. Had I had free access to guns I might have done the same.

Undoubtedly, inexperience in love made me deaf to the messages of love. Undoubtedly, lack of self esteem, self respect and self care withdrew from my reach the only remedy for my pain and loneliness. Truth be told, however, many other aspects of my early life distanced me from the acceptance of God as my inspiration and my savior.

The world in which I grew up did not seem to have much use for God. By then Italy was divided in two major political blocs. On one side communists and socialists were seen as atheists and enemies of religion (though in practice they tried to draw the pope's blessing by opposing the introduction of divorce and endorsing the agreement negotiated by Mussolini with the Holy See that allowed, in the new constitution, the freedom and the predominance of the Catholic Church.) On the other side was everybody else. This included the predominant Christian democracy that professed being inspired by Christian principles and enjoyed clerical support. There were also the so-called liberals divided into a number of small parties who professed agnosticism in facts of religion and belief in a free-market approach to economy. A final group consisted of nostalgics of fascism and monarchy. Though the distinction should have been clear, it was not clear at all. The social message of communists and socialists that wanted to eliminate privilege and slavery was much closer to my understanding of Christianity than the message of the so-called liberals who defended feudal privileges including the wedding-night *ius primae noctis* still widely practiced in rural Italy, especially in the south. In *Seeds of Contemplation*, Thomas Merton, the American Trappist monk and author, wrote, "A person cannot be a perfect Christian—that is a saint—unless he is also a communist."

In the meantime, the Christian democracy did not shy from compromising with organized crime, with the silent support of the United States, concerned about the rise of communism in Italy. The massacre of Portella delle Ginestrea was effected by Sicilian bandits. American money financed them, conveyed by officers of the Christian democracy. Hundreds of sharecroppers congregated at Portella delle Ginestre in a peaceful demonstration asking for more favorable working conditions from Sicilian landowners. They were corralled like beasts in a slaughterhouse and gunned down by the gang led by Salvatore Giuliano. In his 1962 film *Salvatore Giuliano* the Neapolitan director Francesco Rosi details the corruption and the violence of those times.

Likewise in the movie *Le Mani Sulla Città* (*Hands over the City*) starring a very young Rod Steiger, Rosi portrays the real estate corruption that filled the coffers of the Christian democracy and the rightward parties at the expense of the lives and livelihood of the Neapolitan poor. Unfortunately this tradition of corruption keeps infecting Italian politics up until today. Former Prime Minister Silvio Berlusconi's wild parties and monopolization of the media for years amused the Western world. In the 2006 book *Gomorrah* (a not too veiled reference to Camorra, the name of Neapolitan organized crime) an Italian journalist put his own life at risk by detailing current Camorra crimes. But at least these politicians no longer make the claim that they are speaking on behalf of the Christ.

My family as well as many of my acquaintances' families gathered every Sunday for mass at the local parish and eliminated meat from Friday meals. They may also have visited the tombs on the so-called Remembrance Day (November 2). But the influence of God in our daily lives did not go any farther. My father used to spend Sunday afternoon at his club playing cards and making fun of innocent Christian believers with his well-to-do friends. During one of these smoky afternoons Don Oreste was indicted for daring to introduce psychology into his ministry. The sleepy town did not feel the need to be awakened into the twentieth century!

Another topic of conversation was the sexual affairs of other friends, which were looked at with benevolent amusement rather than the condemnation one might expect for the violation of one of God's commandments.

My mother enjoyed the freedom from school and family duties, organizing her own office, and did not care to share her few hours of freedom with children she had grown less and less able to recognize as hers.

My sister and I might have gone to a movie or to a dance party, which was an occasion for most of my friends for petting. Holding a glass of whisky, an older boy warned me with a malicious smile of understanding, "Under no circumstances are you to reveal what you will be witnessing today," as he welcomed me to a party in his mansion. During that very feast I made a fool of myself and got drunk. Everybody felt I was just an inexperienced drinker. The truth was that I had tried to drown in alcohol the pain of what I had witnessed that day. During a dance with the lights dimmed I perceived an older boy, a university student, sucking the breasts of the girl who for years had disdained my courting and even had reported me for harassement to the school principal when my attempts to woo her became too intrusive and insistent. To pretend to have innocent fun with friends when my very flesh had been torn apart, together with my dreams, was more than I could bear.

Later on, as I grew older, in the last high school years, I went on some outing in the nearby mountains during the weekends with the members of the local mountain climbing clubs. But even in those circumstances, in the middle of nature, in God's own garden, people did their best to turn their thoughts away from God. If mentioned at all, religion was derided and the name of God was cursed in an exercise of fun, a statement of one's freedom of thought. I still remember that on a Sunday in 1961 I expressed my discomfort over missing mass that day. One of club members underlined my discomfort with a fart that echoed through the rocky walls of the Gran Sasso. "Listen to God's wrath," exclaimed another climber, to everybody's amusement. "Who is that fathead who mentioned mass?" asked a despondent girl chain-smoking on the bus. An older friend of mine, in his thirties, had the time of his life that Sunday petting with her. He hadn't realized how young she was. At the end of the day he was mortified—he had come perilously close to having sex with a 14-year-old! Definitely God was unwelcome on our outings.

And let's not forget school. Though religion was taught for an hour a week, as part of the so-called *concordato* (the agreement negotiated between Mussolini and the Vatican, which found its way to the new Italian constitution thanks to communist support), the subjects were anything but religious. The school followed a curriculum developed during the years of the Italian reunification, when Christianity was eliminated from public places. People like Giuseppe Garibaldi, who had fought several wars against the pope, were worshipped as heroes, even though (or because) they had died excommunicated by the Catholic Church.

The twentieth of September was a national holiday in Italy, as it commemorated the conquering of Rome in 1870. Italian soldiers, the *Bersaglieri*, destroyed one of the doors to the city (Porta Pia), as papal troops offered just virtual resistance. The pope ordered his troops to surrender to avoid more bloodshed. As a result of the invasion of Rome by royal troops, the king of Italy and all of his followers were excommunicated. Catholics were warned not to participate in national elections, as the power of the king was considered illegitimate by the pope and remained such until the famous *concordato* of 1929. So a Catholic country where Catholicism was the "state religion" was asked to celebrate the anniversary of the date when more than half of the peninsula had been deprived of its Catholic status and condemned to eternal damnation. For one of those ironic coincidences that mark the history of Italy, despite (or maybe thanks to) the Italian themselves, on September 20, 1959, all the whorehouses were made illegal. The national jubilation was turned into national mourning for overheated young men!

Likewise, the centerpiece of our humanities curriculum was study of the classic and the humanistic world that had ignored or rejected Christianity. That world was epitomized by the author Pietro Aretino. An epitaph written for him reads: "Here lies Aretino, the Tuscan poet, who said ill of every one except of Christ, and he excused the omission, saying that he had never heard of him."

But perhaps the most disheartening experience was the inability to talk with my parents about God! I have mentioned how they skirted the topic everytime it came out and tried to use religion as a source of guilt and punishment, thwarting my questions and discouraging my own exploration of life.

With the encouragement of my parents I elected to study medicine at the Catholic University in Rome. There I was hoping to find support for my crumbling faith thanks to a rigorous teaching of Catholic theology and through the allegiance of like-minded young people desiring to develop and witness their faith. I was proved wrong on both accounts. The priest charged with our religious education was no match for the philosophy I and most of my friends learned in high school. Despite his incompetence, he got that position because he was a good friend of the associate bishop of Rome, Monsignor Cunial. The majority of young people who elected to study medicine at the Catholic University did so because they liked the idea of living in Rome, and also because undoubtedly it was by far the best equipped medical school of our time. It was private and therefore a privileged school for the sons of privilege. A Sicilian student, the son of a university professor as well as a member of the house of representatives for the Christian democracy, made it his goal to visit all the brothels of Rome during his first two months in medical school. He had named this activity "live anatomy." The apartments around the school were utilized for orgies during which fiancé swapping was a prized activity. The students who joined the Catholic University because it was Catholic could be counted on the finger of two hands.

And soon the study of medicine proposed problems to my faith on three fronts. The first had to do with the complexity and redundancy in the function of the human body as well as with its vulnerability. By then I had ceased to believe in the literal account of the creation in Genesis. The work of the Jesuit and philosopher Teilhard de Chardin, to whom I had been introduced by a Belgian friend, had convinced me that the evolution of the species was a real possibility and was fully compatible with the work of a loving God. Yet I could not help asking why the utilization of oxygen should occur through so many different and tortuous pathways, or why the disorder in the metabolism of some sugar or amino acid could have devastating consequences for a body destined to glorify God. The more insight I gained in molecular biology, the more difficult it became to accept the fifth proof of God's existence according to Aquinas. This was based on a distinct aim of all natural activities, from the way bees selected the appropriate pollen for honey to the way a horse's instinct led him back to the stable, to the way in which the five senses of the human body work in maintenance of the species. Molecular biology made of the body function a maze whose outlet might never be found.

The second difficulty arose from psychoanalysis and the destructive instinct with which human beings were supposedly supplied, the way the id confused and sometimes overwhelmed the ego. Today the idea that one should hate one's own parents is commonly accepted in some circles. I remember one night driving down the Swiss mountains toward Geneva with a young woman I had just met, the scientific collaborator with the drug company hosting a conference. We were speaking French, a language in which I don't feel nearly as comfortable as I am with Italian, English or Spanish. I was exhausted from the long day and the long drive. Nonetheless in less than two hours I learned that she was married with two children, that her marriage was troubled, and that she would never be able to solve these troubles until she had fully expressed her hatred toward her own father, according to her counselor. To resent one's parents is not more shocking nowadays that it is disposing of an old garment. In the meantime to mention one's feeling of guilt is considered as gross as describing one's bowel movement. A guilt-ridden person is looked at as a child who is not yet potty trained. And to mention God in a casual conversation is considered esoteric and inappropriate, like touching one's testicles in order to dispel bad luck when meeting a priest on the road.

"Talk about these things with Bruce and Glenn, and do not bother me with them during rounds!" snapped a vocal medical resident from Boston. I had just mentioned how during the weekend I had attended a seminar on biblical archeology. "I am concerned about this patient. I don't believe she will ever overcome her chest pain until she acknowledge that she hates her father and she overcomes the guilt of a recent affair," he continued. Undoubtedly psychoanalysis makes a lot of sense. Yet the rationalization of hatred and the outcasting of guilt limits if not excludes any role God plays in everydays lives.

But by far the worst difficulty came from learning neuropsychology. "Excuse me, do you fuck?" asked a 15-year-old as I was descending the stairs of our dormitory, minding my own business. "I always thought that this activity was my personal concern!" I retorted, more stupefied than irritated by this intrusion. "But I need to know!" he insisted, ignoring my protest. Eventually his father, waiting for him in the lobby of the dormitory, explained what had happened. During knee surgery, he had undergone cardiac arrest long enough to destroy from lack of oxygen the left prefrontal lobe of his brain. All inhibitions had waned as a result. At those times, neurosurgeons had started to perform stereotactic brain surgery for the treatment of emotional disorders, such as OCD or severe depression, a practice that has become obsolete. The more insight we gained into neuropsychology, the more difficult it became to believe in an immortal human soul. The dependence of our will and our behavior on the electrochemical reactions of the brain directly contradicted the statement that the soul is "simple" and has no connection with any corporeal functions, hence it must be immortal. Brain tumor sufferers have reported experiences in which their perceptions, behavior and judgment have been altered.

It should be easy to understand how my longing for God had been silenced, almost like a shameful secret. Think of a deer longing for the source of water; she had her thirst quenched momentarily by an alcoholic beverage, but this had the effect of enhancing her thirst and also creating dependence on alcohol. Only pure water would have relieved her thirst, but she had forgotten what pure water tasted like, and she had lost her way to the stream! The last time as a young adult that I indulged my religious yearning probably occurred during the first few months of medical school. Disappointed by the religious teaching I was receiving, disheartened by the religious indifference of most of my colleagues, I spent a few minutes every night in the dark of the chapel, asking for God's guidance. Very soon that feeble search for the truth was suffocated by thorns, and as I had done before I started pretending again to be what I was not, as I did not feel sure of being anything.

## CHAPTER 33

# Encounter with Christ

"Jim, you did it. You sneaked me back into my belief in God, and what is worse you did it despite my resistance. What is done is done, I can't help it, you can't help it. Don't expect a free ride, however. To punish you I will rejoin the Catholic Church!"

"Please don't tell my students!" answered Jim with a mischievous smile.

The head of the chaplaincy at the University of Mississippi Medical Center, Jim Travis was a Baptist minister who had pioneered hospital chaplaincy in the United States. Because of this he was looked upon with suspicion by the Southern Baptist Convention and by the Mississippi legislature that eventually eliminated his job, employing the excuse of budget constraints. Jim ended up at Duke University, where his innovations and his faith received proper recognition. He had just shared with us how he had ministered to a young man with sarcoma that had spread to the lung. The patient and his widowed mother had no religious convictions, and Jim did not even try to mention God. Instead he invited the young man to review his life, to make a distillate of his life, to discover what really had mattered to him. During this process the young man recognized a transcendent extratemporal dimension to his existence, and in that way he died looking at a God that he did not know but in whose love he felt fully accepted.

Maybe I was a little hyperbolic in saying that this experience prompted my return to the Catholic Church. In reality Claudia and I started returning to mass when we found out that we were going to have a baby, though it took a couple of years before we participated in communion. But for me it was a time of discovery, and the experience Jim shared with us gave me the sense of the mystery; that is, of a direct experience of the reality that cannot be circumscribed by words or thoughts, can only be lived. That is the first occasion I can remember in which I was capable of surrendering myself to the mystery. More occasions were to follow, as occurred in the meeting of Grace and her parents. Others included the 6,000 lires paid to Don Oreste for blessing the boat and preventing a woman from selling herself.

For the first time I felt well disposed toward Christianity. Rather than looking for reasons to stay away from it, I was looking forward to exploring a message that appeared congruent with my present needs. Maybe being a husband and a father endowed me with a sense of responsibility that highlighted my unique dignity. Maybe I had learned that medicine, including the technologically sophisticated form of medicine practiced in the United States, had not provided me with any sense of meaning. Maybe because I felt the need to save my relationship with Claudia, as I had a vague but certain feeling that it represented my only chance to find an ongoing meaning to my life. Maybe I just had been charmed by the voice of a young carpenter from Nazareth that sounded like the calls of my childhood friends yelling for me to come play in the garden. It was a feeling of coming home to a home and a family whose treasures I was ready to appreciate fully for the first time.

My friend Mark Frascogna from Jackson described this sensation best. The son of an oil magnate of Italian origin, Mark belonged to the Jackson upper class that congregated around the most exclusive golf and country club in the South. Despite being a son of privilege, he never felt comfortable with his upbringing; somehow he felt like a foreigner in his own country. At age 15 he visited his Italian family for the first time in some small Tuscan village, and that visit was a revelation, He realized that he belonged there in the small farm of his cousins. He found home for the first time. Mark's experience reflects my return to the Catholic Church. I belonged there and I had always belonged there. I found home.

Some of the Gospel images were particularly inspiring to my newly found faith. I could identify with the woman who washed Jesus's feet with her tears and dried them with her hair, according to Luke. Learning that I was loved for myself, in spite of my shortcomings, was the revelation that kept me from taking my life or dissolving it in impersonal sexual affairs at a time when I felt unable to elicit anybody's love. Then the construct of eternal life was all but foreign to me.

Overburdened by guilt, I had not admitted yet to any wrongdoing. I had decided that I myself as well as my fellow men were not responsible for our actions and so I did not have to ask for forgiveness from my spouse, my parents and her parents, or the patients I had abused and deceived, the friends I had betrayed, and more in general all people whose suffering I had caused. I had nothing to apologize for or to forgive: I could not help being who I was. And the way I was I could not be loved until I realized how much Jesus had loved that woman.

And it was the certainty of that love that allowed me to become progressively more aware of the fact that on my own I had only sown the seeds of suffering, disappointment and desperation. Had I faced that reality on my own, without the support of the love of God, I would have been sunk the way a skier is submerged in a ravine. Another trap of the devil is to prevent us from getting rid of our guilt by convincing us that we are not guilty, which of course is a form of denial. In my professional life I have seen many a patient on deathbeds from cancer planning travels and celebrations years ahead. Denial of guilt will not make guilt disappear. The real issue is whether the suffering inflicted on other people is a consequence of our behavior and our actions, not whether we are legally responsible of those actions. The marriage of guilt and responsibility is a figment of one's imagination without correspondence in the emotional world. It does not make any difference to the victim of a car accident how he or she encountered his or her death. He or she remains dead irrespective of whether the driver of the offending car respected traffic rules or was drunk at the wheel or was reckless and inattentive. Irrespective of whether the driver was or not responsible of the accident, he or she cannot help carrying the guilt of another person's death. Any attempt to ignore our guilt based on responsibility is a lie that prevents the acceptance of the reality in which we live. And the acceptance of the truth, the refusal of the lie, was possible for me only at the moment in which I recognized myself in the woman who washed Jesus's feet with her own tears.

At the moment I was struggling to save my marriage, the image of the transfiguration of Jesus on Mount Tabor succored me. I was looking for a reason not to give up on a marriage that appeared on its last legs. I was asking myself why I wanted to stay married to a woman who had told me she had no time for me. In those difficult years after Marco's birth, as she was trying to build her own professional status, she blamed me for having lured her into what appeared a dead-end street. As a consequence Claudia answered my requests for sexual intimacy: "I have time for Marco (we referred to him as "the puppy"); I have time for my work; I don't have time for you." She did not begrudge my presence as long as I did not have any expectations, and today I am grateful to her for her brutal honesty. It provided the opportunity to get in touch with my own lie, to recognize that I had lived forty years trying to conquer the love of my mother and punish her for her desertion at the same time. Claudia's rejection allowed me to get in touch with myself, to learn what I could offer my family and the world, to build my own house in a life I had treaded so far as a mendicant begging for attention and validation.

Both of us became aware of this much later, however, and without the love of God I don't think I would have ever been able to face myself. By then the most important immediate goal was to preserve our marriage that I did not wish to lose, but I did not know how to keep it together. Then the transfiguration of Jesus struck me as the answer. Claudia had transfigured in front of me on the Appennini snow slopes when she led me down a descent I would have never dared to negotiate myself, I declared myself to her and when she introduced me to her intimacy as a unique, sacred gift. Most of all she had transfigured in front of me as she joyfully accepted my proposal of marriage, when she gave me a feeling of my power to bring her happiness. And there my vision was adorned by many other episodes that had revealed her capacity to love, though they were small in themselves.

These episodes were like the ornaments that allowed a beautiful tapestry to shine. They were the expressions of the little people that gave reality to Giotto's paintings of St. Francis of Assisi. As a medical student she had convinced me to go and care for Donatella, a young woman with severe learning disability. Donatella had been a patient in my ward and assigned to me. I could barely wait for her dischatge. She was rowdy, temperamental and often uncontrollable. I was then a young physician who was only preoccupied with his own carreer and disdained human contacts as a waste of time. It was somehow demeaning for me to have to take care of a person that had no predictable use for and in this world. After discharge, Claudia convinced me to to pay weekly visits to Donatella and her mother, control her blood pressure, check her medications and mainly to show her our care. Eventually she became used to us, and was eager for our visit. One day we did not show up she remained very disappointed, and refused to talk for the following week. Our reappearance gave her joy and perked her up. She did not want for us to leave for fear that we may disappear for ever, In ministering to Donatella Claudia provided to me an early demonstration of my own value, of my own sacredness. Unfortunatley I realized it twenty years after Donatella had been dead. .

When we took strolls in the forest outside Rome, as good friends, Claudia never forgot to collect violets for a patient dying of acute leukemia in our hospital ward. She had been diligent in remembering my and all the staff's birthdays, which created a sense of family, captivating even the most cantankerous of my colleagues. That vision was imprinted in me and was the foundation of my commitment to her, even when things appeared to sour.

The discovery of transfiguration was a turning point for all my personal relationships. A friend of mine once highlighted in a letter something I was not aware of. Whenever I made a new acquaintance, I acted as if that person was my best friend, as if a unique understanding had existed between us. As soon as difficulties in the relationship emerged, I engaged in a policy of personal destruction. My best friend became my worst enemy. Another friend told me when we were teen-agers: "The way you act, you make friends very quickly and you lose them as quick."

Finally I came to realize the source of my volubility: I had not discovered the transfiguration. As I thought I had heard from my parents that I was disposable, so I expected everybody else to be. I had been primed to disappointment. In a certain perverse way I felt comfortable only with disappointment and I did not believe in fighting my way to joy and happiness. My life had been filled with precious stones that I had used as pebbles simply because I focused on everyday actions, and I had forgotten what a person really looked like. I missed a lot of forests to concentrate on a few trees.

. Before I faced the possibility of my own divorce and of the terrible consequences it might have implied, I found the idea of divorce reasonable. For the same reason I felt much allegiance to priests and nuns who decided to forfeit their vows and pursue married life. Without the experience of transfiguration, it was impossible for me to foresee a lifelong fidelity to another person or to an ideal. Unfortunately, the idea that change is the only reality and that fidelity is outdated was very pervasive among young people of our generation.

"How can you remain hitched to the same person for a lifetime?" asked a 15-year-old girl from a very religious family , a schoolmate of mine. "She is entitled to change," stated one of my medical students, noting my distress as a church-going young woman engaged in a hot affair with one of the best known ladies men among the medical residents.

"But why with her?" Claudia asked as we discussed the affair of one of our professors with a surgical resident we considered particularly unattractive and unpleasant. "Because she just happened to be there," explained the chief resident, speaking with the paternal attitude of indulging a naïve child. He added with a malicious smirk: "Claudia, a hard dick does not know any consciousness." The cult of change, enshrined by the "make love not war" crowd, eventually became the cult of monotony and boredom. For author Hemingway that boredom became unbearable to the point of suicide.

The discovery of transfiguration also provided me with a taste of eternity. Already I have admitted that conceiving of eternal life is one of my major difficulties in espousing Christian beliefs. Having learned the biology of the central nervous system, I find it all but impossible to conceive that any human experience may persist beyond the dissolution of human brain. By far I feel more motivated in reveling in God's love, in being a partner to redemption in the little I can do, than in pursuing an eternal recompense.

Even so, the experience of transfiguration transported from Jesus to other human beings gave me the certainty of a persisting reality undergoing our multiple changes. Changes may occur only thanks to the persistence of the person; changes make sense only if they are aimed to position the person in his or her unity, in allowing the emergence of the person in his or her ultimate meaning. I cannot decide, and maybe it is not important to understand, whether we build this unitarian person or whether it is there and our action is only aimed to discover it, the way one rediscovers a masterpiece after cleaning the crusts that time and the weather have imposed on the painting. Did Leonardo create Mona Lisa or discover Mona Lisa? Did Beethoven create or discover the Ninth Symphony?

I also found a number of compelling personal references in the sermon of the mountain "Blessed are the poor in spirit," Jesus had proclaimed, and "Blessed are they that suffer persecution for justice's sake." [Douay-Rheims Bible] What I heard him telling me is: "You will be able to enjoy my friendship only if you again find that poverty that you have been escaping from. . When you are again able to marvel at life; when you are able to relinquish that contempt on which you found your self assurance, and which is as stable as a house built on quicksand; when you are able to relinquish the lies that you used as drugs to assuage your pain and let your pain explode — only then will you be able to appreciate my friendship and my allegiance. They have always been there for you. I have been waiting patiently for you, hoping that you might break the circle of lies that imprisoned you and kept you from reaching me. I love you and I am ready to donate my life for you again and again, but I cannot compel you to accept me. That I cannot do.

"You were ashamed to marvel at life, at dawn and at sunset, and the riches of nature, because you were told that you were to conquer life, to submit nature to your whim. When you saw people flaunting their wealth, you became ashamed of enjoying the free running water of a mountain source and you pretended to enjoy expensive champagne that burned your stomach, clouded your mouth and swelled your belly with gas. You became ashamed of thinking of a woman as your wife and life companion in the discovery of life. Instead you started looking at women as merchandise to fulfill your desire. You disdained the lifelong fulfillment of intimacy and started looking for the momentary relief of an orgasm as a sign of belonging. But mainly you were ashamed of experiencing and expressing the pain of your loneliness and your incertitude. You pretended to quench this pain by becoming a respected professional, a wealthy homeowner, a worldwide traveler who could speak several languages and discuss different philosophical and political theories. Your pride was flattered for having deceived the people who looked at you as an example, as a man of means and power. You almost convinced yourself that the supreme joy of life consisted in being high on pride. But you were lucky. The disconcerterd little child thirsty for love never allowed you to drown in your addiction. He screamed within you to be heard, he undermined like a termite all the palaces you were building. Now that you have shed this prison of lies by which you tried to distance yourself from yourself, now that you have come back to that little disconcerted child , now you are ready to accept my friendship and my allegiance."

In addition to the lack of self assurance for not feeling loved, or as part of the same lack of self esteem I had felt for a long time that I had to pretend that my family's assets were much more abundant than in reality they were. In George Bernard Shaw's play "Widowers' Houses" the daughter of the enriched tenants of unsafe popular houses claims she would have hated her grandmother if she had known her. The young woman had been raised as a princess by her father, who had made a fortune by overcharging people of the working class for dwellings that proved to be insalubrious and unsafe. He had speculated on the health of the poorest of the poor in order to build his wealth. As he revealed to his daughter that his own mother, her grandmother, had been one of the working poor living in the same complexes he now was managing, the young woman's reaction was rejection rather than allegiance. She had felt embarrassed by rather than indebted to a grandmother who had spent her life in abject poverty in order to guarantee her son's and her granddaughter's current wealth. The young woman did not want to have anything to do with her, and she said it clearly. To accept that type of grandmother would have jeopardized the status she relished. To complicate matters she was engaged to a member of the British aristocracy who would have retreated in horror from the proposed marriage had he known the humble roots of his fiancée.

Likewise I always felt that there was a skeleton in my closet that I had to keep other people from discovering, even if I did not identify the skeleton all the time. One of my mentors in medical school crystallized my attitude when he stated: "You want everybody to believe that you have plenty of money while everybody knows that you don't." Another way to put it would have been: "You want everybody to believe that in your life you had unlimited choices and you choose to be who you are, while everybody recognizes that you have no idea who you are and what you want." Like my prom date, he was telling me I was phony all over. Anyone who had gotten in touch with me would have recognized it.

One of the most haunting expressions of this attitude was the need to have somebody to despise, the need to feel superior to somebody. I did not care so much for being happy myself as long as I knew that other people existed who were less happy, more uncomfortable than me.

I already described that I espoused the prejudices that were common in Mississippi forty years ago when Claudia and I arrived there. To Claudia's dismay I started calling black people names in everyday conversation. Undoubtedly I craved to be part of the upper echelon of society and to state my belonging by sharing their contempt for people of different ethnic origin. But there was a deeper need that I recognized only much later. I felt the need to differentiate myself from poor black people mainly because I was afraid that I might be identified with them if I had exposed myself. The similarities were too many to be listed.

A few months after we arrived in Mississippi, Claudia and I visited a black nurse who had a bike for sale. At work she wore an immaculate uniform and sported a dentist-grade smile. At home we found her in a cheap bathrobe at noon and with rolling pins in her hair. All the beds were unmade, and the rest of eggs and bacon were decaying in three plates on the kitchen table and in the living room. An old woman, likely a grandmother, was watching two unruly small children playing on the floor and raising a cloud of dirt. Claudia was horrified, but for me it was déjà vu. As a child in post-war Italy, I too had played in the dirt and with the dirt, just like children in the American ghetto. I too had been raised by a grandmother who ignored the rules of hygiene and spent her time talking at the front door with other women of the same extraction, without any ambition of social promotion. Like the black nurse, my parents were always appropriate at work, and nobody might have suspected the confusion and the dirt infesting our house with the complicity of our grandmother. "You have made of my house a heap of manure," complained the lady who had rented us an apartment for eight years before my grandfather bought us our own dwelling. Like black women at a garage sale, my grandmother would look for bargains at the local market, to my embarrassment.

In the movie *The Color Purple* that describes the life of interrelated black families in the South during Jim Crow, a man's wife finds in his lover a most trusted confident. As she exposed to her her marital problems the other woman reflects her talk by saying: "Darling, from what you are telling me it sounds as if he was going to the bathroom on you and within you."

That could certainly be said of the way I used the few girlfriends I had before Claudia, and I didn't have enough intitiative, ambition or imagination to construct sexual relations in any other way. Like the South American dictator described by Gabriel Garcia Marquez in his 1975 masterpiece *The*

*Autumn of the Patriarch*, I had not been able to see sex under any other light than the relief of a corporeal urgency.

But for some reason the episode that impressed me most was encountering a black family in one of the exclusive hotels of the Grand Canyon's South Rim. I visited the place with my wife and my mother-in-law. The family stuck out immediately because they were the only blacks in a dining room crowded by white people. Both parents were overweight in a society that in 1976 still had enshrined slimness as expression of status, education and self discipline. Their clothes had been selected from among the cheapest choices of K-mart or Walmart, while everybody else was flaunting mountain attire bought from a catalog of L.L. Bean or its equivalent. One may say that their clothes were as out of fashion as their color was out of tune. In the middle of all these disproportions, what triggered deja' vu was the cheap camera the young boy sported hanging from his neck. As I grew up in post-war Italy, for some reason I had conceived the possession of a camera as a sign of status. Maybe because cars were so scarce at that time, I saw them out of the reach of my own imagination. In my perception people were divided into two groups: those with and those without a camera. For my first communion my uncle gave me a cheap camera as a present, and somehow I felt promoted in status by that gift. For years I sported that camera at each trip as a sign of belonging to the class of privilege. In that black family I saw the history of my family during my childhood. My parents did their best to introduce us to the resorts of the Italian mountains from the time we were young. Both my sister and I are grateful for that introduction to the beauty of nature and to the enjoyment of long hikes of discovery among forests and rocks.

We generally spent a month in a small apartment we rented from some local farmers. As a lower middle class family we could not afford the expensive establishments that soon started populating those resorts. From time to time we intruded in an expensive restaurant or café,' to listen to a concert or to protect ourselves from a storm. In those situations I could not have felt more out of place. While other children could leave on their plates expensive pastries or cakes filled with cream without regret, my sister and I had to share a juice or a hot chocolate, all that our finances allowed us to afford. We could only afford to eat the panini my mother had packed for us early in the morning. And we were scared to spill any of our drink on the velvet chairs of the cafes, which the children of privilege negotiated with the same confidence with which we would have played in the grass.

Throughout my life I had tried to ignore, and when I could not ignore, to suppress that little destitute child in myself that instead emerged in every social occasion to my embarassment, the way our grandmother, smelling of urine in her later years and letting the fragments of half-chewed food drop on the tablecloths, would embarrass us during a dinner or a party to which we had invited our friends. Now Jesus provided me a way to love and adopt that little destitute boy, to discover him as a treasured legacy of myself.

The Italian priest Primo Mazzolari had conceived his entire ministry as a voice for the voiceless, and his ministry attracted the thunder and condemnation from representatives of the Catholic hierarchy. "Priests do not belong in politics," was the refrain of these prelates, always scared to offend the ruling class, and maybe also afraid of losing their own perks by espousing the claims of the poor. In his book *La Parola ai Poveri* (*Let the Poor Speak*) Mazzolari confronts the prejudices of the " haves" toward the "have nots." His message was summarized in the blunt statement of a friend of mine. There is no way that people with a full belly can speak the language of those with an empty one. Wealthy people, or at least those who do not have to confront daily emergencies such as putting food on the table, by and large try to bestow upon the poor the guilt of their own poverty. Ronald Reagan's characterization of the "truly needy," a reference to the fact that some, or maybe the majority, of poor were freeloaders, still represents a masterful example of oratorical creativity. Espousing a cloack of compassion, he exorcised the wealthy of their own guilt. What he really said was, "We will kick a lot of butts, and we will stop paying a lot of welfare checks. Be heartened: You will see people starving in the streets." As a corollary of this attitude, President Reagan could get away with the most outrageous of statements, that homeless people lived in the street of their own free choice. These coldhearted messages delivered with a warm persuasive voice electrified a crowd that desired an excuse to get rid of the poor, irrespective of whether they were truly needy. But even individuals who are well disposed toward the poor and sincerely desire to help them don't know how to listen to them.

When I lived in Mississippi, a pastor of a black church found laughable our offer of free screenings for breast and cervical cancer in a community infested by drugs and violent crime. In his book Mazzolari described the case of a wealthy lady, a passionate member of the so called Dames of Charity who complained to him about the facts that the poor she wished to serve "lived like beasts." She referred both to their dirt and to their promiscuity and was disheartened from her efforts. "Did you even try to listen to them, ma'am?" asked Mazzolari. "It looks like you feel you need help more than they do. You come to me asking for my attention that in your opinion would be wasted on them. If you let them speak, and if they felt confident enough to talk to you (and it will take a lot of work for you to deserve their trust), they will tell you that they feel so disenfranchised that they don't have any choice. They learned to gather the crumbs of a rich mess wherever they can find them and with whatever means available to them. How do you expect them to clean their house if everybody treats them as dirt, as pigs in a sty? They just reflect the image that you and the likes of you have developed of them. They live up to your expectations. You blame them for being promiscuous. Let me ask you a blunt question: How would you spend your own day if it were not occupied with the activities to which your wealth gives you access: preparing your children for school, visiting with your friends, leisurely meals with abundant food, your dresses, your vacations and all other civic activities with which you hope to immortalize your name in monuments, streets and city squares? Do you realize that by enshrining wealth you have deprived the poor of any dignity, and now you complain because they act the way you made them!"

Unfortunately Mazzolari did not provide any follow-up description of the lady's reaction. Perhaps this disenfranchisement, this loss of dignity of the poor is crystallized best in the words of Dolittle, the father of Eliza Doolittle in George Bernard Shaw's *Pygmalion*. Doolittle is ready to sell his own daughter for five British pounds, When Colonel Pickering asks: "Have you NO morals, man?" Dolittle answers, "Nah. Nah, can't afford 'em, guv'nor. Neither could you, if you was as poor as me." In my opinion this is the most meaningful indictment of a Christless society where morals had become a luxury, possessed by wealth.

Listening to the destitute child in myself means listening to the poor, learning from the poor that faith is an immediate necessity, the only reliable sustenance of life. Listening to the child in myself I learned that a fundamental lie of the society of wealth is to consider religious faith a choice that can be selected at your leisure on a Saturday afternoon when one is in a vein of shopping from a Saks Fifth Avenue catalogue (or Sears if you come from a working class family).

Understanding the redemptive value of suffering represented the most meaningful and lasting message I assimilated from my renewed relation with the Christ. I have already described the four ways by which suffering may redeem the emotional and moral debts another person has contracted.

The first is to say, "The buck stops here: I refuse to pursue revenge for the pain inflicted upon me." The second is to become a lightning rod for the hatred of the world, as prophesized by Isaiah in the songs of the suffering servant and as experienced by Christ at the time of his passion. The third is to use the very cause of our suffering as an instrument to relieve other people's sufferings. The fourth is to learn from one's own mistakes how to prevent somebody else endebtment.

Discovering that my suffering from depression had become a valuable asset as a doctor allowed me to obtain full reconciliation with the people I held responsible for my suffering, especially my parents. I always had felt grateful to them for providing me with life, education and means, and I regretted that the grudges I held against them prevented me from loving them unconditionally. In discovering the redemptive value of suffering, in being able to make treasured assets of my most dreaded liabilities, I overcame my grudges. Thanks to the Christ, I had become free to love. Ultimately the grudges that distanced me from my parents, from my wife and from my friends also separated me from God. The freedom of experiencing unconditional love was really the freedom to encounter God.

Though I cannot identify a specific turning point on my spiritual journey, I recognize in my marriage to Claudia the event that ignited this process.

In the *Chronicles of Narnia*, C.S. Lewis describes how two young people escaping on horseback from the same city are compelled to meet by a lion (Aslan, which in Narnia's alternative world represents the Christ). The lion pursues their horses and scares them into taking the same road. Eventually the two young people will fall in love and get married and continue the dynasty that reigned over Narnia. Unknown to everybody, including himself, the boy was the only son of the King of Narnia who had been kidnapped as an infant and brought up as a slave by his father's enemies. Somehow those two young people represented Claudia and me escaping from the prison of the respective self. Christ compelled us to meet and fall in love with each other.

From the beginning my marriage gave me a sense of the disproportion between my aspiration and my ability to love. On one side I wished to give all of myself to Claudia, wholly and unconditionally. I never believed in the so-called "prenuptial agreements" that established the conditions through which a marriage may be dissolved. Even though I had not discovered agape yet, I knew that love had to be unconditional or otherwise could not be love. At the same time I could not help setting a number of benchmarks with which to gauge the success of my marriage. These included overturning the control of Claudia's father on her life, immigration to the States, the pursuance of our independent professional careers. Undoubtedly my concerns were valid, as they represented my response to the situation in which I had grown up, my remedy for my parents' and my own previous mistakes and shortcomings. My new mistake, however, was the pretense to be in control of my future, my failure to recognize that marriage is a commitment to explore together an unknown land rather than a triumphal march toward preselected ends.

Unconditional love recognizes an opportunity in every obstacle one encounters in the road, instead of bypassing the obstacles through short cutting. History, including personal history, may provide some indication of on how to approach the road ahead of us but can never provide a blueprint for the future. My original attitude toward Claudia's father was the he should be ignored or destroyed if he could not accept our marriage and our departure for the States. Claudia's duty was to support me in the pursuance of my goals, and any hesitation generated by concerns for her father's emotions was nothing less than betrayal of our marriage.

Eventually, the relationship with her father became my best opportunity to learn how to listen, to realize that people may disagree and love each other at the same time, when room is made for the expression of their feelings and concerns. A world of winners and losers is a lie. Once we beat another person we are both losers.

Even if Claudia had rejected her father and followed me, I would have lost Claudia's trust. The burned land we left behind, the humiliation of her father would always have burdened her heart and poisoned love with resentment. This toxic combination might have killed our marriage once my own shortcomings had been fully revealed. To be listened to, I needed to learn how to listen, to be forgiven I had to learn how to forgive! More in general I came to recognize that the gap would have always existed between the love I wished to give (and to receive) and the love I was able to give (and to receive), as I was held back by my own fears and concerns, as I was trying to establish benchmarks to help me establish whether I was really loved. That gap could be replenished only by faith in God. At the time He and She blessed our wedding, God became guarantee of our journey. God gave substance to a love that on our own we could only have dreamed of.

Only through Claudia could I gain insight into my shortcomings and became able to face myself, which means face the lies with which I had tried to justify my shortcomings. When her joyful acceptance became cautious criticism and criticism became open hostility, my choices became clear. I could learn the painful truth about myself or I could escape one more time from myself and try to suffocate my pain in occasional relationships promising a love that inevitably would have waned. And Claudia, for the first time in my life, had given me a taste of unconditional love.

For whatever reason she had agreed joyfully to buy into my unconventional choices, to challenge the world and the environment where we had grown up. Though I did not know at the time whether I would have been able to conquer that love again, I knew that it was impossible for me to find that love again. Had I lost Claudia I would have lost my chance of being loved for myself. So it was a no brainer, even if there were women who seemed to covet my attention. They seemed to want sex and asked nothing in exchange, but I had become experienced enough to recognize the trap, to realize that the excitement of a few days would have been followed by disappointment and guilt. This challenge—to try to revel again in Claudia's love—was the best opportunity, as I said, to face myself. I did not have to fake or feign anymore, my real self had been uncovered. The confused adolescent who was trying at the same time to punish his mother and to conquer her attention and her love in the process had developed anger and suspicion toward the whole world, which covered him like quills cover a porcupine. The awareness that I had been loved for myself by Claudia, the awareness that I was still loved by God, the awareness that a small child was looking to me for unconditional love—all gave me the strength to break free of my prison. As the father of Anne Frank said when the Nazis invaded their refuge: "For the past two years we have lived in fear. Now we can live in hope." Once I was no longer scared to look at myself, I could start hoping to live for myself.

"Christ, where are you?"

" It is here, sarge! He was 33 when he died, so he must have been of the 1884 draft."

This exchange took place between an army sergeant and the army chaplain in the 1959 movie *La Grande Guerra* (*The Great War*) after the defeat of Caporetto where thousands of Italian soldiers were slaughtered in 1917.

Indeed I met Christ many times, as the chaplain implied. I will provide a description of a few of these encounters as experiences of the living Christ entering my human mystery.

With my friends in medical school, after a movie, we stopped at the Delfino Verde, (The Green Dolphin) a fast food restaurant in Piazza Argentina. Though the nuns from our dormitory had packed some food for us, we elected to abandon our little food sacks on a table and enjoy the restaurant food. Out of nowhere a woman dressed in rags appeared, stood at the table and started feeding on the grub we had discarded. To be fed, Christ had depended on our throw- aways.

"My son was a university student and enjoyed his time, but he never begged in the street. What you are doing has given a bad name not just to you, but to all university students," the gray-haired woman said. She wore a dark skirt, a brown sweater and no makeup. She reminded me of one of my pious aunts returning home from church after early morning mass. She had reacted to my request for money on the occasion of the Festa della Matricola (the freshman feast). Tradition warranted that university students invade the streets of Rome to ask shopowners and passersby for money. Most people obliged, probably because that was the way of least resistance. On that occasion Christ stood me up: He reminded me that I was competing with him; that is, with the people in need, for charity. In my oblivion I was robbing the poor.

"Your dad left, slamming the door." Mother appeared unable to cry; she had been taught not to complain and she did not complain. Facing his latest disregard and verbal abuse, she had grown beyond anger. Only her eyes expressed pain. I had seen those eyes before. In the paintings showing Christ in the garden, the eyes were the same, no matter the different styles of Rembrandt, Piero della Francesca, Crivelli, Tiziano, Van Eyck or Petrus Christus. The same eyes even showed up in the work of a modern Brazilan artist who had painted the Via Crucis (stations of the cross) in the cathedral of Lille in France. Christ asked me that evening to help him withstand a solitude that might have lasted forever.

I saw those eyes again. I saw them in Claudia one night when I accused her of lack of love for me because she had been too sensitive to her father's pain. At that time I believed her father was competing with me for my wife's attention.

I saw the eyes in my girlfriend after I reproached her for having wasted a lot of money in hiring a taxi to move her grandmother to a haven away from the people who had been abusing the helpless old lady. And those eyes pierced me when a woman emerging from the waiting room of the hospital ward begged me: "Doctor, please!. . . ."

" I don't have time. Go away," I answered without even looking at her face. As a matter of fact I had plenty of time. I had nothing planned that afternoon. I just felt mean.

"She should have been dead for three years! It is time for her to go." I slammed the phone on the hook. Jeannie, the primary nurse working for a vacationing colleague of mine, whose patients I was covering, had called me about Zadira. Zadira had missed her regular clinic appointment in the morning and at 4 p.m. she called to inform us that she felt shivering rigor and her left arm felt heavy and immobile. She might have had another relapse of her leukemia, but what was I to do? Hospital beds were full, and the place we used for emergencies was on Code Red, which meant they were saturated with patients. No way could I see her. I was meeting with a colleague regarding a scientific publication; one hour later I had a leadership meeting and, after that, a dinner with a potential donor for the hospital. Had she kept her appointment in the morning, we might have been able to take care of her. Late in the afternoon it was all but impossible. I told Jeannie to send her to the Tampa General emergency room, knowing full well that Jeannie would disregard my recommendation. Visiting an emergency room for an undocumented alien is a dangerous proposition. If some politician catering to the religious right had become aware of the situation, he would have tried to hasten her deportation, even if she was dying. What a wonderful opportunity to show lack of compassion cloaked as firmness to a pro-life constituency saturated with hatred for life!

Zadira was a mixed-blood Hispanic woman of 25, illegally in the United States since 2000. In 2003, at 18, still pregnant with her first and only child, she had developed acute lymphoblastic leukemia, a rapidly deadly disease in absence of treatment. While carrying her pregnancy to term she received high doses of chemotherapy, went into complete remission and delivered a healthy baby. After she left the hospital her treatment became difficult. She missed many appointments and experienced no less than ten relapses of her leukemia, seven of which involved the central nervous system ( a condition that is lethal in a few months in 80 percent of cases). Her social situation prevented her from being compliant with medical advice. Challenges included an abusive husband (or live-in boyfriend; it was never clear), no child care, abject poverty (we had to reimburse the taxi driver who took her to the hospital) combined with lack of education and maybe of intelligence. If my colleague, a devout Presbyterian, had not orchestrated the miracle of keeping her alive for seven years, I would not now be faced with an impossible situation, I grumbled to myself. That evening I wished that Christ has died a second time, for my own convenience! I failed to appreciate the unique opportunity to minister to the wounded Christ.

A woman in our medical school always wore long skirts and long-sleeved blouses, and her hair was arranged in a long ponytail that she turned around to cover her scalp. A flat face without any makeup made it all but impossible to guess her age, which might have been as young as 18 and as old as 34. Eventually we learned that she had worked as a waitress and a saleswoman for five years after dropping out of high school to save the money to go to medical school, so she must have been in her mid-twenties. Always sitting on the rearmost benches, she made no effort to toady up to the professors, and her medical grades were barely passing. Though she did not consort with the other students, she was not protected from our pranks nor from our derision. One of the girls in our classes won a meal paid for by three boys for succeeding in stealing her pharmacology textbook, an expensive item that eventually was sold on the used book market, earning threefold the price of the meal. After discovering her loss, she expressed sadness but no anger. Her faith gave her a deep form of wisdom, which made her ready to endure this type of derision and abuse. More than for herself and her loss, she seemed sorry for the thieves, imprisoned in a hell of their own making. From the height of the cross Jesus's worst cause of pain had been the vision of the hell of his persecutors.

Forty years later, she retired, still unmarried, with two adopted children from Africa who are now in medical school. She had spent forty years on that continent, where she had managed to found forty hospitals in the poorest and most battle-ravaged corners of a tormented country. When I think of her I realize that I lived side by side with Christ for six years (the duration of our Italian medical school). Instead of recognizing and honoring him I joined the rank of his persecutors!

"He looks like Christ." A few days before his death, my mother was moved after seeing my father lying exhausted and breathless after an enema administered by the caregiver we had hired. "He is just faking, like the old comedian he has been all his life to attract other people's attention," I mumbled to myself, hoping and praying he would soon get out of the way.

"Since you have done it unto one of the least of these my brethren, you have done it unto me." [King James 2000 Bible] These words ring in my mind as the sounds of the trump of judgment. Every time I succeed in gathering my thoughts, I do thank Christ for the opportunity to assist him, and I ask for forgiveness of my betrayals.

These and many other encounters have been my personal experience of Christ. I have concluded after almost 70 years of life that the only meaning of life is to partake of the redemptive suffering of Christ, by taking part of Christ's own suffering every time we have the opportunity to encounter him on our road. All the rest is a lie.

But from where do I derive this certainty? How do I know that the Christ I pretend to see is not a product of my imagination? Maybe I am right: All there is to life is to share other people's pain, is to make the pain of living bearable for everybody with whom we get in touch. After all, the Buddha and Mohammed and all the prophets and authors of the wisdom literature in the Old Testament preached the same message. And in modern times many thoughtful people who had become skeptical of ideologies and representative democracies expressed with their own lives a commitment to human solidarity that was not rooted in any specific religious belief or ideology.

Jesus, in a depressed mood, asked his disciples why they decided to stick with him instead of abandoning him as everybody else had done. Peter replied, "Lord, to whom would we go? You have the words of eternal life." [International Standard Version] This statement encapsulates the uniqueness of Jesus. I do not fathom what eternal life is, but to me Peter's declaration means, "Only you allow us to partake of the life of God. Through you we become God's partners in His work of redemption." Only when it is engrafted in God does our work of redemption have a chance to succeed. Without this certainty it becomes a Sisyphean effort; that is, an exercise in futility. Only after he discovered his allegiance to God did Silvio, my father-in-law, learn that his suffering had meaning. He could then abandon stoicism and find an outlet for the love he carried in himself.

But let's not dismiss historical reality. Despite the inconsistencies of the Gospel accounts, it is clear that something happened around 2,000 years ago that gave origin to a *petit noyau* (little nucleus) of embattled men and women who underwent persecutions, torture and death from which sprouted the universal Christian church. By and large these people were uneducated peasants who could not read or write. They did not have the fantasy or the ambition, let alone the imagination, to make up the experience of encountering Jesus, nor could they have made up what they had witnessed and heard from Jesus. And considering that the majority of them were martyred, they certainly had no secondary gain in pretending to have met Jesus.

With all of its infights, contradictions, shortcomings and crimes, the universal Christian church upheld these truths:

Christ was the Son of God, and in Christ we met God. Irrespective of whether one believes in the transubstantiantion, consubstantiation, or no susbstantiation at all, Christ proclaimed the intercourse of humankind with God

Christ revealed a God who made Himself and Herself vulnerable in order to be loved by the humans He and She cherishes. I'll let philosophers and theologians dispute how God may be at the same time almighty and needy of human love. The New Testament as well as the tradition of the church tells me that God depends on my love and support in order to be God. As Jean Delannoy put it in the title of his forgotten movie *Dieu A Besoin des Hommes God Needs Men*!

In our communion with Christ we become children of God, we become brothers and sisters, and we are responsible for each other. Everybody's problem is our problem!

Regardless of our free will, we do carry a inheritance of debts that needs to be paid (redeemed) in order to gain the freedom to be ourselves. The passion and death of Christ has given us the opportunity to make currency able to pay our own and everybody else's debts out of our own suffering.

Rudolf Bultmann, the founder of modern theology, said that we cannot know the historical Christ, and this message was echoed by the participants of the Jesus seminars who went through a painstaking effort to decide which of the statements reported in the Gospel were authentically Jesus's.

I beg to disagree. The three synoptic Gospels (Mark's, Matthew's and Luke's) were meant to bring solace to the Christain communities confused by persecution and the delay of the second coming. They were never meant as historical texts. John's Gospel was meant as a rebuttal of the Gnostic philosophy that had infected the Christian message. Though they do not provide a detailed account of Jesus's everydays life and indeed may reveal inconsistencies in the details they describe, the four Gospels, as well as the apostolic letters and the Book of Revelation could not be more consistent in revealing Christ's message of love expressed in the redemptive suffering of a God who had become man.

There are two other aspects of the historicity of Jesus that I wish to highlight.

First, in his book "The Case for Christ," an American journalist interviewed some prominent biblical scholars and theologians who demonstrated beyond doubt, in my opinion at least, how Christ fulfilled all the prophecies and expectations of the Old Testament related to the messiah.

Second, in the last two thousand years, many indisputable miracles were operated by God through the intercession of the Virgin Mary and of his saints, and Christ Himself has appeared to prayerful people, including St. Francis of Assisi, whom he asked to rebuild his church. At the beginning Francis felt he was talking about the building of a small church in disrepair in the countryside. To that end he invested the resources of his father, a wealthy merchant known as Pietro di Bernardone. Only later did he realize that Christ meant the universal church devastated by sin and avarice caused by wealth. This is another example of how Christ keeps speaking to us in a human way and trusts to our human comprehension the diffusion of his message.

At the end of this book I ask again the reader to answer for himself or herself Father Clarke's question: Who is crazier? The one who hears thunder and believes it is the voice of God or the one who hears the voice of God and believes it is thunder?

www.ingramcontent.com/pod-product-compliance
Lightning Source LLC
Chambersburg PA
CBHW071235230426
43668CB00011B/1451